SOCIAL JUSTICE, EQUALITY AND EMPOWERMENT

VULNERABLE YOUTH AND EMPLOYMENT ISSUES

SOCIAL JUSTICE, EQUALITY AND EMPOWERMENT

VULNERABLE YOUTH AND EMPLOYMENT ISSUES

CHRISTOPHER E. PERRY

EDITOR

Nova Science Publishers, Inc.

New York

For permission to use material from this book please contact us:
Telephone 631-231-7269; Fax 631-231-8175
Web Site: http://www.novapublishers.com

NOTICE TO THE READER

The Publisher has taken reasonable care in the preparation of this book, but makes no expressed or implied warranty of any kind and assumes no responsibility for any errors or omissions. No liability is assumed for incidental or consequential damages in connection with or arising out of information contained in this book. The Publisher shall not be liable for any special, consequential, or exemplary damages resulting, in whole or in part, from the readers' use of, or reliance upon, this material. Any parts of this book based on government reports are so indicated and copyright is claimed for those parts to the extent applicable to compilations of such works.

Independent verification should be sought for any data, advice or recommendations contained in this book. In addition, no responsibility is assumed by the publisher for any injury and/or damage to persons or property arising from any methods, products, instructions, ideas or otherwise contained in this publication.

This publication is designed to provide accurate and authoritative information with regard to the subject matter covered herein. It is sold with the clear understanding that the Publisher is not engaged in rendering legal or any other professional services. If legal or any other expert assistance is required, the services of a competent person should be sought. FROM A DECLARATION OF PARTICIPANTS JOINTLY ADOPTED BY A COMMITTEE OF THE AMERICAN BAR ASSOCIATION AND A COMMITTEE OF PUBLISHERS.

Additional color graphics may be available in the e-book version of this book.

LIBRARY OF CONGRESS CATALOGING-IN-PUBLICATION DATA
Vulnerable youth and employment issues / editor, Christopher E. Perry.
p. cm.
Includes index.
ISBN 978-1-61122-020-9 (hardcover)
1. Youth--Employment--United States. 2. Occupational training. I. Perry, Christopher E.
HD6273.V85 2010
331.3'40973--dc22
2010038657

Published by Nova Science Publishers, Inc. † New York

CONTENTS

PREFACE

In an increasingly global economy, and with retirement starting for the Baby Boomer generation, Congress has indicated a strong interest in ensuring that today's young people have the educational attainment and employment experience needed to become highly skilled workers, contributing taxpayers, and successful participants in civic life. Challenges in the economy and among certain youth populations, however, have heightened concern among policymakers that some young people may not be prepared to fill these roles. The employment levels for youth under age 25 have declined markedly in recent years, and the current recession may cause these levels to decrease further. This book explores the vulnerable youth population with regard to schooling, employment and job training programsbg

Chapter 1- In an increasingly global economy, and with retirement starting for the Baby Boomer generation, Congress has indicated a strong interest in ensuring that today's young people have the educational attainment and employment experience needed to become highly skilled workers, contributing taxpayers, and successful participants in civic life. Challenges in the economy and among certain youth populations, however, have heightened concern among policymakers that some young people may not be prepared to fill these roles.

The employment levels for youth under age 25 have declined markedly in recent years, and the current recession may cause these levels to decrease further. Certain young people—including high school dropouts, current and former foster youth, and other at-risk populations—face challenges in completing school and entering the workforce. While the United States has experienced a dramatic increase in secondary school achievement in the past several decades, approximately 9% of youth ages 18 through 24 have not attained a high school diploma or its equivalent. In addition, millions of young people are out of school and not working.

Chapter 2- The Workforce Investment Act of 1998 (WIA, P.L. 105-220) is the primary federal law that provides job training and related services to unemployed and underemployed individuals, including vulnerable young people with barriers to employment. All youth job training programs and related services are authorized under Title I of WIA and administered by the Department of Labor (DOL). These programs include the WIA Youth Activities (Youth) formula program, Job Corps, YouthBuild, and the Youth Opportunity Grant (YOG) program. Under the pilot and demonstration authority in Title I, DOL has also carried out the Reintegration of Ex-Offenders program for both youth and adults. Together, these programs make up the federal job training and employment system for disadvantaged youth. Although the programs have distinct activities and goals, each of them seeks to connect eligible youth to educational and employment opportunities, as well as leadership development and community service activities.

Chapter 3- For decades, the federal government has played a role in helping vulnerable young people secure employment and achieve academic success through job training and employment programs, including summer youth employment opportunities. The enactment of the Workforce Investment Act (WIA, P.L. 105-220) in 1998 marked the first time since 1964 that states and localities did not receive funding specifically designated for summer employment programs for vulnerable youth. Although WIA does not authorize a stand-alone summer program, the law requires that local areas funded under its Youth Activities (Youth) program provide summer employment opportunities as one of 10 elements available to eligible low-income youth with barriers to employment. Together, these elements are intended to provide a comprehensive year-round job training and employment program for youth. Approximately one-quarter of youth in the program participate in summer employment activities, which are required to be directly linked to academic and occupational learning. Funding authorization for WIA expired in FY2003, but Congress has continued to appropriate funds for WIA, including the Youth program.

Chapter 4- The study team would like to thank the many individuals who contributed to the development of this evaluation report. We truly appreciate all of their efforts.

Most importantly, this study would not have been possible without the patience and generosity of the administrators, staff members, employers, and youth who participated in the study's 20 site visits. They took the time to share their experiences and respond to our requests for information during a period of intense activity and demands from many stakeholders in the workforce investment community. We appreciate the help offered by program staff in coordinating the visits, and the willingness of local employers and youth to share their personal stories with us.

In: Vulnerable Youth and Employment Issues
Editor: Christopher E. Perry

ISBN: 978-1-61122-020-9
© 2011 Nova Science Publishers, Inc.

Chapter 1

VULNERABLE YOUTH: EMPLOYMENT AND JOB TRAINING PROGRAMS

Adrienne L. Fernandes

SUMMARY

In an increasingly global economy, and with retirement starting for the Baby Boomer generation, Congress has indicated a strong interest in ensuring that today's young people have the educational attainment and employment experience needed to become highly skilled workers, contributing taxpayers, and successful participants in civic life. Challenges in the economy and among certain youth populations, however, have heightened concern among policymakers that some young people may not be prepared to fill these roles.

The employment levels for youth under age 25 have declined markedly in recent years, and the current recession may cause these levels to decrease further. Certain young people— including high school dropouts, current and former foster youth, and other at-risk populations—face challenges in completing school and entering the workforce. While the United States has experienced a dramatic increase in secondary school achievement in the past several decades, approximately 9% of youth ages 18 through 24 have not attained a high school diploma or its equivalent. In addition, millions of young people are out of school and not working.

Since the 1930s, federal job training and employment programs and policies have sought to connect vulnerable youth to work and school. Generally, these young people have been defined as being at-risk because they are economically disadvantaged and have a barrier to employment. During the Great Depression, the focus was on employing young men who were idle through public works and other projects. The employment programs from this era included an educational component to encourage youth to obtain their high school diplomas. Beginning in the 1960s, the federal government began funding programs for low-income youth that address their multiple needs through job training, educational services, and supportive services.

Today's primary federal youth employment and job training programs are authorized under the Workforce Investment Act of 1998 (WIA, P.L. 105-220), and are carried out by the Department of Labor's (DOL) Employment and Training Administration (ETA). Although these programs are funded somewhat differently and have varying eligibility requirements, they generally have a common purpose—to connect youth to educational and employment opportunities, as well as to leadership development and community service activities. Many of the programs target the most vulnerable youth, including school dropouts, homeless youth, and youth offenders. Based on funding and the number of youth served, the WIA Youth Activities (Youth) formula program and Job Corps are the largest. The Youth formula program provides an array of job training and other services for youth through what are known as local workforce investment boards (WIBs). Job Corps provides training in a number of trades at centers where youth reside. Another program, YouthBuild, engages youth in educational services and job training that focus on the construction trades. Separately, WIA's pilot and demonstration authority has been used to carry out the Reintegration of Ex-Offenders program, which provides job training and other services to juvenile and adult offenders. Finally, the Youth Opportunity Grant (YOG) program, which was funded until FY2003, was targeted to youth who lived in select high-poverty communities.

INTRODUCTION

In an increasingly competitive economy, and with retirement starting for the Baby Boomer generation, Congress has indicated a strong interest in ensuring that today's young people have the educational attainment and employment experience necessary to become highly skilled workers, contributing taxpayers, and successful participants in civic life. Challenges in the economy and among vulnerable youth populations, however, have heightened concern among policymakers that many young people may not be prepared to fill these roles.

The employment levels for youth under age 25 have declined markedly in recent years, and the current recession may cause these levels to decrease further. Certain young people in particular— including those from low-income families, high school dropouts, foster youth, and other at-risk populations—face barriers to completing school and entering the workforce. Since the 1960s, federal job training programs and policies have sought to connect these youth to education and employment pathways. Contemporary federal youth employment programs with this same purpose are authorized under the Workforce Investment Act (WIA) of 1998 (P.L. 105-220). These programs provide a range of services and supports to youth. They include the Youth Activities (Youth) formula grant program; Job Corps; YouthBuild; the Reintegration of Ex-Offenders program, which includes a youth component; and the Youth Opportunity Grant (YOG) program. Some of the programs concentrate on specific job trades and/or serve targeted at-risk populations. Based on funding, Job Corps and the Youth program are the largest.

This chapter provides an overview of federal employment programs for vulnerable young people. It begins with a discussion of the current challenges in preparing all youth today for the workforce. The report then provides a chronology of job training and employment programs for at-risk youth that began in the 1930s and were expanded or modified from the

1960s through the 1990s. It goes on to discuss the five youth programs currently authorized under WIA, and draws comparisons between these programs. Following this section is a detailed discussion of each of the programs. This chapter accompanies two CRS reports—CRS Report R40930, *Vulnerable Youth: Issues in the Reauthorization of the Workforce Investment Act*; and CRS Report R40830, *Vulnerable Youth: Federal Funding for Summer Job Training and Employment*.

CONTEXT

The current economic recession has focused attention on the role of the federal and state governments in supporting workers who have been laid off or are at risk of being laid off. During economic downturns, youth are particularly vulnerable to job loss. From 2000 through 2009, the rate of employment among teens steadily declined.[1] During the summer, when teens are most likely to have jobs, the rate of employment has decreased most steeply. In June 2000, nearly half (45.9%) of all teens were employed, compared to 29.3% in June 2009.[2] The June 2009 employment rate is the lowest it has been during the post-World War II period. Young men have experienced the greatest losses in summer employment. Among males ages 16 through 19, less than one-third (27.6%) were employed in June 2009, compared to 46.1% in June 2000. Rates of employment among teens vary based on income.[3] Since the summer of 2000, employment rates of teens in every income category have decreased; however, the lowest-income youth have experienced the sharpest declines. In June 2008 (the latest data analysis available), just over one- quarter (26.5%) of teens in households with incomes of less than $20,000 were employed. This is compared to almost half of all youth in households with incomes of $60,000 to $150,000.

The declining rate of teen employment overall appears to be attributable to rising levels of joblessness and not to a declining interest in employment among teens.[4] According to the research literature, possible consequences of reduced work among teens are reduced employment earnings, labor productivity in the future, and output in the economy. Similarly, the employment rates of young adults ages 20 through 24 have declined steadily.[5] Among males in this age group, the average employment-to-population ratio was 65.1% in January through June of 2009, which represents about a 12 percentage point decrease from the same period in 2000. The 2009 employment-to-population ratio for these youth is the lowest it has been in the post-World War II period.

Even in periods of relative economic stability, some youth do not complete school and/or make the transition to the workforce. While the majority of young people graduate from high school by age 18 or shortly thereafter,[6] about 9% of youth ages 18 through 24 have dropped out and have not earned a high school diploma or its equivalent.[7] This figure is higher among black and Hispanic youth.[8] Further, estimates of youth who are not working or in school (i.e., "disconnected") for at least a year are approximately two million.[9] Certain youth face barriers to remaining in school or securing employment, including poverty, their parents' level of education, and whether the youth are pregnant or parenting, among other factors. For example, youth ages 16 through 24 who are parenting are far more likely to be disconnected than their counterparts who are not.[10] Youth in or aging out of foster care, runaway and homeless youth, and youth offenders, among other groups of youth, are particularly vulnerable to not completing high school, going on to college, or securing employment.[11] For example, in a study of youth who had been in foster care and were, on average, about age 25, most had obtained a high school diploma or passed the general education development (GED) test at about the same rate as young people ages 18 to 29 in the general population. However, they were much less likely to have a bachelor's degree—1.8% versus 22.5% of all young people.[12] Further, the employment rate for these foster care alumni was 80%, while the employment rate for their counterparts in the general population was 95%.

As they leave high school, either through graduation or by dropping out, young people can pursue various options. Youth with a high school diploma may attend a two- or four-year college, enlist in the armed services, or secure part-time or full-time employment (sometimes paired with attending school). Youth without a high school diploma can do some of these same things, but their opportunities are more limited. They cannot enroll in a four-year college or, in most cases, enlist in the military. These youth will likely have difficulty supporting themselves if they do work. For example, adults ages 18 and older who worked during 2007 earned an average of $42,064, with earnings ranging from $21,484 for high school dropouts to $31,286 for high school graduates and $57,181 for college graduates.[13]

Federal youth employment and job training programs have long targeted services to young people who leave school before graduating or are in school and may be vulnerable to dropping out. The purpose of these programs, as they currently exist, is to provide job training, employment, educational services, and social services that can help youth become economically self-sufficient and achieve their career and academic goals. These contemporary programs also emphasize leadership development and community service. Note that while youth employment and job training programs are also enhanced with state workforce and other dollars, the extent to which this support is provided is unclear.

HISTORY OF FEDERAL YOUTH EMPLOYMENT AND JOB TRAINING PROGRAMS[14]

For more than 70 years, the federal government has played a role in helping young people secure employment and achieve academic success. Generally, these young people have been defined as being vulnerable in some way—either because they are economically disadvantaged and/or have a barrier to securing employment or completing their education. During the Great Depression, the focus was on employing idle young men in public works and other projects. The employment programs from this era included an educational component to encourage youth to obtain their high school diplomas. Beginning in the 1960s, the federal government started funding programs for low-income youth, such as Job Corps, that address their multiple needs, including job training, educational services, housing, and supportive services. During the 1970s and 1980s, Job Corps was expanded and the federal government funded additional programs for both in-school and outof-school youth. Funding was also appropriated to test the efficacy of some of these programs. The Workforce Investment Act of 1998 extended earlier programs and created new ones, with the intention of providing more seamless job training and education services for youth year-round. Generally, these programs are targeted to teenagers and young adults, usually not beyond age 24, who are at risk of dropping out or have already done so.

Depression Era

Prior to the 1930s, the federal government's involvement in youth employment was primarily limited to regulating child labor.[15] The Great Depression served as a catalyst for the creation of federal programs to employ and educate young people who were out of work or at risk of dropping out of school due to financial difficulties. The Civilian Conservation Corps (CCC) began in 1933 as an employment program for unemployed males ages 18 to 25 (and veterans, Indians, and residents of territories of any age) to participate in projects planned by the Departments of the Interior and Agriculture. These projects focused on creating and improving infrastructure, transportation, and recreational services, among other categories. The young men lived in camps and were provided with an allowance, food, and medical care. The CCC also included an educational component, which taught nearly 35,000 participants to read and write and assisted a smaller number with attaining their high school and college degrees. Until the program ended in 1945, it served nearly three million men, of whom approximately 10% were veterans.

Other Depression era programs—the Student Aid program, Works Project program, and Guidance and Placement program—were administered by the National Youth Administration, which was created as part of the now-defunct Works Progress Administration by an Executive Order in 1935. The programs provided funds for part-time employment of needy high school, college, and graduate students to assist them in completing school, as well as funds for part-time employment for unemployed out-of-school youth. These young people, all of whom were ages 16 through 25, were employed in a number of broad areas, including construction, clerical work, and research. These programs served hundreds of thousands of youth before they were discontinued in the early 1940s.

War on Poverty Programs

The 1960s marked a period of federal efforts to assist poor and disadvantaged children, adolescents, and their families through job training and other programs. In response to concerns about high unemployment, the Manpower Development and Training Act of 1962 (P.L. 87-4 15) and subsequent amendments to it authorized funding for employment training. Specifically, amendments to the act in 1963 (P.L. 88-214) encouraged the Department of Labor to provide assistance to youth so that they might be able to successfully enter the labor force, and expanded the share of job training funds that could be used to train youth under age 22 from 5% to 25%. Further, federal funding was first authorized through the 1963 amendments to provide employment opportunities to youth from low-income families.

President Lyndon B. Johnson's subsequent War on Poverty established new youth-targeted programs in job training and educational assistance under an initiative known as the Neighborhood Youth Corps (NYC). The NYC was comprised of work training programs, the Work Study program, and Job Corps. The work training programs provided work experience, job training, and supportive services to low-income unemployed youth ages 16 through 21 who were in school or out of school, including dropouts. The Work Study program was modeled on the Depression-era Student Aid program and provided money to high school and college students from low-income families who needed earnings to stay in school. The program continues today for college students. Job Corps, which also continues today, was established under the Economic Opportunity Act of 1964 (P.L. 88-452) to provide educational and job training opportunities to disadvantaged youth at residential and non-residential centers. (See "Job Corps," below, for further information.)

Expanding Youth Programs

The 1973 Comprehensive Employment and Training Act (CETA, P.L. 93-203) was the first of four laws enacted during the 1970s and 1980s that focused greater federal attention on youth employment and training. The second law, the Youth Employment and Demonstrations Project Act (YEDPA, P.L. 95-93) was enacted in 1977 and established a variety of employment, training, and demonstration programs for youth. The 1982 Job Training Partnership Act (JTPA, P.L. 97- 300) repealed CETA. JTPA was subsequently repealed by WIA. Separately, the School-to-Work Opportunities Act of 1994 (STWOA, P.L. 103-239) supported the development of programs that encouraged students to pursue learning opportunities and experiences that incorporated occupational skills. Activities authorized under these acts were administered by DOL. STWOA was additionally carried out by the Department of Education (ED).

CETA and YEDPA

As amended through 1978, CETA authorized a range of employment and training programs for adults and youth. Job Corps and the Summer Program for Economically Disadvantaged Youth (SPEDY) were the primary youth programs authorized under CETA. SPEDY provided funding to employers to hire low-income youth ages 14 through 21 during the summer months. Youth served as assistants in hospitals, libraries, community service organizations, and schools, among other settings.

The Youth Employment and Demonstrations Project Act (YEDPA), signed into law in 1977, amended CETA.[16] YEDPA increased authorization of appropriations for Job Corps and SPEDY and authorized three additional programs targeted to "economically disadvantaged" (defined under the act) youth ages 14 through 21: Youth Employment and Training Programs (YETP), Youth Community Conservation and Improvement Projects (YCCIP), and Youth Incentive Entitlement Pilot Projects (YIEPP).[17] YEDPA was passed in response to high levels of unemployment among youth relative to adults, even during periods of economic expansion, and growing gaps in youth unemployment among whites and blacks, males and females, and in- school and out-of-school youth. The programs were carried out during the Carter Administration, from 1977 through 1981. Over this period, YEDPA served 6.1 million youth.

YETP and YCCIP were intended to meet the immediate employment needs of youth, and funding for the programs was allocated primarily on a formula basis. YETP activities include work experience, pre-employment skills, and an emphasis on the transition from school to work. YCCIP was intended to assist unemployed, out-of-school youth obtain a high school degree, conditional on satisfactory performance in work and school. Further, it was aimed at improving coordination between the job training and educational systems as a means of addressing the dropout problem.[18] Finally, YIEPP funded evaluations to test the efficacy of demonstration programs; the other two programs included funding for demonstration programs. During the YEDPA years, more than 60 major demonstrations were funded in about 300 sites, operated by DOL in cooperation with six other federal agencies and private nonprofit intermediaries.

JTPA[19]

CETA was repealed in 1982 by the Job Training Partnership Act. JTPA was distinct from its predecessor because it emphasized that states and localities, rather than the federal government, had the primary responsibility for administering job training and employment programs. Funding was appropriated under JTPA through FY1 999. JTPA programs focused on the training needs of "economically disadvantaged" (defined under the act) youth and adults facing significant barriers to employment. These programs were frequently referred to as "second chance" programs because most of them were intended to train individuals who had not sufficiently benefitted from traditional secondary and post-secondary education. They included the Summer Youth Employment and Training program, the Youth Training Program, and Job Corps (discussed in the next section).

The Summer Youth Employment and Training program provided employment and training activities during the summer months for low-income youth ages 14 through 21 to strengthen basic educational skills, encourage school completion, provide work exposure, and enhance citizenship skills. In the summer of 1997, an estimated 500,000 youth participated. The Youth Training Program was established by the Job Training Reform Amendments of 1992 (P.L. 102-367), which amended JTPA to address concerns that school dropouts were not being reached by the then- existing combined program for disadvantaged adults and youth, and that the program primarily served youth who were the easiest to place in jobs and required the fewest services.[20] The program was year-round and provided direct services, such as on-the-job training, tutoring and study skills training, and school-to-work transition services. It also provided training-related and supportive services, including job search assistance, drug and alcohol abuse counseling, and cash incentives based on attendance and performance in a program. Economically disadvantaged in- school and out-of-school youth ages 16 through 21 were eligible, but 50% of participants in service delivery areas (SDAs), comprised of the state or one or more units of local government, had to be out of school. Further, at least 65% of youth had to be hard to serve, meaning they were school dropouts (if out of school), pregnant or parenting, or offenders, among other qualifications. In program year 1997, an estimated 107,000 youth participated. As discussed below, JTPA was repealed by WIA, the current law that authorizes youth job training and employment programs.

STWOA

The School to Work Opportunity Act of 1994 authorized the School-to-Work (STW) program administered jointly by DOL and the Department of Education through the National School-toWork Office. The program was funded from FY1994 through FY2000.[21] The law supported the development of programs with three main elements: work-based learning to provide participating students with work experience and on-the-job training; school-based learning, involving upgrading and integrating the occupational skills participating students learn in school and the workplace; and program coordination to aid the planning, implementation, and operation of the program. STWOA grants were competitively awarded to states, local partnerships, programs for Indian youth, and U.S. territories to implement school-to-work systems. In addition, STWOA authorized national activities, such as research and demonstrations. Some school-to-work programs that received seed money from the federal program continue to operate today.

WIA

The Workforce Investment Act of 1998 replaced JTPA. WIA includes titles that authorize programs for job training and related services (Title I), adult education and literacy (Title II), employment services (Title III), and vocational rehabilitation (Title IV). Title I of WIA authorizes job training programs for youth, adults, and dislocated workers.[22] As described by DOL in a 2000 Training and Employment Guidance Letter (TEGL) to state and local workforce development boards, WIA places "new emphasis on serving youth within a comprehensive statewide workforce development system." The programs for youth are discussed in further detail below.

OVERVIEW OF YOUTH PROGRAMS AUTHORIZED UNDER TITLE I OF THE WORKFORCE INVESTMENT ACT

Job training and employment services for youth under WIA include

- *WIA Youth Activities*, a formula grant program for states that includes employment and other services that are provided year-round;
- *Job Corps*, a program that provides job training and related services primarily at residential centers maintained by contractor organizations;
- *YouthBuild*, a competitive grant program that emphasizes job training and education in construction;
- *Reintegration of Ex-Offenders*, a demonstration program for juvenile and adult offenders that provides job training and other services and is authorized under WIA's pilot and demonstration authority; and
- *Youth Opportunity Grants* program, a multi-site demonstration program funded through FY2003 that created centers in low-income communities where youth could receive employment and other services.

WIA's authorization of appropriations expired at the end of FY2003. However, Congress continues to appropriate funds, including those for youth job training programs—except for the Youth Opportunity Grants program, which has not been funded since FY2003. All of the programs are carried out by DOL's Employment and Training Administration (ETA).[23] As mentioned above, Job Corps was enacted as part of the Economic Opportunity Act of 1964 (P.L. 88-452), and was later incorporated into CETA and JTPA. YouthBuild was originally authorized under the Cranston-Gonzalez National Affordable Housing Act of 1992 (P.L. 102-550). The program was administered by the Department of Housing and Urban Development (HUD) until it was transferred to DOL in 2007 under the YouthBuild Transfer Act (P.L. 109-281) and incorporated into WIA. Unlike other youth programs authorized under WIA, regulations have not yet been promulgated for YouthBuild as authorized under WIA. DOL expects the rules to be promulgated in the near future.[24]

All of the programs offer employment, job training, and educational services. For example, local areas must provide 10 specific elements, including mentoring and follow-up, to youth who receive services under the Youth Activities formula grant program. YouthBuild program participants engage in employment and other activities primarily related to housing and other types of construction work. Job Corps is the only one of the programs that provides residential services; youth can live onsite and receive health care services, child care, and other supports. As with Job Corps, the YOG program established centers, albeit non-residential, where youth could receive employment and other services. Further, the programs generally serve vulnerable youth, but some have more targeted eligibility criteria. Participants in the Youth Activities formula grant program, YouthBuild, and Job Corps must be low-income and have specific employment barriers. The Youthful Offender component of the Reintegration of Ex-Offenders serves youth who have become involved in the juvenile justice or criminal justice system or youth at risk of becoming involved. When the YOG program was in operation, youth automatically qualified for the program if they lived in low-income communities. Finally, the programs are funded somewhat differently. DOL allocates funding for Youth Activities to states based on a formula, while Job Corps enters into agreements with nonprofit and for-profit organizations and other federal agencies. The other programs competitively award grants to nonprofit and other organizations and local communities.

Coordination

Together, the WIA Youth program and other WIA programs collectively make up a job training and workforce system for youth. In some cases, WIA includes provisions that encourage or require the programs to coordinate with one another. In submitting their state workforce investment plans to DOL, states must specify how they will coordinate Youth Activities programming with services provided by Job Corps centers in places where they exist. In addition, youth councils, comprised of stakeholders with an interest in the employment and other needs of youth, must include representatives from Job Corps, where applicable. Further, Youth Activities, Job Corps, and YouthBuild are required partners at one-stop centers. One-stop centers include approximately 20 federal programs that coordinate employment and other services in a community for all youth and adults.

The White House Task Force for Disadvantaged Youth, convened in 2002 under President George W. Bush, sought to improve coordination of youth programs across the federal government and use federal resources to assist the neediest youth, including those who would be eligible for programs under Title I of WIA. In response, ETA established the Shared Youth Vision, which is intended to connect the most at-risk youth to work and school.[25] As part of these efforts, DOL has partnered with other federal agencies, including the U.S. Departments of Education, Health and Human Services, and Justice to improve communication and collaboration across programs that target at-risk youth groups under an initiative called the "Shared Youth Vision."[26] Together, the agencies convened an Interagency Work Group and conducted regional forums to develop and coordinate policies and research on the vulnerable youth population. The purpose of these forums was to create and implement plans to improve communication and collaboration between local organizations that serve at-risk youth. DOL competitively awarded grants totaling $1.6 million to 16 states to assist them in developing strategic plans to link their systems that serve youth.

Funding

Funding authorization for the youth programs under WIA expired in FY2003.[27] Although funding authorization has expired, Congress has continued to appropriate funds for most programs authorized under the law. **Table 1** summarizes funding for FY2000 through FY20 10, as well as funding appropriated under the American Recovery and Reinvestment Act (ARRA, P.L. 111-5) and funding proposed by the Obama Administration for FY20 11. **Table A-1** in **Appendix A** presents Youth Activities funding allocated to the states and outlying areas for PY2008 and PY2009, and under ARRA (the most recent years for which funding data are available).

As shown in **Table 1,** Congress appropriated a total of $2.7 billion in FY2000, a total of $2.8 billion in FY2009 (not including ARRA), and slightly higher amounts in intervening years. The figure for FY20 10 is not yet final because the amount of funding for the youth component of the Reintegration of Ex-Offenders program has not yet been announced.

Job Corps has received the largest appropriation each year, followed by the Youth Activities formula grant program, Youth Opportunity Grants (funded only through FY2003), YouthBuild, and the youth component of the Reintegration of Ex-Offenders (although in two years, YouthBuild has received less funding than the Reintegration of Ex-Offenders' youth component). Funding for Job Corps has increased over time, from $1.4 billion in FY2000 to $1.7 billion in FY2009. In contrast, funding for Youth Activities has decreased, from $1.0 billion in FY2000 to $924.1 million in FY2009. Funding has fluctuated for the other two major programs, YouthBuild and the youth component of the Reintegration of Ex-Offenders Program. Funding for YouthBuild in FY20 10 is $102.5 million, the highest level to date. In FY2009, the youth component of the Reintegration of Ex-Offenders program was $88.5 million, the highest level to date (the FY20 10 funding for the youth component is not yet final).

ARRA provided additional funding to states and localities for the youth programs. As stated in the law, its purposes are to stimulate economic activity in selected industrial sectors to save existing jobs and create new jobs, reduce taxes, invest in future technologies, and fund infrastructure improvements. The law appropriated $1.2 billion for grants for Youth Activities, $250 million for Job Corps, and $50 million for YouthBuild.

Section 1 89(g)(1)(A) of WIA requires that funds obligated for a program or activity carried out under Title I of the act are available for obligation only on the basis of a program year.[28] The program year begins on July 1 in the fiscal year for which the appropriation is made and ends June 30 of the following year. Under Section 1 89(g)(1)(B), funds for Youth Activities may first become available for a new program year in the preceding April. In addition, Congress has tended to specify that funds appropriated for YouthBuild and the youth component of the Reintegration of Ex-Offenders program are available for obligation beginning in the April preceding a given program year.

Table 1. Funding for DOL Job Training Programs, FY2000-FY2009, Including the American Recovery and Reinvestment Act (P.L. 111-5) and Proposed Funding for FY2011 (Nominal Dollars) (Dollars in Thousands)

Fiscal Year	Youth Activities	Job Corps	YouthBuild[a]	Youthful Offender (Reintegration of Ex-Offenders)[b]	Youth Opportunity Grants[c]	Total Funding, All Programs
FY2000	$1,000,965	$1,357,776	$43,000	$13,907	$250,000	$2,665,648
FY2001	1,127,965	1,399,148	60,000	55,000	250,000	2,892,113
FY2002	1,127,965	1,458,732	65,000	55,000	225,100	2,931,797
FY2003	994,459	1,509,094	59,610	54,643	44,211	2,662,017
FY2004	995,059	1,541,151	65,000	49,705	0	2,650,915
FY2005	986,288	1,551,861	62,000	69,440	0	2,669,589
FY2006	940,500	1,564,180	62,000	49,104	0	2,615,784
FY2007	940,500	1,566,178	49,500	49,104	0	2,605,282
FY2008	924,069	1,610,506	58,952	55,000	0	2,648,527
FY2009	924,069	1,683,938	70,000	88,500	0	2,766,507
ARRA	1,200,000	250,000	50,000	0	0	1,500,000
FY2010	924,069	1,708,205	102,500	[108,493][d]	0	2,734,779[e]
FY2011	1,025,000	1,707,363	120,000	[98,000][d]	0	2,852,363[e]

Source: Compiled by the Congressional Research Service (CRS) from Department of Labor (DOL) budget justifications, Department of Housing and Urban Development (HUD) budget justifications, DOL Employment and Training Administration budget information at http://www.doleta.gov/budget.

a. YouthBuild was transferred from HUD to DOL under the YouthBuild Transfer Act (P.L. 109-281).

b. Prior to FY2008, the Reintegration of Youthful Offenders program was a stand-alone program. It is now part of the Reintegration of Ex-Offenders program, which includes funding for juvenile and adult activities. Funding for the program is authorized under Section 171 (Demonstration and pilot projects) of WIA and Section 112 (Responsible reintegration of offenders) of the recently enacted Second Chance Act (P.L. 110- 199). Section 112 authorizes DOL to make grants to nonprofit organizations for the purpose of providing mentoring, job training and job placement services, and other comprehensive transitional services to assist eligible offenders ages 18 and older in obtaining and retaining employment.

c. The Youth Opportunity Grants program was funded from FY1999 (not shown in the table) through FY2003, and was operational through FY2005.

d. The Department of Labor has not specified how much funding is available for the Youthful Offender component of the Reintegration of Ex-Offenders program.

e. The total excludes the amount for the Youthful Offender component of the Reintegration of Ex-Offenders program.

Pursuant to Section 1 89(g)(2), funds obligated for any program year for a program or activity carried out under Title I may be expended by each state receiving such funds during that program year and the two succeeding program years.[29] Local areas may expend funds received from the state during the program year and the succeeding program year. Congress has generally required that obligated funds for Job Corps are made available for one program year, although funding for certain purposes can be obligated through later dates.

The next section of the report provides further discussion about the five youth programs authorized under Title I of WIA.

YOUTH ACTIVITIES FORMULA GRANT PROGRAM[30]

Overview and Purpose

The Youth Activities formula grant program is one of three state formula grant programs authorized by WIA. The other two programs target adults (Adult Activities) and dislocated workers (Dislocated Worker Activities), although youth ages 18 or older are eligible for services provided through the Adult Activities program. These programs provide core funding for a coordinated system of employment and training services overseen by a state workforce investment board (WIB) and the governor, and comprised of representatives of businesses and other partners. The WIA Youth Activities formula grant program is arguably the centerpiece of the federal youth job training and employment system. As specified in the law, the program has several purposes: to provide assistance in achieving academic and employment success through activities that improve educational and skill competencies and foster effective connections to employers; to ensure ongoing adult mentoring opportunities for eligible youth; to provide opportunities for training, continued supportive services, and participation in activities related to leadership, citizenship, and community service; and to offer incentives for recognition and achievement to youth.

Unlike JTPA, which had two separate programs for summer and year-round activities, WIA funds both under the Youth formula program. WIA also mandates that certain elements be made available to all youth participants through Youth Activities, including summer opportunities linked to academic and occupational learning (see **Table 2**). Under JTPA, several of these elements were either optional or not present. In addition, the Youth program requires that 30% of WIA youth funds be spent on out-of-school youth. While JTPA's Youth Training Program required half of all youth to be out of school, the larger summer youth program did not set any requirements for this population.

Program Structure

DOL provides funding to state WIBs based on their relative[31] unemployment and youth poverty status.[32] In turn, the state WIBs distribute 85% of funds, also based on unemployment and poverty factors, to local workforce areas that are designated by the governor. The state retains as much as 15% for statewide activities.[33] A local area is overseen by the local WIB. Membership of the local WIB includes representatives of businesses, local education entities, labor organizations, community-based organizations, and economic development agencies, among others. Local WIBs, in coordination with their youth councils (discussed below), competitively award funds to local organizations and other entities to provide employment and job training services to youth. A 2004 report by the Government Accountability Office

(GAO) examined the entities that local WIBs contract with to provide these services. Based on a survey of all local WIBs, the report found that about half of all youth received Youth Activities services through community-based organizations, secondary schools, and colleges or universities.[34] A smaller share of youth received services through one-stop centers (discussed below) and other entities, such as local or state governments and private employers.

With assistance from the state WIB, the governor develops a five-year plan that addresses several items related to employment and training needs, performance accountability, and employment and training activities. The plan must address items specific to Youth Activities (Section 112), including a description of the factors used to distribute funds to local areas for Youth Activities; the state's strategy for providing comprehensive services to eligible youth, particularly those who have significant barriers to employment; the criteria used by local boards in awarding and assessing providers for youth activities' grants; and a description of how the state will coordinate Youth Activities with services provided by Job Corps and Youth Opportunity grants, where applicable.

The local WIB develops a local plan that discusses items similar to those in the state plan, except that the plan describes the local area's one-stop delivery system, which is comprised of partners that collaborate to provide coordinated employment and training services in the community. Nearly 20 federal programs must provide services through the one-stop system, either by co- location, electronic linkages, or referrals. A local program funded by the Youth Activities formula grant program and the one-stop workforce system are encouraged to work together to facilitate the coordination and delivery of comprehensive, longer-term workforce services for youth.[35] In fact, as a required partner in the one-stop system, a local program must use a portion of its funds to create and maintain the one-stop delivery system and enter into a memorandum of understanding with the local WIB relating to the operation of the one-stop, among other requirements.[36]

Youth Councils

Each local WIB is required under law to establish a local youth council (Section 117(h)). Together, the WIB and the youth council oversee a local youth program funded by Youth Activities. The purpose of the youth council is to provide expertise in youth policy and to assist the local board in developing portions of the local plan relating to eligible youth. As specified in the law, the councils must coordinate youth activities in a local area, develop portions of the local plan related to eligible youth, recommend eligible providers of youth activities to be competitively awarded grants or contracts, oversee the activities of the providers, and carry out other duties specified by the local WIB.

The youth council is comprised of members of the local board with special interest or expertise in youth policy; representatives of youth service, juvenile justice, and local law enforcement agencies; representatives of local public housing authorities; and parents of eligible youth seeking assistance through the adult activities or dislocated workers activities, among others. A 2002 study by GAO of the Youth Activities program included survey data about the membership of local youth councils. At the time, 92% of youth councils included participants from youth-serving agencies and 93% included people who had experience in youth activities. Seventy-five percent of youth councils had personnel from public housing authorities and 71% included parents of WIA-eligible youth. Most youth councils expanded their membership to include optional representatives, such as local educators.[37]

Elements of Local Programs

Local programs are responsible for carrying out the purposes of the act. In addition to assessing the skills of youth who receive services, local programs must provide 10 activities or "elements" to youth, as summarized in **Table 2**. DOL classifies elements based on whether they are targeted to educational achievement, summer employment, employment services, leadership development activities, or additional support for youth services. In addition, programs must provide follow-up services.[38] Note that although local WIBs must make all 10 program elements available to youth, each individual youth does not need to participate in all elements. Further, local programs that receive Youth Activities funding need not provide all 10 program elements if certain services are already accessible for all eligible youth in the area; however, these other services must be closely coordinated with the local programs.[39] Local WIBs must provide to each youth information on the fully array of applicable or appropriate services available through the local board, other eligible providers, or one-stop partners, and they must also refer youth to appropriate training and educational programs, among other activities.

What Elements Mean in Practice

As part of a 2004 survey of local WIBs, GAO found that most local programs used multiple service providers to deliver youth services, although some used a small number. For example, a single WIA provider in rural Wisconsin delivered all 10 elements in a long-term, year-round program for out-of-school youth. Youth participants worked in teams to build or refurbish low- income housing. At the building sites, youth received paid employment, occupational training, leadership training, and mentoring from an adult supervisor. Off site, youth received classroom instruction to prepare for their high school equivalency exam; career counseling; and support services, such as meals and health care. Upon exiting, they received monthly follow-up services for at least two years.

According to the GAO report, schools were also used as youth service providers. Many of the schools provided youth services directly or collaborated with other education providers. For instance, an education provider in New Jersey collaborated with local school districts, universities, and private businesses to operate a program designed to help youth explore careers in the food industry. During the summer, 30 in-school youth ages 14 through 16 learned basic job skills in the classroom, visited farms and food businesses, and worked at local food businesses and restaurants. During the school year, students were placed in paid internships in the food industry and received mentoring services from employers.

The 2004 report also discusses that local areas developed partnerships with the business community to deliver services. Over one-third of local WIBs reported that businesses subsidized work experience for WIA youth. Examples of the types of services provided to youth through these partnerships include work readiness training, in issues such as punctuality, teamwork, respect for others, and appropriate dress, that businesses assisted with; and financial management curricula provided by businesses.

Table 2. Elements of Youth Programs Funded by WIA Youth Activities Formula Grant Program

Educational achievement
• Tutoring, study skills training, and instruction leading to completion of secondary school, including dropout prevention strategies. • Alternative secondary school services, as appropriate.
Summer employment opportunities
• Summer employment opportunities that are directly linked to academic and occupational learning.
Employment services
• As appropriate, paid and unpaid work experiences, including internships and job shadowing. • Occupational skill training, as appropriate.
Leadership development activities
• Leadership development opportunities, which may include, but are not limited to, community service and peer-centered activities encouraging responsibility and other positive social behaviors during non-school hours, as appropriate; community and service learning projects; organizational and teamwork training, including team leadership training; and citizenship training, including life skills training such as parenting, work behavior training, and budgeting of resources, among other activities.
Additional support for youth services
• Supportive services. • Adult mentoring for the period of participation and a subsequent period, for a total of not less than 12 months. • Comprehensive guidance and counseling, which may include drug and alcohol abuse counseling and referral, as appropriate.
Follow-up services
• Follow-up services for not less than 12 months after the completion of participation, as appropriate; follow-up services for youth include regular contact with a youth participant's employer, including assistance in addressing work-related problems that arise; assistance in securing better jobs, career development, and further education; work-related peer groups; adult mentoring; and tracking the progress of youth in employment after training.

Source: Congressional Research Service, based on Section 1 29(c)(2) of the Workforce Investment Act and Department of Labor, *PY 2008 WIASRD Data Book*, Appendix B.

Finally, a 2004 report for DOL by Social Policy Research Associates drew on data from site visits to a small number of states and local areas in 2000 and 2001 to understand how the elements are carried out.[40] For example, paid and unpaid work experience entailed work experience in conjunction with other services to increase a youth's education and occupational skills. For instance, in Du Page County, IL, the local WIB developed paid and unpaid work experiences in information technology occupations, such as web design and computer maintenance.

Participants

A youth is eligible for the Youth Activities formula grant program if he or she is age 14 through 21,[41] is a low-income individual, and has one or more of the following barriers:

- deficient in basic literacy skills;
- a school dropout;
- homeless, a runaway, or a foster child;
- pregnant or parenting;
- an offender; or
- requires additional assistance to complete an educational program or to secure and hold employment.[42]

At least 30% of all Youth Activities formula grant funds must be used for activities for out-ofschool youth, *or* youth who have dropped out or received a high school diploma or its equivalent but are basic skills deficient, unemployed, or underemployed.[43]

Older and Out-of-School Youth

Youth ages 18 through 21 may enroll in the Youth Activities formula grant program or Adult Activities program, or may co-enroll in both programs. Less than 1% of youth tend to enroll in both programs.[44] Participation in the adult program is based on a "sequential service" strategy that consists of three levels of services. Any individual may receive "core" services (e.g., job search assistance). To receive "intensive" services (e.g., individual career planning and counseling), an individual must have received core services and need intensive services to become employed or to obtain or retain employment that allows for self-sufficiency. To receive training services (e.g., occupational skills training), an individual must have received intensive services and need training services to become employed or obtain or retain employment that allows for self- sufficiency.

Allocations

Funding for the Youth Activities formula grant program is allocated from DOL to states, including Washington, DC, and territories. Under current law, not more than 0.25% is reserved for outlying areas[45] and not more than 1.5% is reserved for youth activities in the Native American programs (Section 166). The remainder of the funds are allocated to states by a formula based one-third on the relative number of unemployed individuals residing in areas of substantial unemployment (an unemployment rate of at least 6.5%), one-third on the relative "excess" number of unemployed individuals (an unemployment rate of at least 4.5%), and one-third on the relative number of low-income youth. In addition, states receive, at minimum, the higher of 90% of their relative share of the prior year's funding or 0.25% of the total allocation, or at maximum, 130% of their relative share of the prior year's funding.[46]

Of the funds allocated to states for the Youth Activities formula grant program (as well as for the Adult and Dislocated Worker programs), not more than 15% can be reserved for statewide activities (Section 128(a)). States may use some of this funding for certain purposes related to youth activities, such as disseminating a list of eligible providers of youth activities and providing additional assistance to local areas that have high concentrations of eligible youth, among other activities. Funds may not be used to develop or implement education curricula for school systems in the state.

The balance of funding is allocated to local areas on the same basis that Youth to take into account the relative numbers of unemployed individuals and low-income youth in that area compared to other local areas of the state (Section 128(b)). Local WIBs may reserve no more than 10% of funds allotted under the Youth program (and Adult and Dislocated Worker programs) for administrative costs. The local WIBs are responsible for competitively awarding grants or contracts to youth providers, based on the recommendations of the youth council and the criteria listed in the state plan (Section 117(d)(2)(B) and Section 123).

MIGRANT AND SEASONAL FARMWORKER PROGRAMS FOR YOUTH

Migrant and Seasonal Farmworker programs are authorized under Section 167 of WIA. Of appropriations exceeding $1 billion for Youth Activities, 4% is to be allocated to youth activities for farmworkers. The law specifies that every two years, DOL must, on a competitive basis, make grants or enter into contracts to carry out workforce investment activities (including those for youth) and provide related assistance for eligible migrant and seasonal farmworkers. These activities may include employment; training; educational assistance; literacy assistance; an English language program; workers' safety training; housing; supportive services; dropout prevention activities; follow-up services for those placed in employment, self-employment, and related business enterprise development; and technical assistance to build capacity in management information technology.

Funds were allocated in FY 1999 through FY2003 for workforce investment activities targeted to youth from migrant and seasonal farmworker families. The projects provided a variety of educational, employment, and youth development activities to migrant youth.

Migrant youth can qualify for education and other services as dependents under the Adult Migrant and Seasonal Farmworker program authorized under Section 167 of WIA. Youth ages 18 and older can also be served as adults under the program.

Source: Congressional Research Service correspondence with the U.S. Department of Labor, Employment and Training Administration, September 2009.

When funds exceed $1 billion, DOL is to reserve a portion for Youth Opportunity grants, discussed in more detail below, and the Migrant and Seasonal Farmworkers program (see text box above) before allocating funds to states. In addition, if appropriations exceeded $1 billion for youth activities for FY1999, DOL was to make available such sums as necessary for the Role Model Academy Project. Funds have not been appropriated for the Youth Opportunity grants and Migrant and Seasonal Farmerworkers program since FY2003, the last year that Congress appropriated more than $1 billion for Youth Activities. The Role Model Academy Project received $10 million in FY1 999 to establish a training academy for youth on an old military base. However, the project operated for only one year due to problems with the grant and the project did not enroll youth.[47]

Table 3. Statutory and Common Measures for WIA Youth Programs

	WIA Statutory Measures	Common Measures
Youth (ages 14 through 18)	• *Skill Attainment Rate:* (Number of basic skills goals attained + Number of work readiness skills goals attained + Number of occupational skills goals attained)! (Number of basic skills goals set + Number of work readiness skills goals set + Number of occupational skills goals set). • *Diploma or Equivalent Attainment Rate:* Number of younger youth attaining secondary school diploma or equivalent by end of [1st] quarter after exit ! Number of younger youth exiters during exit quarter. • *Retention Rate:* Number of youth in postsecondary education, advanced training, employment, or apprenticeships ! Number of younger youth exiters during exit quarter.	• *Placement in Employment and Education:* Number of youth in employment (including the military) or enrolled in post-secondary education and!or advanced training or occupational skills training in the first quarter after the exit quarter ! Number of youth exiters during the exit quarter. • *Attainment of a Degree or Certificate:* Number of youth participants who attain a diploma, GED, or certificate by the end of the third quarter after the exit quarter ! Number of youth exiters during the exit quarter. • *Literacy or Numeracy Gains:* Number of youth participants who increase one or more educational functional levels ! Number of youth participants who have completed a year in the program (i.e., one year from the date of first youth program service) + the number of youth participants who exit before completing a year in the program.
Youth (ages 19 through 21)	• *Entered Employment Rate:* Number of older youth employed in [1st] quarter after exit quarter ! Number of older youth exiters during the exit quarter. • *Employment Retention Rate at Six Months:* Number of older youth employed in 3rd quarter after exit ! Number of older youth exiters during the exit quarter. • *Earnings Change in Six Months:* Earnings in 2nd and 3rd quarter after exit minus earnings in 2nd and 3rd quarter prior to participation ! Number of older youth exiters during the exit quarter. • *Credential/Certificate Rate:* Number of older youth employed, in postsecondary education, or in advanced training after 1st quarter of exit and received credential by end of [3rd] quarter ! Number of older youth exiters during the exit quarter.	

Source: Congressional Research Service, based on the Workforce Investment Act of 1998 (P.L. 105-220), ETA Training and Employment Guidance Letter No. 7-99 ("Core and Customer Satisfaction Performance Measures for the Workforce Investment System "), March 3, 2000, and ETA Training and Employment Guidance Letter No. 17-05 ("WIA Title IB Performance Measures and Related Clarifications," Attachment D), February 17, 2006.

Note: Some of the terms, such as "basic skills goals," "credential," and "certificate" are defined in Appendix B.

Performance

Section 136 of WIA sets forth state and local performance measures as part of the accountability system. The measures, or "core indicators," for youth ages 14 through 18 are different than the indicators for youth ages 19 through 21, as shown in Table 3. The measures for younger youth focus on skill attainment and educational attainment. The older youth outcomes focus on employment. For each of the core indicators, the states negotiate with DOL to establish a level of performance. That is, the "measures" are identified in WIA Section 136, but the "levels" are determined by negotiation between states and DOL.[48] Measures are reported as part of the Workforce Investment Act Standardized Record Data (WIASRD), which also collects demographic and other information about youth, adults, and dislocated workers who exit the program.

ETA implemented a "Common Measures" policy for several workforce programs and revised the reporting requirements for WIA Title I programs.[49] Specifically, ETA introduced three youth measures, as listed in **Table 3**. It is important to note, however, that ETA specifically indicated that the Common Measures were not to supersede the existing statutory performance reporting requirements for WIA. Despite this, DOL has granted waivers to more than half of all states to permit implementation of and reporting on only the Common Measures rather than on the current, fuller array of measures in WIA for youth, adults, and dislocated workers.[50]

The next section of the report discusses, in less detail, four additional programs for youth that are authorized under WIA.

JOB CORPS[51]

Overview and Purpose

The Job Corps program is carried out by the Office of Job Corps within the Office of the DOL Secretary,[52] and consists of residential centers throughout the country. The purpose of the program is to provide disadvantaged youth with the skills needed to obtain and hold a job, enter the Armed Forces, or enroll in advanced training or higher education. In addition to receiving academic and employment training, youth also engage in social and other services to promote their overall well-being.

Program Structure

Currently, 123 Job Corps centers operate throughout the country.[53] Of the 123 centers, 28 sites are known as Civilian Conservation Corps Centers, which are jointly operated by DOL and the Department of Agriculture or the Department of the Interior.[54] Programs at these sites focus on conserving, developing, or managing public natural resources or public recreational areas. Most Job Corps centers are located on property that is owned or leased long-term by the federal government.

Job Corps centers may be operated by a federal, state, or local agency; an area vocational education school, or residential vocational school; or a private organization. Authorization and funding for new Job Corps centers are contained in appropriations law. DOL initiates a competitive process seeking applicants that are selected based on their ability to coordinate activities in the workforce system for youth, their ability to offer vocational training opportunities that reflect local employment opportunities, past performance, proposed costs, and other factors.

Job Corps campuses include dormitories, classrooms, workshops for various trades, wellness (or health) centers, a cafeteria, a career services building, and administrative buildings. Each Job Corps center must develop standards for student conduct and implement a zero tolerance policy for violence and drug and alcohol use. Students are dismissed from the program if they violate this policy. Centers also follow detailed guidelines about all aspects of the program as they are outlined in the Policy and Requirements Handbook.[55]

Services

Students may participate in the Job Corps program for up to two years. While at a Job Corps center, students receive the following services:

- academic, vocational, employment, and social skills training;
- work-based learning, which includes vocational skills training and on-the-job training; and
- counseling and other residential support services, including transportation, child care, a cash clothing allowance or clothing that is needed for participating in the program, and living and other allowances.

Students tend to experience the program in four stages.[56] In the *first phase*, students learn about the program and center through orientation sessions and other outreach efforts conducted by the center and its contractor for outreach and admissions. Students who decide they want to pursue the program and are selected participate in the *second phase,* which emphasizes career preparation, in the first few weeks of the program. Students learn about life at the center and focus on personal responsibility, social skills, and career explanation. Students also receive assessments of their abilities in math and reading, and they work with staff to develop and commit to what is known as a Personal Career Development Plan (PCDP). This plan includes the students' personal, academic, and career goals, which are evaluated as they progress through the program.

The *third phase* focuses on career development and is the stage at which most youth spend the majority of their time in the program. During this period, students learn and demonstrate career technical, academic, and employability skills. Training focuses on academic subject matters and how they are applied to specific trades or occupations. Students who did not graduate from high school can pursue a high school diploma or GED. Most Job Corps centers have developed a high school diploma program for their students through partnerships with public, private, and/or charter schools. Students who have already graduated focus on developing their technical skills at the center and on work sites under the direction of Job Corps' employer partners. Job Corps centers offer several technical training clusters. The clusters that are most commonly offered are construction, business and finance, health care, hospitality, manufacturing, automotive and machine repair, information technology services, renewable resources and energy, retail, and transportation.[57] During this period, students also begin to look for a job and learn how to identify and access the support services that are needed to live independently.

Finally, in the *fourth phase,* students participate in a period of career transition, in which they receive placement services that focus on placing them in full-time jobs that are related to their vocational training and pay wages that allow them to be self-sufficient, or placing them in higher education or advanced training programs, including apprenticeship programs. For one year after exiting the program, graduates must receive services that include transition support and workplace counseling. Some graduates may go on to participate in advanced training. These students continue to remain in the program for another year while obtaining additional training and education, such as an Associate's Degree.

Job Corps centers provide services both on-site and off-site, and contract some of these services. Centers rely on outreach and admissions contractors to recruit students to the program. These contractors may include a one-stop center, community action organizations, private for-profit and nonprofit businesses, labor organizations, or other entities that have contact with youth. Contractors seek out potential applicants, conduct interviews with applicants to identify their needs and eligibility status, and identify youth who are interested and likely Job Corps participants. Similarly, centers rely on placement agencies—organizations that enter into a contract or other agreement with Job Corps—to provide placement services for graduates and, to the extent possible, former students. Services such as vocational training are sometimes provided by outside organizations, such as the Home Builders Institute.

In addition, each Job Corps center must have a business and community liaison designated by the center director to establish relationships with employers, applicable one-stop centers and local boards, and other stakeholders. Each center must also establish an Industry Advisory Council, comprised of employers; representatives of labor organizations, where present, and employees; and Job Corps students and graduates. A majority of the members must be local and distant business owners, chief executives or chief operating officers of non-governmental employers, or other private sector employers, and they must have substantial management and other responsibilities and represent businesses with employment opportunities for youth in the program. The council must work with local WIBs and review local market information to provide recommendations to the center director about the center's education and training offerings, including emerging occupations that would suitable for training.

Finally, each center must establish a Community Relations Council to serve as a liaison between the center and the surrounding communities.[58] The councils are to be comprised of representatives of business, civic, and educational organizations; elected officials; representatives from law enforcement agencies; other service providers; students; and staff. Centers must provide opportunities for students and staff to participate in community service activities on a regular basis.

Participants

Job Corps participants must be ages 16 through 24,[59] low-income, and facing one or more of the following barriers to education and employment: (1) basic skills deficient; (2) homeless, a runaway, or a foster child; (3) a parent; or (4) in need of additional education, vocational training, or intensive counseling and related assistance in order to participate in regular schoolwork or to secure and maintain employment.[60] Notably, the program does not impose an upper age limit for students with disabilities. Job Corps centers take additional factors into consideration when selecting participants, such as whether the program can best meet their educational and vocational needs and whether the youth can engage successfully in group situations and settings. The applicant must also pass a background check that demonstrates he or she is not on probation or parole, or subject to similar findings. When selected for the program, students are usually placed at the site closest to their home. No more than 20% of participants may live off the grounds of the Job Corps center. Priority in non-residential placements is to be given to participants who are single parents.

Allocations

DOL enters into contracts with nonprofit and for-profit organizations, the Department of Agriculture, and the Department of Labor to operate the centers. Contracts are competitively awarded to organizations based on ranked scores, in conjunction with other factors. The contract period is two years, with three one-year-option renewals.

Performance

WIA specifies that Job Corps collect data on 25 measures related to performance and retention in the program. These measures pertain to graduation rates, graduates' entry into full-time or part- time unsubsidized employment, the average wage received by graduates at certain points in time, job retention at select points in time, entry into post-secondary education or advanced training programs, attainment of job readiness and employment skills, and the share of dropouts from the program, among other data. The program also collects information to assess performance through the Common Measures. As explained above, DOL introduced the Common Measures for WIA Title I programs in 2005. The Common Measures for Youth are placement in employment and education, attainment of a degree or certificate, and literacy and numeracy gains.[61] The measures in WIA and the Common Measures are interwoven into the Job Corps' performance management system that is used by the Job Corps Office to evaluate student performance and how well students are served at each of the centers.[62]

YOUTHBUILD[63]

Overview and Purpose[64]

In 2007, YouthBuild was transferred from the Department of Housing and Urban Development to DOL under the YouthBuild Transfer Act (P.L. 109-28 1). The program is authorized under WIA. As stated in the law, the purpose of YouthBuild is to (1) enable disadvantaged youth to obtain the education and employment skills necessary to achieve economic self-sufficiency in occupations in demand and post-secondary education and training opportunities; (2) provide disadvantaged youth with opportunities for meaningful work and service to communities; (3) foster the development of employment and leadership skills and commitment to community development among youth in low-income communities; and (4) expand the supply of permanent affordable housing for homeless individuals and low-income families by utilizing the energy of disadvantaged youth.

Program Structure

DOL competitively awards YouthBuild funds to organizations, which carry out the program in cooperation with subgrantees or contractors or through arrangements made with local education agencies and certain other entities. Entities that are eligible to apply for funding include a public or private nonprofit agency or organization, including a consortium of such agencies or organizations; community-based or faith-based organizations; entities that carry out activities authorized under certain other parts of WIA; community action agencies; state or local housing development agencies; an Indian tribe or agencies primarily serving Indians; state or local youth service or conservation corps; or any other entity eligible to provide education or employment training under a federal program.

While in the program, youth participate in a range of education and workforce investment activities, as listed in **Table 4**. These activities include instruction, skill building, alternative education, mentoring, and training in rehabilitation or construction of housing. Notably, any housing unit that is rehabilitated or reconstructed may be available only for rental by, or sale to, homeless individuals or low-income families; or for use as transitional or permanent housing to assist homeless individuals achieve independent living. In addition to construction activities, programs can support career pathway training targeted toward other high-demand occupations and industries offered within a YouthBuild program. All educational programs, including programs that award academic credit, and activities supported with YouthBuild funds must be consistent with applicable state and local educational standards.

At least 40% of the time, youth must participate in certain work and skill development activities (these activities are denoted by footnote a in **Table 4**). At least an additional 50% of the time, participants must be engaged in education and related services and activities designed to meet their educational needs (these activities are denoted by footnote b in **Table 4**). Youth are offered positions in the program for a period of six months to two years, and are provided with a year of follow-up services.

Table 4. Eligible Activities Funded by YouthBuild

Education and Workforce Investment Activities, Generally
• Work experience and skills training, coordinated, to the maximum extent feasible, with pre-apprenticeship and registered apprenticeship programs, in the rehabilitation and construction activities (see below).[a]   • Occupational skills training.[a]   • Other paid and unpaid work experiences, including internships and job shadowing.a   • Services and activities designed to meet the educational needs of participants, including skills instruction and remedial education, language instruction educational programs for individuals with limited English proficiency, assistance in obtaining postsecondary education and required financial aid, and alternative secondary school services.[b]   • Counseling services and related activities.[b]   • Activities designed to develop employment and leadership skills, including community service and peer-centered activities encouraging responsibility and other positive social behaviors, and activities related to youth policy committees that participate in decision-making related to the program.[b]   • Supportive services and provision of need-based stipends to enable individuals to participate in the program, and supportive services to assist individuals, for a period not to exceed 12 months after the completion of training, in obtaining or retaining employment, or applying for and transitioning to postsecondary education.[b]   • Job search assistance.[a]
Rehabilitation or Construction of Housing
• Supervision and training for participants in the rehabilitation or construction of housing, including residential housing for homeless individuals or low-income families, or transitional housing for homeless individuals.   • Supervision and training for participants in the rehabilitation or construction of community and other public facilities, except that not more than 10% of funds appropriated to carry out this section may be used for such supervision and training.
Administrative Costs
• Payment of administrative costs of the applicant, except that not more than 15% of the amount of assistance provided under this subsection to the grant recipient may be used for such costs.
Other
• Adult mentoring.   • Provision of wages, stipends, or benefits to participants in the program.   • Ongoing training and technical assistance that is related to developing and carrying out the program.   • Leadership development opportunities, which may include, but are not limited to, community service and peer-centered activities encouraging responsibility and other positive social behaviors during non-school hours, as appropriate; community and service learning projects; organizational and teamwork training, including team leadership training; and citizenship training, including life skills training such as parenting, work behavior training, and budgeting of resources, among other activities.   • Follow-up services.

Source: Congressional Research Service, based on Section 1 73A of the Workforce Investment Act of 1998.

a. This activity counts toward the requirement that at least 40% of the time, youth must participate in certain work and skill development activities.

b. This activity counts toward the requirement that at least 50% of the time, youth must participate in education and related services and activities.

Participants

Youth are eligible for the program if they are (1) ages 16 through 24; (2) a member of a low- income family, a youth in foster care, a youth offender, an individual with a disability, a child of incarcerated parents, *or* a migrant youth; *and* (3) a school dropout.[65] However, up to 25% of youth in the program are not required to meet the income or dropout criteria, so long as they are basic skills deficient despite having earned a high school diploma, GED, or the equivalent; *or* have been referred by a high school for the purpose of obtaining a high school diploma.

Allocations

Grants are competitively awarded to organizations based on ranked scores, in conjunction with other factors, such as the applicant's potential for developing a successful YouthBuild program; the need for the program in the community; the applicant's commitment to providing skills training, leadership development, and education to participants; regional distribution of grantees; and the applicant's coordination of activities to be carried out with certain other stakeholders, including employers, one-stop partners, and national service and other systems; among other criteria.

DOL makes awards for three years (two years of program operations with a one-year period of follow-up). Awards range from approximately $700,000 to $1.2 million annually.[66] Applicants must provide cash or in-kind resources equivalent to at least 25% of the grant award amount as matching funds. Prior investments and federal resources do not count toward the match.

Performance

YouthBuild grantees report the Common Measures and two additional performance measures for all youth in the program through a management information system (MIS) designed specifically for the program.[67] The two other measures are retention in employment or education and recidivism. Retention in employment and education tracks the share of young people who are employed or in an educational placement for each of the three quarters after exiting. The recidivism measure tracks the share of youth arrested and convicted of a new crime or parole violation within one year of enrollment.

REINTEGRATION OF EX-OFFENDERS[68]

Overview and Purpose

Section 171 of WIA authorizes DOL to conduct pilot and demonstration programs. The purpose of these programs is to develop and evaluate innovative approaches to providing employment and training services. In recent years, two programs have been specified in appropriations language and funded under the authority of Section 171. One of the programs—Reintegration of ExOffenders—is targeted, in part, to youth. The youth component of the program is known as the Youthful Offender program. (Other, shorter-term programs that do not focus on youth offenders, per se, but do specifically target vulnerable youth have also been funded, as described in the text box below.) The Youthful Offender program is comprised of related initiatives that seek to assist youth and young adults returning from prison or juvenile justice facilities with pre-release, mentoring, housing, case management, and employment services; to reduce violence within persistently dangerous schools through a combination of mentoring, educational, employment, case management, and violence prevention strategies; and to provide alternative education and related services for youth at risk of involvement with the justice system.[69]

The Youthful Offender program has operated under WIA since FY2000.[70] The program was a stand-alone program until FY2008, when it was made a part of the Reintegration of Ex-Offenders program. It also supports the Prisoner Reentry Initiative (PRI) for adults. Funding for the program is authorized under both WIA and Section 112 (Responsible Reintegration of Offenders) of the Second Chance Act (P.L. 110-199), enacted on April 9, 2008. The Second Chance Act authorizes DOL to make grants to nonprofit organizations for the purpose of providing mentoring, job training and job placement services, and other comprehensive transitional services to assist eligible offenders ages 18 and older in obtaining and retaining employment. DOL is currently conducting a review of current grants for ex-offender programs, and plans to work with the Department of Justice to carry out programs for ex-offenders.[71]

Program Structure

The earliest Youthful Offender initiatives, from FY1999 through FY2004, operated under what is known as the Youth Offender Demonstration Project (YODP).[72] The pilot funded 52 grantees to assist youth at risk of court or gang involvement, youth offenders, and gang members ages 14 to 24 in finding long-term employment. The more contemporary Youthful Offender program has funded five types of projects in recent years that have a focus similar to the earlier projects under YODP. Recent projects have included the School District Youth Offender Initiative; Persistently Dangerous Schools Initiative; Categorical Grants (Youth Offender Registered Apprenticeship, Alternative Education, and Project Expansion Grants); Beneficiary-Choice Demonstration; High Growth Youth Offender Initiative; and Planning, State/Local Implementation, and Replication Grants. Grantees include local and state governments, nonprofit organizations, including faith- based organizations; school districts; and community colleges.[73] These programs have been funded in at least one year since PY2006.[74] The projects are grouped below based on their focus. While the projects each have a distinct purpose, their overall aim is to provide employment and other assistance to youth who are involved in the justice system, or are at risk of becoming involved.

Education

The School District Youth Offender Initiative, also known as the School District Gang Reduction grants, intends to develop strategies for reducing youth involvement in gangs using a workforce development approach. The initiative is aimed at helping five public school districts—Baltimore; Chicago; Milwaukee; Orange County, FL; and Philadelphia—reduce the involvement of youth in gangs and violent crimes. Grant funds can be used for a range of education and employment interventions for youth who are involved, have been involved, or have a high risk of being involved in gangs or the juvenile justice system. Youth are eligible if they are in school and in grades 8-12, or are high school dropouts under the age of 21. School districts are required to partner with the local juvenile justice system, the mayor's office, the local WIB, the police department, and the U.S. Attorney's office in carrying out the program.

The Persistently Dangerous Schools Initiative provides funding to three school districts—Berkshire Union Free School District in Canaan, NY; Baltimore; and Philadelphia—to improve outcomes of students in nine high schools that have been identified as persistently dangerous by the states' department of education, pursuant to the Elementary and Secondary Education Act. The grants fund a combination of new initiatives at each school, including reduced class size in core 9th and 11th grade English and math, which have a history of high rates of failure; a mentoring program using adult and peer mentors; career academies with particular themes; and a summer bridge program with remediation in English and math.

Apprenticeships, Alternative Education, and Expansion Grants

The Categorical Grants project funds programs that provide apprenticeship opportunities and alternative education to youth who have been adjudicated (i.e., cases have been judicially determined) or are at risk of involvement in the justice system. The programs with apprenticeship opportunities prepare young adult offenders for in-demand careers in fields such as construction, welding, masonry, and advanced manufacturing. Programs with an alternative education focus are creating or enhancing schools to help young offenders earn diplomas and continue on to postsecondary education or jobs. Some grantees received funding to expand their programs to additional sites because of their records of successfully providing assistance to juvenile offenders. Grantees include state departments of corrections, schools boards, and nonprofit organizations.

Reentry[75]

The Beneficiary Choice Demonstration has provided funding to grantees to assist ex-offenders ages 18 through 29 transition from prison to the workplace. Participants may choose service providers from pools of faith-based and community groups. The grantees include the Arizona Women's Education and Employment, Inc., of Phoenix; the Colorado Department of Labor and Employment; the City of Chicago; the Indianapolis Private Industry Council, Inc.; and the Director's Council of Des Moines, IA. For example, Colorado's project focuses on delivering individualized, comprehensive offender reentry strategies through partners such as the Department of Corrections, Salvation Army, Grant Valley Catholic Outreach, one-stop centers, and Goodwill, among other entities. The project offers mentoring, counseling, housing, education, and training and employment opportunities in industries with high growth.[76] The project is working to increase its network to include all organizations that choose to provide offender services.

The High Growth Youth Offender Initiative has funded efforts to help former offenders gain the skills necessary to enter industries with high growth. Projects have focused on addressing the workforce needs of growing industries that provide employment opportunities and potential for advancement. Among the grantees are nonprofit organizations and workforce boards.

Finally, the Planning, State/Local Implementation and Replication Grants have funded four state juvenile justice agencies in the District of Columbia, Maryland, Texas, and Washington to serve all youth returning from juvenile correctional facilities to one county in the state; five counties to develop plans for serving all youth returning from correctional facilities to the local area; and YouthBuild Newark to develop YouthBuild programs serving juvenile offenders in four additional cities in New Jersey.

FOSTER CARE YOUTH DEMONSTRATION PROJECT

DOL awarded demonstration grants in 2005 and 2006 to five states—California, Illinois, Michigan, New York, and Texas—to design and implement programs to improve the self sufficiency, education attainment, and employment skills of youth aging out of foster care. The purpose of the grant, known as the Foster Care Youth Demonstration Project, was to encourage states to develop best practices around serving foster youth in the workforce investment system, and to integrate these practices across the state. The five states were required to target the programs to youth in areas with the largest foster care populations. DOL awarded each state $800,000 total; states were required to provide 100% matching funds. The programs served over 1,000 youth.

Source: Congressional Research Service, based on Institute for Educational Leadership, Foster Care Youth Demonstration Project, *Final Evaluation Report, Executive Summary*, July 2008.

Participants

Each of the initiatives targets select groups of at-risk youth. However, the projects generally serve youth ages 14 and older (or 18 or older) who have been involved with or have a high risk of involvement in gangs or the juvenile justice system, or attend "persistently dangerous" schools, as reported by select states.

Allocations

Grants are competitively awarded to entities based on ranked scores and other factors, depending on the project. Notably, only schools that meet the criteria of "persistently dangerous," as specified by the states and as permitted under the Elementary and Secondary Education Act (ESEA), are eligible to apply for funds under the Persistently Dangerous Schools Initiative.[77] Allocations vary for each of the projects, but, generally, grantees have received grants of $1 million to $5 million for one or more years.

Performance

DOL has performance measures for each Youth Offender initiative. The standards vary for each initiative depending on the focus of the grants and the population of youth served. However, the program has uniform measures for the program overall: (1) percentage of youth ages 18 and older entering employment or enrolling in post-secondary education, the military, or advanced training/occupational skills training; (2) percentage of youth offenders ages 14 through 17 who recidivate; and (3) percentage of youth offenders ages 18 and older who recidivate.[78]

MULTIPLE EDUCATION PATHWAYS BLUEPRINT

The Multiple Education Pathways Blueprint is a one-time grant program funded under WIA's pilot and demonstration authority. In FY2007, DOL provided $3.4 million to seven midsize cities "to 'blueprint' and implement a system that can reconnect youth [who have dropped out of high school] to a variety of high quality, innovative multiple education pathways." Each city has built a partnership among multiple stakeholders to study the scope of the dropout problem, map the service and resources in their community, and assess efforts to reform high schools. Partners are currently planning or pilot testing new approaches to education, including identifying youth at risk of dropping out, launching new supports during the summer or first semester of high school, offering Saturday school programs that get youth back on track with their peers, and providing sector-based education and training programs.

Source: U.S. Department of Labor, Employment and Training Administration, Multiple Education
    Pathways Initiative.

YOUTH OPPORTUNITY GRANTS

Overview and Purpose

The Youth Opportunity Grants program was funded from FY1999 through FY2003, and operated until 2005. As stated in WIA, the program was intended to provide employment, educational, and youth development activities to increase the long-term employment of youth who live in enterprise communities, empowerment zones, and high-poverty areas and who seek assistance. By definition, enterprise communities and empowerment zones are in low-income areas. The program enrolled 92,263 participants over the course of the grant period, of whom 52.7% were female; 51.9% were in school and 48.1% were out of school; and 58.9% were black, 22.4% Hispanic, and 11.2% American Indian or Native Alaskan. At enrollment, just over half of all participants were attending school (54.3%). This is compared to 68.3% of youth in the community overall who were attending school.

Program Structure

YOG funds were awarded to 36 communities, 24 in urban areas, six in rural areas, and six on tribal lands.[79] A local WIB was eligible to receive funding if it had been designated as an empowerment zone or enterprise community; was in a state without such a zone or community and was designated as a high-poverty area by the governor; or was one of two areas in a state designated by the governor as areas for which a local board could apply for the grant and that met certain poverty guidelines. Entities other than a local board were eligible to receive funding if they were a recipient under WIA's Native American programs (Section 136); served a community that met certain poverty guidelines; and were located on an Indian reservation or served Oklahoma Indians or Alaska Native villages or Native groups.

According to a December 2005 report by GAO about the YOG program, recipients of the funds included states, local WIBs, counties, cities, and other entities. These entities either provided services directly to youth, or entered into contracts with organizations. As required under WIA, grantees were required to provide a broad range of education, employment, and other related activities that are currently provided under WIA Youth Activities (see Table 2). In addition, grantees were required to implement youth development activities that addressed leadership development, citizenship and community service, and recreational activities.

The programs were carried out at centers in each community. YOG communities had as few as one or as many as 40 centers.[80] Centers included at least a couple of the following amenities: classrooms, recreational facilities, computer labs, career centers, health centers, and staff offices. Some centers operated out of local high schools. At least one of the programs established a charter school to provide alternative educational services to youth, while another had a recording studio for youth to record music. Program staff included case managers to help identify youth's needs and connect them to services and activities, as well as employment specialists to help youth look for, secure, and retain employment or help them transition to college. Program staff also followed up with youth. WIA required grantees to provide intensive placement services, as well as follow-up services for not less than two years after the youth completed the program.

A key feature of YOG was the networks that the grantees created in each community. According to the GAO report, the networks were often comprised of educational, occupational, and other providers for youth services. The networks were facilitated by formal arrangements among the partners and referrals to other organizations, such as those that provided GED preparation and clothing for interviews. Some participants at some of the centers had the opportunity to enroll part time at a community college to earn academic credit. Partners also provided referrals to the grantees.

Participants

Unlike other youth programs authorized under WIA, youth could participate in the YOG program as long as they lived in a community receiving funds. Therefore, youth did not have to show that they met income and other eligibility criteria.

Allocations

Funds were awarded to communities for a one-year period, with renewals in each of the four succeeding years. WIA required that grants were distributed equitably among local boards and other entities serving urban and rural areas, taking into account the poverty rate in these areas. Grant applicants were required to describe how the activities carried out at the YOG center(s) would be linked to the activities under the WIA Youth Activities program and the type of community support for the activities, among other requirements.

Performance Measures

As specified under Section 167(f) of WIA, DOL set performance measures for the Youth Opportunity grants and negotiated with grantees on the levels expected to be achieved for each measure. The performance measures included a completion rate, placement rate, retention rate, participation rate, and enrollment rates for in-school and for out-of-school youth.

APPENDIX A. WORKFORCE INVESTMENT ACT FUNDING FOR YOUTH PROGRAMS

Table A- 1. WIA Youth Activities State Allotments, PY2008-PY2010, Plus Funding Under the American Recovery and Reinvestment Act (ARRA, P.L. 111-5)

State	PY2008 (P.L. 110-161)	ARRA (P.L. 111-5)	PY2009 (P.L. 111-8)	PY2010 (P.L. 111-117)
Total	$924,069,465	$1,188,000,000[a]	$924,069,000	$924,069,000
Alabama	10,066,414	11,647,403	9,059,768	11,777,698
Alaska	3,401,753	3,936,018	3,061,576	2,755,418
Arizona	15,410,351	17,830,637	13,869,309	15,982,731
Arkansas	10,427,807	12,065,555	9,385,022	8,446,520
California	131,478,160	186,622,034	145,161,310	136,875,948
Colorado	10,263,091	11,874,970	9,236,777	11,132,070
Connecticut	7,422,406	11,034,723	8,583,204	8,869,254
Delaware	2,269,746	2,918,025	2,269,744	2,269,744
District of Columbia	3,430,967	3,969,821	3,087,869	2,779,082
Florida	25,652,600	42,873,265	33,348,363	43,352,872
Georgia	20,223,508	31,361,665	24,394,229	28,251,785
Hawaii	2,404,095	2,918,025	2,269,744	2,690,193
Idaho	2,290,478	2,918,025	2,269,744	2,950,667
Illinois	41,245,377	62,203,400	48,384,035	43,545,632
Indiana	20,463,638	23,677,573	18,417,265	19,697,136
Iowa	4,091,704	5,172,183	4,023,109	4,750,212
Kansas	6,155,030	7,121,714	5,539,524	5,930,458
Kentucky	14,567,756	17,709,821	13,775,333	14,303,105
Louisiana	17,295,855	20,012,271	15,566,262	14,009,636
Maine	3,280,785	4,293,710	3,339,802	3,476,520

Table A-1 (Continued)

Maryland	10,013,008	11,585,610	9,011,703	11,311,383
Massachusetts	21,466,585	24,838,038	19,319,917	17,387,925
Michigan	57,931,951	73,949,491	57,520,566	51,768,509
Minnesota	10,984,461	17,789,172	13,837,056	14,264,509
Mississippi	15,536,771	18,687,021	14,535,436	13,081,892
Missouri	19,654,610	25,400,077	19,757,091	17,781,382
Montana	2,269,746	2,918,025	2,269,744	2,344,418
Nebraska	2,544,921	2,944,616	2,290,428	2,518,508
Nevada	4,529,527	7,570,212	5,888,382	7,654,897
New Hampshire	2,269,746	2,918,025	2,269,744	2,269,744
New Jersey	16,249,272	20,834,103	16,205,512	20,938,294
New Mexico	5,389,263	6,235,678	4,850,334	4,365,301
New York	54,654,801	71,526,360	55,635,768	51,835,670
North Carolina	19,061,803	25,070,698	19,500,888	25,351,154
North Dakota	2,269,746	2,918,025	2,269,744	2,269,744
Ohio	48,535,694	56,158,510	43,682,103	39,313,893
Oklahoma	7,526,029	8,708,036	6,773,423	6,970,582
Oregon	13,022,777	15,068,081	11,720,493	13,707,810
Pennsylvania	32,746,691	40,647,780	31,617,301	31,871,328
Puerto Rico	36,693,982	42,456,987	33,024,567	29,722,110
Rhode Island	3,357,319	5,611,097	4,364,513	4,531,698
South Carolina	21,357,908	24,712,293	19,222,108	17,299,897
South Dakota	2,269,746	2,918,025	2,269,744	2,269,744
Tennessee	19,653,705	25,099,116	19,522,993	18,716,506
Texas	70,870,137	82,000,708	63,783,091	57,404,782
Utah	4,379,351	5,067,154	3,941,414	3,547,273
Vermont	2,269,746	2,918,025	2,269,744	2,269,744
Virginia	9,462,211	12,982,612	10,098,341	13,127,843
Washington	20,263,008	23,445,432	18,236,698	17,997,280
West Virginia	4,618,029	5,343,318	4,156,224	3,924,261
Wisconsin	11,934,438	13,808,812	10,740,989	13,963,286
Wyoming	2,269,746	2,918,025	2,269,744	2,269,744
State Total	907,898,249	1,167,210,000	907,897,792	907,897,792
American Samoa	131,813	170,030	131,813	131,813
Guam	1,072,924	1,383,998	1,072,924	1,072,924
Northern Mariana Islands	397,036	512,149	397,035	397,035
Palau	75,000	86,779	75,000	75,000
Virgin Islands	633,401	817,044	633,401	633,401
Outlying Areas Total	2,310,174	2,970,000	2,310,173	2,310,173

Source: Congressional Research Service presentation of U.S. Department of Labor, Employment and Training Administration, *State Statutory Formula Funding*, available at http://www.doleta .gov/budget/statfund.cfm.

Note: The program year for Youth Activities is July 1 through June 30, although funds may be made available on April 1, pursuant to Section 1 89(g)(1)(B) of the Workforce Investment Act. Funds for the program are available for two program years, including funds appropriated under ARRA. ARRA funds are available for two program years—PY2009 and PY2010, which extends through June 30, 2011. For purposes of the summer youth component, youth may participate in summer activities from May 1 through September 30, though it would appear that youth could participate only through the end of June in 2011.

a. ARRA appropriated $1.2 billion for the Youth Activities program. Section 801 of ARRA permits DOL to use 1% ($12 million) of funds for administration, management, and oversight of the program.

APPENDIX B. DEFINITIONS OF TERMS USED IN WIA YOUTH PROGRAMS

- *Advanced training* refers to an occupational skills employment/training program, not funded under Title I of WIA, that does not duplicate training received under Title I. It includes only training outside of the one-stop, WIA, and partner system (i.e., training following exit). This measure is used as part of WIA statutory youth measures. (Training and Employment Guidance Letter 17-05, Attachment B, February 17, 2006.)

- *Advanced training/occupational skills training* refers to an organized program of study that provides specific vocational skills that lead to proficiency in performing actual tasks and technical functions required by certain occupational fields at entry, intermediate, or advanced levels. Such training should (1) be outcome-oriented and focused on a long-term goal as specified in the Individual Service Strategy, (2) be long-term in nature and commence upon program exit rather than being short-term training that is part of services received while enrolled in ETA-funded youth programs, and (3) result in attainment of a certificate (defined below). This measure is used as part of WIA youth common measures. (Training and Employment Guidance Letter 17-05, Attachment B, February 17, 2006.)

- *Basic skills goal* refers to a measurable increase in basic education skills, including reading comprehension, math computation, writing, speaking, listening, problem solving, reasoning, and the capacity to use those skills. This measure is used as part of WIA statutory youth measures. (Training and Employment Guidance Letter 17-05, Attachment B, February 17, 2006.)

- *Certificate* refers to a document awarded in recognition of an individual's attainment of measureable technical or occupational skills necessary to gain employment or advance within an occupation. These technical or occupational skills are based on standards developed or endorsed by employers. Certificates awarded by workforce investment boards are not included in this definition. Work readiness certificates are also not included in this definition. A certificate is awarded in recognition of an individual's attainment or technical or occupational skills by specified entities, such as a professional, industry, or employment organization, Job Corps Centers, etc. This measure is used as part of WIA youth Common Measures. (Training and Employment Guidance Letter 17-05, Attachment B, February 17, 2006.)

- *Credential* refers to a nationally recognized degree or certificate or state/locally recognized credential. Credentials include, but are not limited to, a high school diploma, GED, or other recognized equivalents, post-secondary degrees/certificates, recognized skill standards, and licensure or industry- recognized certificates. States should include all state education agency- recognized credentials. In addition, states should work with local workforce investment boards to recognize successful completion of the training services listed above that are designed to equip individuals to enter or re-enter employment, retain employment, or advance into better employment. This measure is used as part of WIA youth statutory measures. (Training and Employment Guidance Letter 17-05, Attachment B, February 17, 2006.)

- *Deficient in basic literacy skills* may be defined at the state or local level. The definition must include criteria to determine that an individual (1) computes or solves problems, reads, writes, or speaks English at or below the 8th grade level on a generally accepted standardized test or would receive a comparable score on a criterion-referenced test, or (2) is unable to compute or solve problems, read, write, or speak English at a level necessary to function on the job, in the individual's family, or in society. If the definition is established at the state level, the policy must be included in the state plan. (20 C.F.R. 664.205).
- *Ever in foster care* refers to a person who is in foster care or has been in the foster care system (as defined in WIASRD Data Book, Appendix B).
- *Individual with a disability* refers to an individual with any disability as defined in section 3 of the Americans with Disabilities Act of 1990. The act defines "disability" with respect to an individual as (1) a physical or mental impairment that substantially limits one or more major life activities of such individual; (2) having a record of such an impairment; or (3) being regarded as having such an impairment. "Being regarded as having such an impairment" refers to whether the individual establishes that he or she has been subjected to an action prohibited under the Americans with Disabilities Act because of an actual or perceived physical or mental impairment, whether or not the impairment limits or is perceived to limit a major life activity.

  Low-income individual means an individual who:
  (1) receives, or is a member of a family that receives, cash payments through a federal, state, or local income-based public assistance program;
  (2) received an income, or is a member of a family that received a total family income (excluding unemployment compensation and certain other payments), for the six-month period prior to applying for youth employment and training activities, that, in relation to family size, did not exceed the higher of the poverty line, for an equivalent period, or 70% of the lower living standard income level, for an equivalent period;
  (3) is a member of a household that receives food stamps[81] (or has been determined to be eligible for food stamps within the six-month period prior to applying for youth employment and training activities);
  (4) qualifies as a homeless individual, as defined by the McKinney-Vento Homeless Assistance Act; or
  (5) is a foster child on behalf of whom state or local government payments are made.

  In cases permitted by DOL in regulations, an individual with a disability, whose own income meets the standards specified in the first two criteria but who is a member of a family whose income does not meet such requirements, may qualify (WIA Section (101)(25)).
- *Occupational skills goal* refers to a measurable increase in primary occupational skills encompassing the proficiency to perform actual tasks and technical functions required by certain occupational fields at entry, intermediate, or advanced levels. Secondary occupational skills entail familiarity with and use of set-up procedures, safety measures, work-related terminology, record keeping and paperwork formats, tools, equipment and materials, and breakdown and clean-up routines. This measure

is used as part of WIA statutory youth measures. (Training and Employment Guidance Letter 17-05, Attachment B, February 17, 2006.)

- *Out-of-school youth* means a youth eligible for services under Youth Activities who is a school dropout; or an eligible youth who has received a secondary school diploma or its equivalent but is basic skills deficient, unemployed, or underemployed (WIA Section (101)(33) and 20 C.F.R. 664.300).

- *Offender* means any adult or juvenile who (1) is or has been subject to any stage of the criminal justice process, for whom services under this act may be beneficial; or (2) requires assistance in overcoming artificial barriers to employment resulting from a record of arrest or conviction (WIA Section (101)(27)).

- *Pregnant or parenting youth* is an individual who is under 22 years of age and pregnant, or a youth (male or female) who is providing custodial care for one or more dependents under age 18 (as defined in WIASRD Data Book, Appendix B).

- *Requires additional assistance* refers to an individual who needs help in completing an educational program or securing and holding employment. The term may be defined at the state or local level. If the definition is established at the state level, the policy must be included in the state plan (20 C.F.R. 664.2 10).

- *School dropout* refers to an individual who is no longer attending any school and has not received a high school diploma or its equivalent. A youth's dropout status is determined at the time he or she registers for youth activities. An individual who is not in school at the time of registration and is subsequently placed in an alternative school may be considered an *out-of-school youth.*

- *Supportive services* means services such as transportation, child care, dependent care, housing, and needs-related payments that are necessary to enable an individual to participate in services provided by the Youth Activities program and other programs authorized under Title I of WIA. In addition, supportive services for youth also includes linkages to community services, referrals to medical services, and assistance with uniforms or other appropriate work attire and work- related tools, including such items as eyeglasses and protective eye gear (Section 10 1(46) of WIA, and as defined in WIASRD Data Book, Appendix B).

- *Work readiness skills goal* refers to a measurable increase in work readiness skills, including world-of-work awareness, labor market knowledge, occupational information, values clarification and personal understanding, career planning and decision making, and job search techniques (resumes, interviews, applications, and follow-up letters). They also encompass survival/daily living skills such as using the phone, telling time, shopping, renting an apartment, opening a bank account, and using public transportation; and include positive work habits, attitudes, and behaviors such as punctuality, regular attendance, presenting a neat appearance, getting along and working well with others, exhibiting good conduct, following instructions and completing tasks, accepting criticism from supervisors and co-workers, showing initiative and reliability, and assuming the responsibilities involved in maintaining a job. This category also entails developing motivation and adaptability, obtaining effective coping and problem-solving skills, and acquiring an improved self image. This measure is used as part of WIA statutory youth measures. (Training and Employment Guidance Letter 17-05, Attachment B, February 17, 2006.)

End Notes

[1] Andrew Sum, Joseph McLaughlin, and Sheila Palma, *The Collapse of the Nation's Male Teen and Young Adult Labor Market, 2000-2009: The Lost Generation of Young Male Workers*, Center for Labor Market Studies, Northeastern University, prepared for C.S. Mott Foundation, July 2009, http://www.nyec.org/content/documents/ThecollapseoftheNation'sMaleTeenandYoungAdult.pdf. (Hereafter, Sum, McLaughlin, and Palma, *The Collapse of the Nation's Male Teen and Young Adult Labor Market, 2000-2009.*) See also U.S. Department of Labor, Bureau of Labor Statistics, *The Employment Situation*, http://www.bls.gov/schedule/archives/empsit_nr.htm.

[2] Ibid.

[3] Andrew Sum et al., The Historically Low Summer and Year Round Teen Employment Rate: The Case for an Immediate National Public Policy Response to Create Jobs for the Nation's Youth, Center for Labor Market Studies, Northeastern University, September 15, 2008, http://www.nyec.org/content/documents/The_Historically_Low_Summer_2008_Teen_Employment_Rate.pdf. (Hereafter, Sum et al., The Historically Low Summer and Year Round Teen Employment Rate.)

[4] Ibid.

[5] Sum, McLaughlin, and Palma, *The Collapse of the Nation's Male Teen and Young Adult Labor Market, 2000-2009.*

[6] The average freshman graduation rate (AFGR) is an estimate of the percentage of an entering public school freshman class graduating in four years. For the most recent school years, the AFGR has been about 75%. Of the 25% of youth who do not graduate in four years, some continue in school because they have a learning disability or for other reasons; however, many of these youth drop out, with some returning to school at a later time while they are working or are idle. U.S. Department of Education, National Center for Education Statistics, *Dropout and Completion Rates in the United States: 2006*, Table 13, September 2008, http://nces.ed.gov/pubs2008/dropout06/.

[7] Ibid, Table 8.

[8] Ibid.

[9] CRS Report R40535, *Disconnected Youth: A Look at 16- to 24-Year Olds Who Are Not Working or In School*, by Adrienne L. Fernandes and Thomas Gabe.

[10] Ibid.

[11] For further information about the challenges certain groups of youth face while making the transition to adulthood, see CRS Report RL33975, *Vulnerable Youth: Background and Policies*, by Adrienne L. Fernandes.

[12] Peter J. Pecora et al., *Improving Foster Family Care: Findings from the Northwest Foster Care Alumni Study*, Casey Family Programs, 2005, http://www.casey.org/Resources/Publications/ImprovingFamilyFosterCare.htm.

[13] CRS Report RS22792, *Education Matters: Earnings and Employment Outcomes by Educational Attainment*, by Linda Levine. This chapter also discusses changes in wages based on educational attainment from 1980 onward. It shows that the wage premium of workers with bachelor's degrees compared to workers with lower levels of education has grown over this period.

[14] Unless otherwise noted, this section draws heavily on an archived report by the Congressional Research Service, *Youth Employment: A Summary History of Major Federal Programs*, 1933-1976. Available upon request.

[15] John H. Bremner, Tamara K. Hareven, and Robert M. Mennel, eds., *Children & Youth in America*, Vol. II: 1866-1932, Parts 1-6 (Cambridge, MA: Harvard University Press, 1971), pp. 687-749.

[16] Much of this section on YEDPA was drawn from Charles L. Betsey, Robinson G. Hollister, and Mary R. Papageorgiou, eds., *Youth Employment and Training Programs: The YEDPA Years*, National Research Council, Washington, DC, 1985, http://www.eric.ed.gov/ERICWebPortal/custom/portlets/recordDetails/detailmini.jsp?_nfpb=true&_&ERICExtSearch_SearchValue_0=ED265245&ERICExtSearch_SearchType_0=no&accno=ED265245. (Hereafter, Betsey, Hollister, and Papageorgiou, *Youth Employment and Training Programs.*)

[17] A fourth, the Young Adult Conservation Corps (YACC), was operated by the Department of Agriculture and Department of the Interior, in cooperation with DOL, and targeted unemployed youth ages 16 to 23 who were not necessarily disadvantaged. This program operated year-round and was separate from a similarly named program, the Youth Conservation Corps (YCC). YCC was permanently authorized by the Youth Conservation Corps Act of 1970 (P.L. 91-378) and continues to operate.

[18] Other parts of YEDPA required close coordination with the school system. According to an assessment of the act's implementation, the schools maintained their focus on in-school youth and provided essentially the same set of educational services as usual. The lack of influence of YEDPA on schools may be largely attributed to the schools' resistance to allocating services according to income and the schools' perception that their mission was exclusively to educate students. Betsey, Hollister, and Papageorgiou, *Youth Employment and Training Programs*, pp. 84-87.

[19] Unless otherwise noted, this section was drawn heavily from an archived report by the Congressional Research Service, *The Job Training Partnership Act: A Compendium of Programs*. Available upon request.

[20] Archived report by the Congressional Research Service, *Job Training Partnership Act: Legislation and Budget Issues*. Available upon request.

[21] Archived report by the Congressional Research Service, *The School-to-Work Opportunities Act*. Available upon request.

[22] For further information about the Adult and Dislocated Worker programs, see CRS Report RL33687, *The Workforce Investment Act (WIA): Program-by-Program Overview and Funding of Title I Training Programs*, by David H. Bradley.

[23] The Office of Job Corps is being transferred from the Office of the Secretary to ETA pursuant to the Consolidated Appropriations Act, 2010 (P.L. 111-117).

[24] U.S. Department of Labor, Employment and Training Administration, *YouthBuild General Program Questions*, http://www.doleta.gov/youth_services/youthbuild/Updated_05_29_07/REVISED%20YouthBuild%20General %20Program%20Questions%206-13-07.pdf.

[25] U.S. Department of Labor, Employment and Training Administration, Training and Employment Guidance Letter No. 3-04 ("The Employment and Training Administration's (ETA's) new strategic vision to serve out-of-school and at-risk youth under the Workforce Investment Act (WIA)"), July 16, 2004.

[26] U.S. Department of Labor, Employment and Training Administration, "Shared Youth Vision, Mission and Objectives," http://www.doleta.gov/ryf/whitehousereport/vmo.cfm.

[27] Congress may sometimes choose to appropriate funds even after the expiration of the funding authorization.

[28] Section 173(h)(2), which pertains to authorization for YouthBuild, states that notwithstanding Section 189(g), appropriations for any fiscal year for programs and activities carried out under this section are to be available for obligation only on the basis of a fiscal year.

[29] Funds obligated for any program year for a pilot or demonstration program (Section 171) are to remain available until expended.

[30] Title I, Chapter 4 of the Workforce Investment Act and 20 CFR 664.

[31] The word "relative" as used in this chapter means the number of individuals in a state compared to the total number in all states.

[32] Under WIA, of the funds appropriated for Youth Activities, not more than 0.25% is reserved for outlying areas and not more than 1.5% is reserved for Youth Activities for Native Americans. The remainder of funds are allocated to states by a formula based one-third on the relative number of unemployed individuals residing in areas of substantial unemployment (an unemployment rate of at least 6.5%), one-third on the relative "excess" number of unemployed individuals (an unemployment rate more than 4.5%), and one-third on the relative number of low-income youth. Section 127(b) of WIA.

[33] Alternatively, a state may distribute to local areas a portion equal to not less than 70% of the funds they would have received using the employment and poverty factors, with the remaining portion of funds allocated on the basis of a formula that incorporates additional factors relating to excess youth poverty in urban, rural, and suburban local areas and excess unemployment above the state average in these areas. Such a formula must be developed by the state WIB and approved by the DOL Secretary as part of the state plan. Section 128(b)(3) of WIA.

[34] The report found that in-school youth were most likely to receive services through—in this order—community organizations, secondary schools, colleges or universities, youth one-stop centers, adult one-stop centers, and other providers, such as local or state governments. Out-of-school youth were most likely to receive services through—in this order—community organizations, colleges or universities, secondary schools, adult one-stop centers, youth adult one-stop centers, and other providers, such as local or state governments. U.S. General Accounting Office, *Workforce Investment Act: Labor Actions Can Help States Improve Quality of Performance Outcome Data and Delivery of Youth Services*, GAO-04-308, February 2004, pp. 17-19. (GAO is now know as the Government Accountability Office.) (Hereafter, Government Accountability Office, *Workforce Investment Act: Labor Actions Can Help States Improve Quality of Performance Outcome Data and Delivery of Youth Services*, February 2004.)

[35] U.S. Department of Labor, Employment and Training Administration, Training and Employment Guidance Letter (TEGL) No. 9-00, ("Workforce Investment Act of 1998, Section 129—Competitive and Non-competitive Procedures for Providing Youth Activities Under Title I"), January 31, 2001; and U.S. Department of Labor, Employment and Training Administration, Training and Employment Guidance Letter (TEGL) No. 16-00 ("Availability of Funds to Support Planning Projects that Enhance Youth Connections and Access to the One-Stop System"), March 19, 2001. (Hereafter, U.S. Department of Labor, Employment and Training Administration, TEGL No. 16-00, March 19, 2001.)

[36] U.S. Department of Labor, Employment and Training Administration, Training and Employment Guidance Letter No. 16-00, March 19, 2001.

[37] U.S. General Accounting Office, *Workforce Investment Act: Youth Provisions Promote New Service Strategies, but Additional Guidance Would Enhance Program Development*, GAO-02-213, April 2002, pp. 20-21. (GAO is now know as the Government Accountability Office.) (Hereafter, Government Accountability Office,

Workforce Investment Act: Youth Provisions Promote New Service Strategies, but Additional Guidance Would Enhance Program Development.)

[38] These elements are classified in the PY2008 Workforce Investment Act Standardized Record Data (WIASRD) Data Book. See *PY2008 Data Book*, January 19, 2010, http://www.doleta.gov/Performance/Results/pdf/ PY_2008_WIASRD_Data_Book_FINAL_1 1920 10.pdf.

[39] Department of Labor, Employment and Training Administration, Training and Employment Guidance Letter (TEGL) No. 9-00, January 23, 2001; and Department of Labor, Employment and Training Administration, Training and Employment Guidance Letter (TEGL) No. 18-00, April 23, 2001. Local WIBs are advised to establish ongoing relationships with non-WIA funded activities that provide services for WIA-eligible youth.

[40] Social Policy Research Associates, *The Workforce Investment Act After Five Years: Results from the National Evaluation of the Implementation of WIA*, prepared for the U.S. Department of Labor, June 2004, http://www.doleta.gov/reports/searcheta/occ/papers/SPR-WIA_Final_Report.pdf. (Hereafter, Social Policy Research Associates, *The Workforce Investment Act After Five Years: Results from the National Evaluation of the Implementation of WIA*, June 2004.)

[41] ARRA effectively authorizes programs funded by Youth Activities via the law to temporarily extend the age of eligibility from 21 to 24.

[42] These terms are defined in **Appendix B**. Up to 5% of youth participants in a local area may be individuals who do not meet the income criteria, but have at least one barrier to employment, some of which are not identical to those listed above: (1) deficient in basic literacy skills; (2) a school dropout; (3) homeless or a runaway; (4) an offender; (5) one or more grade levels below the grade level appropriate to the individual's age; (6) pregnant or parenting; (7) possess one or more disabilities, including learning disabilities; or (8) face serious barriers to employment as identified by the local WIB (20 C.F.R. 664.220).

[43] Title I, Section 10 1(33) of the Workforce Investment Act.

[44] Ibid, Table II-14.

[45] The outlying areas comprise the U. S. Virgin Islands, Guam, American Samoa, the Commonwealth of the Northern Mariana Islands, the Republic of the Marshall Islands, the Federated States of Micronesia, and the Republic of Palau.

[46] In years where appropriations exceed $1 billion, the minimum allotments are the higher of (1) 90% of a state's relative share of the previous year's funding, (2) the amount the state received in 1998, or (3) 0.3% of the first $1 billion plus 0.4% of the amount over $1 billion.

[47] According to the U.S. Department of Labor, Employment and Training Administration, the grantee spent all of the grant funds except for $12,355. An audit by the Office of the Inspector General (OIG) resulted in $262,258 in disallowed costs. The grantee appealed the determination, and the Department of Labor and the grantee entered into a settlement agreement in which the grantee agreed to pay $90,000. This is based on Congressional Research Service correspondence with the Department of Labor, Employment and Training Administration in October 2009.

[48] In their state plans, states must identify the expected (adjusted) level of performance for each of the core indicators for the first three program years of the plan, which covers five program years. In order to "ensure an optimal return on the investment of Federal funds in workforce investment activities," the Secretary and the governor of each state shall "reach agreement on the levels of performance" for all youth and other indicators identified in Section 136(b)(2)(A). This agreed-upon level then becomes the "state adjusted level of performance" that is incorporated into the plan.

[49] U.S. Department of Labor, Employment and Training Administration, Training and Employment Guidance Letter (TEGL) No. 18-04 ("Announcing the Soon-to-be Proposed Revisions to Existing Performance Reporting Requirements ... "), February 28, 2005.

[50] U.S. Department of Labor, Employment and Training Administration, "Workforce Investment Act (WIA) Waiver Summary Report: WIA Inception—December 16, 2008," http://www.doleta.gov/waivers/pdf/ WIA_Waivers_Summary.pdf.

[51] Title I, Subtitle J of the Workforce Investment Act and 20 C.F.R. 670.

[52] Since FY2006, Congress has directed DOL to operate the Job Corps Office in the Office of the Secretary. Federal regulations established the Office of Job Corps within the Office of the Secretary, pursuant to Secretary's Order 09- 2006. U.S. Department of Labor, "Establishment of the Office of Job Corps Within the Office of the Secretary; Delegation of Authority and Assignment of Responsibility to Its Director and Others," 71 *Federal Register* 16192, March 30, 2006.

[53] U.S. Department of Labor, Education and Training Administration, Office of Job Corps, *Budget Justification of Appropriation Estimates for Committees on Appropriations, FY2011*, vol. III, p. OJC-17.

[54] Ibid.

[55] U.S. Department of Labor, Office of Job Corps, *Policy and Requirements Handbook*, July 15, 2009, http://www.jobcorps.gov/Libraries/pdf/prh.sflb.

[56] Ibid.

[57] U.S. Department of Labor, Office of Job Corps, *Job Corps Annual Report: Program Year July 1, 2006—June 30, 2007*, pp. 18-21, http://www.jobcorps.gov/Libraries/pdf/py06report.sflb.

[58] Ibid.

[59] No more than 20% of participants may be ages 22 through 24 on the date of enrollment.

[60] Some of these terms are defined in Appendix B.

[61] See Table 3 for a definition of these terms.

[62] The performance management system is comprised of four outcome measure systems: Outreach and Admissions (OA) Report Card, Center Report Card, Career Technical Training Reporting and Improvement System, and Career Transitions Services (CTS) Report Card.

[63] Title I, Subtitle D, Section 173A of the Workforce Investment Act.

[64] For an overview of the differences between the YouthBuild Program as administered by HUD and DOL, see U.S. Department of Labor, Employment and Training Administration, *YouthBuild Transfer Act: Synopsis and Section-bySection Analysis,* http://www.doleta.gov/youth_services/YouthBuildSec-bySec%20Analysis%20 FINAL.pdf.

[65] Some of these terms are defined in Appendix B.

[66] This is based on a review of grants awarded in 2007 and 2008. U.S. Department of Labor, Employment and Training Administration, *YouthBuild Grantee Information,* http://www.doleta.gov/you th_services/youthbuildgrantee.cfm.

[67] U.S. Department of Labor, Employment and Training Administration, *YouthBuild Reporting Requirements and Common Measures,* available at http://www.doleta.gov/youth_services/youthbuild/Updated_05_29_07/ REVISED%20YouthBuild%20Common%20Measure%20Questions%205-29-07.pdf; and U.S. Department of Labor, Employment and Training Administration and Workforce3 One, *Understanding and Using YouthBuild Performance Measures* webinar, January 6, 2009.

[68] Title I, Subtitle D, Section 171 of the Workforce Investment Act.

[69] This is based on a review of initiatives funded by the Reintegration of Ex-Offenders program. U.S. Department of Labor, Employment and Training Administration, *Youth Services Discretionary Grants,* http://www.doleta.gov/ Youth _services/Discretionary.cfm.

[70] This program was known as the Youth Offender Pilot Program, and funded 14 communities that provided educational, employment, re-entry, and other services to youth.

[71] U.S. Department of Labor, Employment and Training Administration, *Budget Justification of Appropriation Estimates for Committees on Appropriations, FY2010,* volume I, TES-74.

[72] The earliest funding for the program was authorized under Title IV of the Job Training Partnership Act. See U.S. Department of Labor, Employment and Training Administration, *Notice Inviting Proposals for Youth Offender Demonstration Projects,* August 28, 1998, http://www.doleta.gov/grants/sga/01-101sga.cfm.

[73] For a list of grantees and grant funding amounts, see U.S. Department of Labor, Employment and Training Administration, *Youth Services Discretionary Grants,* http://www.doleta.gov/Youth_services/D iscretionary.cfm.

[74] Between PY2000 and PY2006, DOL used Youthful Offender funding to support the Serious and Violent Reentry Initiative at the Department of Justice; to award competitive grants to serve youthful offenders in 29 communities; to award non-competitive grants to several nonprofit organizations to serve young offenders and youth at risk of becoming offenders; and to award grants to eight states to improve the academic and workforce preparation programs in one juvenile correctional facility in each state.

[75] Youth ages 18 and older may also be eligible to participate in the Prisoner Reentry Initiative (PRI), which seeks to reduce recidivism by helping former inmates find work when they return to their communities.

[76] For further information about DOL's recent efforts to fund initiatives that promote employment in high-growth industries, see CRS Report RL338 11, *The President's Demand-Driven Workforce Development Initiatives,* by Ann Lordeman and Linda Levine.

[77] ESEA requires each state receiving funds under the act to establish and implement a statewide policy requiring that a student attending a persistently dangerous school, as determined by the state in consultation with a representative sample of local education agencies (LEAs), or a student who becomes a victim of a violent criminal offense on school grounds be allowed to attend a safe school within the LEA.

[78] U.S. Department of Labor, Employment and Training Administration, *Budget Justification of Appropriation Estimates for Committees on Appropriations, FY2010,* vol. I, p. TES-78.

[79] U.S. Government Accountability Office, *Youth Opportunity Grants: Lessons Can Be Learned from Program, but Labor Needs to Make Data Available,* GAO-06-53, December 2005.

[80] Ibid.

[81] The Food Stamp program was recently renamed the Supplemental Nutrition Assistance Program (SNAP).

In: Vulnerable Youth and Employment Issues
Editor: Christopher E. Perry

ISBN: 978-1-61122-020-9
© 2011 Nova Science Publishers, Inc.

Chapter 2

VULNERABLE YOUTH: ISSUES IN THE REAUTHORIZATION OF THE WORKFORCE INVESTMENT ACT

Adrienne L. Fernandes

SUMMARY

The Workforce Investment Act of 1998 (WIA, P.L. 105-220) is the primary federal law that provides job training and related services to unemployed and underemployed individuals, including vulnerable young people with barriers to employment. All youth job training programs and related services are authorized under Title I of WIA and administered by the Department of Labor (DOL). These programs include the WIA Youth Activities (Youth) formula program, Job Corps, YouthBuild, and the Youth Opportunity Grant (YOG) program. Under the pilot and demonstration authority in Title I, DOL has also carried out the Reintegration of Ex-Offenders program for both youth and adults. Together, these programs make up the federal job training and employment system for disadvantaged youth. Although the programs have distinct activities and goals, each of them seeks to connect eligible youth to educational and employment opportunities, as well as leadership development and community service activities.

WIA authorized funding through September 30, 2003; however, WIA programs continue to be funded through annual appropriation acts. In the 111th Congress, policymakers have signaled that the law may be reauthorized in the near future. A focus of recent congressional hearings and forums on reauthorization has been the WIA Youth Activities formula program. The Youth program provides funding for a coordinated system of youth employment and training services overseen by a state workforce investment board (WIB) and the governor, in coordination with local WIBs and community organizations. The program targets youth ages 14 through 21 who are low-income and have one or more barriers to employment.

This chapter provides an overview of issues that have been raised by stakeholders about the Youth formula program. Since the start of the program, stakeholders have discussed the extent to which youth have had to prove their eligibility for the program, and separately, how much of an emphasis the program should place on serving older youth. In addition, policymakers and others have raised issues about the youth population in the Youth Activities program; specifically, whether the program should focus more on out-of-school youth, including those who are not working. Related to this is the age of youth who ought to be eligible for the program. The American Recovery and Reinvestment Act (ARRA, P.L. 111-5) has temporarily enabled youth ages 22 through 24 to access WIA Youth services. Whether WIA ought to target these older youth, particularly in light of the possible cost of doing so, could be addressed in any reauthorization legislation.

Another reauthorization issue is the perceived lack of coordination between the workforce system and other systems that serve youth, such as the education system. Stakeholders have suggested that greater coordination can help meet the multiple needs of youth, as intended by WIA, and that existing WIA infrastructure can facilitate better coordination. Finally, Members of Congress and others have continued to inquire about the effectiveness of the Youth formula grant in meeting its objectives and serving the most at-risk youth. To date, an impact evaluation of the Youth program has not been completed; however, DOL recently awarded a contract to a private research organization to conduct an evaluation of the WIA Youth, Adult, and Dislocated Worker formula grant programs authorized under Title I of WIA.

INTRODUCTION

Since the 1930s, federal job training and employment programs and policies have sought to connect vulnerable youth to work and school. Generally, these young people have been defined as being vulnerable because they are low-income and have a barrier to employment, such as having dropped out of school or spent time in foster care. The Workforce Investment Act of 1998 (P.L. 105-220) is the most recent federal law to provide job training and related services to unemployed and underemployed individuals, including youth. WIA includes titles that authorize programs for job training and related services (Title I), including for youth, adults, and dislocated workers; adult education and literacy (Title II); employment services (Title III); and vocational rehabilitation (Title IV).

All youth job training programs and related services are authorized under Title I of WIA and are carried out by the Department of Labor (DOL). These programs include the WIA Youth Activities (Youth) formula program, Job Corps, YouthBuild, and the Youth Opportunity Grant (YOG) program. Under the pilot and demonstration authority in Title I, DOL has carried out the Reintegration of Ex-Offenders program. Together, these programs make up the federal job training system for youth. Although the programs have distinct activities and goals, each program seeks to connect youth to educational and employment opportunities, as well as leadership development and community service activities.

WIA authorized funding through September 30, 2003; however, WIA programs continue to be funded through annual appropriation acts. In the 111th Congress, policymakers have signaled that the law may be reauthorized in the near future. A focus of recent congressional hearings and forums on reauthorization has been the WIA Youth Activities formula program. The Youth program provides funding for a coordinated system of youth employment and training services overseen by a state workforce investment board (WIB) and the governor, in coordination with local WIBs and community organizations. The program targets youth ages 14 through 21 who are low-income and have one or more barriers to employment. Relevant reauthorization issues are the population of youth served, including issues related to eligibility and out-of-school youth; coordination with other systems that serve youth, particularly the education system; and the measures used to assess the performance of the program, and whether they adequately capture progress made by youth.

YOUTH PROGRAMS AUTHORIZED UNDER TITLE I OF THE WORKFORCE INVESTMENT ACT

Job training and employment services for youth under WIA include

- *WIA Youth Activities*, a formula grant program that includes employment and other services that are provided year-round;
- *Job Corps*, a program that provides job training and related services primarily at residential centers maintained by contractor organizations;
- *YouthBuild*, a competitive grant program that emphasizes job training and education in construction;
- *Reintegration of Ex-Offenders*, a demonstration program for juvenile and adult offenders that provides job training and other services and is authorized under WIA's pilot and demonstration authority; and
- *Youth Opportunity Grants (YOG)*, a multi-site demonstration program funded through FY2003 that created centers in low-income communities where youth could receive employment and other services.

Although WIA's authorization of appropriations expired at the end of FY2003, Congress continues to appropriate funds, including those for youth job training programs—except for the YOG program, which has not been funded since FY2003. All of the programs, except Job Corps, are (or were) carried out by the Division of Youth Services in DOL's Employment and Training Administration (ETA), Office of Workforce Investment. The Office of Job Corps is under the Office of the Secretary, although DOL has signaled that it intends to transfer the office to ETA, where it was previously housed.[1]

Table 1 summarizes key features of the five youth programs. Each of the programs has a similar purpose—to connect youth to educational and employment opportunities, and to offer similar services for doing so. All of the programs offer employment, job training, and educational services. However, these services are carried out differently and by distinct entities. For example, local areas must provide 10 specific elements, including mentoring and follow-up, to youth who receive services under the Youth Activities formula grant program. YouthBuild program participants engage in employment and other activities primarily related to housing and other types of construction work. Job Corps is the only one of the programs that provides residential services, where youth can live onsite and receive health care services, child care, and other supports. As with Job Corps, the YOG program established centers, albeit non-residential, where youth could receive employment and other services.

The programs generally serve vulnerable youth, but some have more targeted eligibility criteria. Participants in the Youth Activities formula grant program, YouthBuild, and Job Corps must be low-income and have specific employment barriers. The Youthful Offender component of the Reintegration of Ex-Offenders serves youth who have become involved in the juvenile justice or criminal justice system or youth at risk of becoming involved. When the YOG program was in operation, youth automatically qualified for the program if they lived in low-income communities. Finally, the programs are funded somewhat differently. DOL allocates funding for Youth Activities to states based on a formula, while Job Corps enters into agreements with nonprofit and for-profit organizations and other federal agencies. The other programs competitively award grants to nonprofit and other organizations and local communities.

For further information about the programs, see CRS Report R40929, *Vulnerable Youth: Employment and Job Training Programs*, by Adrienne L. Fernandes.

ISSUES

The 111th Congress has begun to take steps toward reauthorizing WIA.[2] In April 2009, the Senate Health, Education, Labor, and Pensions (HELP) Committee held a series of listening sessions to address the positive aspects of WIA and to increase understanding of the issues that can be addressed as part of any reauthorization legislation. One of the listening sessions focused on the Youth formula grant program. Youth advocates, researchers, and other stakeholders spoke about the ways the committee could consider refining the law to improve the program. The Senate HELP Subcommittee on Employment and Workplace Safety subsequently conducted a hearing in July 2009 to discuss how WIA can be updated to help workers and employers meet the demands of a changing economy.[3] In October 2009, the House Education and Labor Committee held a hearing on declining youth employment.[4]

A primary focus of these forums has been the Youth Activities program. The WIA Youth Activities formula grant program is arguably the centerpiece of the federal youth job training and employment system. As specified in the law, the program has several purposes: to provide assistance in achieving academic and employment success through activities that improve educational and skill competencies and foster effective connections to employers; to ensure ongoing adult mentoring opportunities for eligible youth; to provide opportunities for training, continued supportive services, and participation in activities related to leadership, citizenship, and community service; and to offer incentives to youth for recognition and achievement. Employment and training services for youth are overseen by a state workforce investment board and the governor, in coordination with local WIBs and community organizations. The program targets youth ages 14 through 21 who are low-income and have one or more barriers to employment.

Table 1. Features of Youth Programs Authorized under Title I of WIA

Key Feature	Youth Activities Formula Program	Job Corps	YouthBuild	Youthful Offenders (Reintegration of Ex-Offenders)[a]	Youth Opportunity Grants (no longer funded)
Purpose	To provide eligible youth with assistance in achieving academic and employment success through activities that improve educational and skill competencies and foster effective connections to employers; ensure on-going adult mentoring opportunities for eligible youth; provide opportunities for training, continued supportive services, and participation in activities related to leadership, citizenship, and community service; and offer incentives for recognition and achievement to eligible youth.	To provide disadvant-aged youth with the skills needed to obtain and hold a job, enter the Armed Forces, or enroll in advanced training or higher education.	To enable disadvantaged youth to obtain the education and employment skills necessary to achieve self-sufficiency; foster leadership skills; provide work and service opportu-nities; and expand the supply of permanent affordable housing for the homeless.	Among other purposes, to assist adults and youth returning from prison or juvenile justice facilities with pre-release, mentoring, housing, case management, and employment services; to reduce violence within "persistently dangerous" schools through a combination of mentoring, educational, employment, case management, and violence prevention strategies; and to provide alternative education and related services for youth at risk of involvement with the justice system.	To increase the longterm employment of youth who live in enterprise commu-nities, empowerment zones, and high-poverty areas.
Target Population	Youth age 14 through 21 who are low-income and have one or more of the following barriers: (1) deficient in basic literacy skills; (2) a school drop-out; (3) homeless, a runaway, or a foster child; (4) pregnant or parenting; (5) an offender; (6) or require additional assistance to complete	Youth ages 16 through 24 who are low-income and meet one or more of the following criteria: (1) basic skills deficient; (2) homeless, a runaway, or a foster child; (3) a parent; or (4) an individual who requires additional education, vocational training, or intensive counseling and related	Youth ages 16 through 24 who are members of low-income families, in foster care, offenders, disabled, the children of incarcerated parents, or migrants; *and* are school dropouts.	Generally, youth ages 14 through 28 who have been involved in the juvenile justice or criminal justice systems; have been involved with or have a high risk of involvement in gangs or the juvenile justice system; or reside in "persistently dangerous" school districts.	Youth ages 14 thr-ough 21 who reside in enterprise communities, empowerment zones, and high-poverty areas and who seek assistance.

Table 1. (Continued)

Key Feature	Youth Activities Formula Program	Job Corps	YouthBuild	Youthful Offenders (Reintegration of Ex-Offenders)[a]	Youth Opportunity Grants (no longer funded)
	an educational program or to secure and hold employment. At least 30% of funds are to be used for out-of-school youth.				
Funding Mechanism	Funds are allocated by formula to state workforce investment boards (WIBs), based on a formula that accounts for a state's relative share of unemployment and economically disadvantaged youth. In turn, state boards make awards to local WIBs using certain factors. Local WIBs competitively contract with local entities, such as nonprofit organizations and community coll-eges, to provide services.	DOL enters into an agreement with a federal, state, or local agency; an area vocational education school or residential vocational school; or a private organization to operate Job Corps centers.	Grants are competitively awarded to community based organizations, community action agencies, state or local youth service or conservation corps, and other organizations that provide the services directly.	Grants are competitively awarded to local governments, state and local government partnerships, schools, and community-based organizations.	Grants were competitively awarded on a one-time basis to 36 low-income communities who established one or more centers where youth could participate in activities and receive services.
Types of Activities for Youth	Each local WIB must provide 10 "elements," which include academic activeties, summer employment opportunities, supportive services, follow-up servi-ces and other activities.	Youth generally live at the Job Corps centers, which provide youth with a program of education, vocational training, work experience, recreational activities, physical rehabi-litation and development, and counseling.	Grantees may carry out a number of activities, including education and employment activities, supervision in rehabili-tating or constructing housing and facilities; adult mentoring; provision of wages or other benefits; and follow-up services.	Grantees carry out a variety of youth activities, including employment services, mentoring, case management, education services, restorative justice projects, and efforts in the community to reduce violence.	Grantees carried out a number of activities, including education and workforce investment activities; and leadership development, citizenship, community service, and recrea-tional activities.

Table 1. (Continued)

Key Feature	Youth Activities Formula Program[b]	Job Corps	YouthBuild	Youthful Offenders (Reintegration of Ex-Offenders)[a]	Youth Opportunity Grants (no longer funded)
Youth Served	108,418 (PY2007)[b]	60,900 (PY2008)	2,401 (PY2007)	6,898 (across all programs in PY2007)	92,263 (cumulative FY2000-FY2005)
Authorized Funding	Such sums as necessary for FY1999-FY2003.	Such sums as necessary for FY1999-FY2003.	Such sums as necessary for FY2007-FY2012.	Such sums as necessary for FY1999-FY2003 (for pilot and demonstration programs, generally).	Such sums as necessary for FY1999-FY2003.

Sources: Congressional Research Service, based on correspondence with the U.S. Department of Labor, Employment and Training Administration; the Workforce Investment Act (P.L. 105-220), as amended; U.S. Department of Labor, Employment and Training Administration, "Workforce Investment Act; Final Rules," 65 *Federal Register*, August 11, 2000; U.S. Department of Labor, *Budget Justifications of Appropriation Estimates for Committee on Appropriations*, FY20 10 (for the Reintegration of Ex- Offenders program); U.S. Government Accountability Office, *Youth Opportunity Grants: Lessons Can Be Learned from Program, but Labor Needs to Make Data Available*, GAO- 06-53, December 2005; and Decision Information Resources, Inc., *Youth Opportunity Grant Initiative: Impact and Synthesis Report*, December 2007.

a. The Youthful Offenders component of the Reintegration of Ex-offenders program is authorized under WIA's pilot and demonstration authority. Prior to FY2008, the program was a stand-alone program. It is now part of the Reintegration of Ex-Offenders program, which includes funding for juvenile and adult activities.

b. This is the number of youth who exited the program. An exiter is a participant who received a service funded by WIA or a partner program, has not received the service for 90 consecutive calendar days, and is not scheduled to receive future services.

Issues surrounding reauthorization of the program are the eligibility and populations of youth served; coordination among the workforce and other systems, including the education system, and entities that ought to coordinate workforce services; and the accountability of the program and performance of youth participants.[5]

Youth Served by the Program

Since the start of the Youth program, stakeholders have discussed the extent to which youth have had to prove their eligibility for the program, and separately, how much of an emphasis the program should place on serving out-of-school youth and older youth.

Eligibility

A youth is eligible for the Youth Activities formula grant program if he or she is age 14 through 21,[6] a low-income individual, and has one or more of the following barriers:

- deficient in basic literacy skills;
- a school dropout;
- homeless, a runaway, or a foster child;
- pregnant or parenting; or
- requires additional assistance to complete an educational program or to secure and hold employment.[7]

An ongoing point of discussion about the WIA Youth program is the extent to which youth should be required to prove their eligibility—particularly, that they are low-income. Although dated, the Government Accountability Office's (GAO) 2002 research on the implementation of the program found that a majority of state and local officials who were interviewed or visited told GAO that documenting a youth's income eligibility was challenging. State and local officials reported that many potentially eligible youth were unable or unwilling to provide pertinent documentation of their eligibility, such as their parents' paycheck stubs or tax returns.[8] The officials said obtaining necessary documentation diverted financial and staff resources away from direct service delivery. More recently, GAO has examined how states and localities are carrying out their WIA Youth program and nine other federal programs using funding appropriated under the American Recovery and Reinvestment Act (ARRA, P.L. 111-5). According to GAO, state and local workforce officials commented that youth had difficulty providing the documents required to prove WIA program eligibility, and that the income eligibility requirements for the program may exclude some needy youth.[9]

Separately, youth may also face challenges in obtaining documentation to prove that they are eligible under other WIA criteria, such as documentation that they are or were involved in foster care or the juvenile justice or criminal justice system, or were runaways or homeless youth.[10] For example, youth may be reticent to furnish their previous criminal records. Youth who have run away or are homeless may not be connected to family, and may have difficulty in providing their records.

Some states have appealed to DOL to waive certain eligibility criteria for youth. Under WIA, DOL is authorized to waive certain statutory or regulatory requirements for states or local areas (Section 189 (i)(4)(A)(i)). However, DOL cannot allow waivers for participant eligibility, among other categories. Therefore, this would not be an option for the states and localities that wish to waive certain eligibility criteria. It appears that DOL has denied requests from at least four states (Indiana, Louisiana, Massachusetts, and Ohio) to waive the youth eligibility requirements related to income. Nonetheless, DOL allows states to have some flexibility in documenting eligibility. For example, in its letter to Louisiana, DOL pointed to the regulations (20 CFR 661.120) that give states and local governments authority to establish their own policies and guidelines relating to verifying and documenting eligibility.[11]

Still, stakeholders have asserted that WIA does not allow flexibility in documenting income and other eligibility factors. As part of GAO's work in 2002, some states and localities reported that they preferred using certain eligibility criteria under WIA's predecessor, the Job Training Partnership Act (JTPA).[12] In-school youth were eligible if they qualified for the federal free lunch program or they participated in a program authorized under Title I of the Elementary and Secondary Education Act, which is targeted to low-income school districts. Alternatively, youth were eligible if they met the definition of "economically disadvantaged," which was nearly the same as the current definition of "low-income" under WIA. Out-of-school youth were eligible if they met the definition of "economically disadvantaged."

Other stakeholders support adding eligibility based on a youth's residency in a high-poverty census tract.[13] Youth who lived in Youth Opportunity grant program sites were automatically eligible based solely on their residency in low-income communities. Some stakeholders have also suggested that certain groups of at-risk youth—such as dropouts, youth in foster care, homeless and runaway youth, and youth who are not working or in school—should be categorically eligible without regard to income.

It is unclear the extent to which changing the eligibility requirement to make it based on a means tested program (such as the free lunch program), residency of youth, or certain risk factors would change the number of youth who would be eligible.

In-School and Out-of-School Youth

Stakeholders have raised another issue about the youth population in the Youth Activities program; specifically, whether the program should focus more on out-of-school youth, including those who are not working. WIA requires that at least 30% of all Youth Activities funds must be used for activities for out-of-school youth, *or* youth who have dropped out or received a high school diploma or its equivalent but are basic skills deficient, unemployed, or underemployed. Yet, GAO found, as part of its 2002 and 2004 reports, that while local youth programs may meet this goal, they still reported challenges in recruiting and retaining out-of-school youth.[14] GAO cited a DOL estimate that serving an out-of-school youth under the program is about twice as costly as serving an in-school youth. In addition, local officials reported that they had more difficulty maintaining contact with out-of-school youth. These youth also faced particular difficulties with transportation.

Some stakeholders have suggested that a greater share of WIA Youth funding should be devoted to dropouts, and other youth in high-risk categories, even those youth who are in school.[15] For example, one policy organization that focuses on workforce development issues has asserted that youth who are not in school, and in-school youth who are overage or under-credited, should be the first priorities for use of WIA funds.[16] Past legislation in Congress would have required local WIBs to serve primarily out-of-school youth; the accompanying conference reports to some of these bills cite that several federal programs already serve in-school youth.[17] Others have argued for maintaining the current share of funding for out-of-school youth but increasing technical assistance to states and localities to meet the needs of these youth.[18] Some observers have asserted that localities need flexibility in determining the optimal share of funding.[19]

DOL has provided some guidance to states and localities about serving out-of-school youth and in-school youth who are at risk of dropping out. In direct response to the concerns raised in the 2004 GAO report about recruiting and retaining out-of-school youth, DOL issued what is known as a Training and Guidance Letter (TEGL) recommending that WIBs provide strong alternative education programs for out-of-school youth, including dropouts and youth at risk of dropping out.[20] Separately, DOL is funding the Multiple Education Pathways Blueprint Grants under WIA's pilot and demonstration authority. In FY2007, DOL provided $3.4 million to seven midsize cities to "blueprint" and implement a system that can reconnect youth who have dropped out to multiple education pathways. These projects may provide insight into the ways that WIA, as a whole, can address the needs of out-of-school youth.

Finally, a 2004 contracted report from DOL addressed the implementation of WIA programs and identified the ways that local areas were successful in serving out-of-school youth.[21] For example, some states provided technical assistance to local areas through a training and technical assistance network. Minnesota prepared a list of resources for out-of-school youth, which included relevant articles and guides and a brief description of strategies used by Job Corps centers to attract these youth. Further, some local areas reported contracting with service providers who had experience working with out-of-school youth, and their services focused on a GED or high school diploma program and vocational training.

Older Youth

Currently, youth are eligible for WIA if they are ages 14 through 21 and meet other criteria. The temporary changes made to the program by the American Recovery and Reinvestment Act enable youth through age 24 to access WIA Youth services for the first time. Extending the program to this older age appears to reflect the growing amount of research literature that suggests that many young people are taking much longer to transition to adulthood. Multiple factors—including the delayed age of the first marriage, the high cost of living independently, and additional educational opportunities—have extended the period of transition from adolescence to adulthood.[22] For vulnerable youth populations, the transition to adulthood is further complicated by a number of challenges, including family conflict or abandonment and obstacles to securing employment that provides adequate wages and health insurance. The research literature has shown that older youth are more likely to be disconnected—that is, not working or in school—than their younger counterparts.[23] Whether WIA ought to target these older youth, particularly those who are disconnected, could be addressed in any reauthorization legislation.

On the other hand, increasing the age of youth in the program could strain the program's resources if funding remains stable (at least in nominal dollars), as it has over the past several years.[24] According to a recent report by GAO on oversight of Recovery Act activities, 7% of the approximately 300,000 youth participating in the Youth program as funded by ARRA are ages 22 through 24.[25] This translates to about 21,000 youth. In other words, the usual Youth program might see an influx in the number of youth who would like services if the age is expanded.

As allowed under WIA, DOL has advised workforce investment systems that they may co-enroll older youth in both the Youth program and Adult program (also authorized under Title I) to meet their individual needs. For example, older youth can receive mentoring services under the Youth program and can be eligible under the Adult program for what is known as an individual training account (ITA), from which they can fund occupational skills training.[26] DOL has also offered webinars on the topic, including one that addresses how to transition older youth into workforce activities, including the Adult program, after they have participated in the Youth program during the summer.[27]

It is unclear the extent to which youth ages 18 through 21 self-select or are encouraged to participate in the Youth program, Adult program, or both. Exiters ages 18 through 21 in the Youth program have increased from about 30% to 45% of all youth exiters.[28] This is compared to youth ages 18 through 21 in the Adult program, who have made up 10% of the program's exiter population during the same time period (although in terms of numbers, there are generally more older youth in the Adult program than in the Youth program, as based on exiter data). Major distinctions between the programs appear to be that the Youth program includes more opportunities for academic services, such as tutoring and alternative secondary school services, although the Adult program provides individuals with information about available dropout services during the core phase, which involves job search assistance.[29] The Adult program also provides programs that combine workplace training with related instruction, including "cooperative education programs" (not defined), during the training phase. The Youth program also focuses on developing the leadership skills of youth in the program and engaging them in community service activities. The Adult program does not have this same emphasis.

While both programs provide opportunities for occupational skills training and links to employment, these activities tend to be available only to those Adult program participants who are in the training component of the program. Training activities include on-the-job training, programs that combine workplace training with related instruction, training programs operated by the private sector, skill upgrading, and entrepreneurial training. And while the Youth program provides supportive services, such as child care and transportation, the Adult program provides referrals to these services. Finally, the Youth program focuses on adult mentoring and job and other counseling, including drug and alcohol abuse counseling. This is compared with the Adult program's primary focus on job counseling, which tends to occur during the intensive phase.

Coordination with Other Systems

An issue raised at the Senate HELP Committee's listening session on WIA youth and elsewhere has been the perceived lack of coordination between the workforce system and other systems that serve youth, such as the education system.[30] Stakeholders have suggested that greater coordination can help meet the multiple needs of youth, as intended by WIA, and that existing WIA infrastructure (youth councils and one-stop centers) can facilitate coordination.

The 2004 GAO report documented some of the ways in which the workforce and education systems have collaborated, and where improvements are needed. Among other items, the report examined the entities that local WIBs contract with to provide services to youth. The report found that about half of all youth received Youth services through community-based organizations, secondary schools, and colleges or universities.[31] (A smaller share of youth received services through one-stop centers for adults or youth and other entities, such as local or state governments and private employers.) Nonetheless, GAO found that education entities in some locations were cautious about partnering.[32] According to GAO, some educators believed WIA's vision for providing comprehensive youth development services to at-risk youth was inconsistent with the mission of schools to provide academic services to all youth. For example, in Wisconsin, some schools were hesitant to allow WIA youth services to be provided on school grounds because of the perceived stigma associated with WIA being targeted to at-risk youth and not all youth generally.

Some stakeholders at the Senate HELP listening session presented options for promoting collaboration between workforce and education entities, and other systems. These stakeholders suggested that WIA Youth funds could be used to bring in partners from the school systems, employer and industry groups, the criminal justice system, and the mental health system.[33] Specifically, they would be responsible for developing a local "youth plan" that sets goals and benchmarks, coordinating activities, and allocating funds for different populations of disadvantaged youth. Localities would be encouraged to consolidate multiple funding streams where possible.

Separately, at the July 2009 hearing conducted by the Senate HELP Subcommittee on Employment and Workplace Safety, Assistant Secretary of Labor Jane Oates and Under Secretary of Education Martha Kanter testified that the Department of Labor and Department of Education are committed to working together to better ensure that youth—whether in-school or out-ofschool—receive the services and supports they need.[34] A past example of collaboration between DOL and ED on education and workforce activities is the School-to-Work program, which authorized a variety of competitive and non-competitive grants. A joint STW office was administered by both agencies. The grants supported the development of programs that combined work-based learning in schools, school-based learning in the workplace, and job training. Congress could look to lessons from the STW program to learn more about the successes and challenges associated with partnerships between the school and work systems.[35]

Role of Youth Councils

Related to the issue of greater coordination among various systems are questions about the body that would be charged with facilitating this coordination. Currently, each local WIB has a youth council, which is responsible for developing parts of the local workforce plan related to eligible youth and coordinating services on behalf of eligible youth, in consultation with the local board.[36] Members of the youth council include members of the local board with special interests or expertise in youth policy; representatives of youth service, juvenile justice, and local law enforcement agencies; representatives of local public housing authorities; and parents of eligible youth seeking assistance through WIA's formula grant programs for adults and dislocated workers.

The National Youth Employment Coalition (NYEC), a nonpartisan national organization that represents the interests of youth employment and youth development organizations, has documented that some youth councils have experienced difficulty developing beyond being advisory bodies to their WIBs.[37] Also in its 2002 report, GAO identified challenges with establishing youth councils.[38] The report found that some councils could not get youth or parents to participate due to a lack of transportation or conflicting work and school schedules. For these reasons, reauthorization legislation from previous Congresses would have made youth councils optional.[39]

NYEC and others have recommended that changes to WIA ought to facilitate stronger linkages between the workforce system, education system, and business community by promoting the inclusion of education and business representatives on the council, among other related changes. Similarly, stakeholders have suggested a stronger role for the youth councils that would enable them to have greater flexibility in configuring their partners and priorities.[40] Stakeholders have also recommended that the councils be required to develop a comprehensive youth plan that coordinates activities and consolidates multiple funding streams for youth.[41]

Regardless of whether Congress decides to make youth councils optional, it may wish to look to best practices for developing youth councils that provide strong leadership. A 2002 report prepared for DOL identified "enabling conditions" that have allowed innovative youth councils to develop a more comprehensive system for carrying out youth activities under the Youth program.[42] Some of these conditions include the presence of an established intermediary organization that has built a strong reputation with critical stakeholders and has an infrastructure to facilitate youth, provider, and business engagement; a strong school-to-career partnership that creates connections between K- 12 institutions, businesses, and institutions of higher education; and a pre-existing, community-wide planning process that has mapped key players and initiatives in a community, identified key indicators around which stakeholders might coalesce, and then determined how WIA dollars can leverage other funds to address relevant issues.

Role of One-Stop Centers

Congress may also wish to consider the role of one-stop centers in facilitating greater coordination, if this should, in fact, become a goal of WIA. One-stop centers are intended to facilitate connections to job training, employment, and other services for all youth in a community, even those who are ineligible for the WIA Youth program. Nearly 20 federal programs must provide services through the one-stop system, either by co-location, electronic linkages, or referrals. Generally, one-stops provide services to youth, as discussed in the 2002 GAO report. These centers reported using a variety of methods to attract youth to the centers, such as actively recruiting youth (75% of local WIB directors polled by GAO), placing youth program staff at the one-stop (64%), training one-stop staff in youth programs (45%), and making the facility more attractive to youth (35%).[43] Yet GAO found that some local areas face challenges attracting youth to one-stop centers. In some areas, youth did not typically come into the centers on their own, unless they were referred or brought to them by schools or other service providers. As part of the April 2009 Senate HELP listening session on the WIA Youth program, one stakeholder explained that one-stops should cater more to youth and do a better job of training service professionals on youth matters.[44]

DOL has encouraged one-stop centers to target youth by providing funding to support planning projects for local WIBs and youths to enhance youth connections to the one-stop delivery system, and providing guidance on this topic.[45] Through written guidance, DOL has explained that local areas can enhance youth access through methods such as co-locating youth program staff at the one-stop center or designating staff to coordinate outreach and services for youth, including cross-training youth program and one-stop staff; and customizing one-stop centers for youth to make the facilities more "youth-friendly," for example, by establishing separate satellite centers for youth at places where youth tend to frequent.

Youth Opportunity Grants

One youth program authorized under WIA, the Youth Opportunity Grant program, focused on coordinating services among multiple providers in a community to meet the needs of youth in those communities. The ways in which they partnered were documented in a 2005 GAO study.[46]

Accountability

Congress and other stakeholders have continued to inquire about the effectiveness of the Youth formula grant in meeting its objectives and serving the most at-risk youth.

Impact Evaluation

Section 172 of WIA requires DOL to continuously evaluate programs and activities authorized under Title I of WIA. The evaluations are to address several aspects of these programs and activities, including their effectiveness relative to their cost. The law also required that DOL conduct at least one multi-site control group evaluation by the end of FY2005.

To date, an impact evaluation of the Youth program has not been completed; however, DOL awarded a contract in 2008 to Mathematica to conduct an evaluation of the WIA Youth, Adult, and Dislocated Worker programs. According to DOL, the complete evaluation will be conducted over seven years, and an initial set of evaluation data on the Youth program will be available in 2012.[47]

Performance Measures

Section 136 of WIA sets forth performance measures as part of the accountability system to determine whether states and localities are "achieving continuous improvement of workforce investment activities" funded under the Youth, Adult, and Dislocated Worker programs. Of the 17 measures, or "core indicators," three are for youth ages 14 through 18 and four are for youth ages 19 through 21. Both sets of measures address educational attainment and employment, except that the measures for older youth focus more on employment. For each of the core indicators, the states negotiate with DOL to establish a level of performance. That is, the measures are identified in WIA Section 136, but the levels are determined by negotiation between states and DOL.[48] Measures are reported as part of the Workforce Investment Act Standardized Record Data (WIASRD), which also collects demographic and other information about youth, adults, and dislocated workers who exit their respective programs.

ETA implemented a "Common Measures" policy for several workforce programs and revised the reporting requirements for WIA Title I programs.[49] Specifically, ETA introduced three youth measures that address education and employment gains, and are applicable to younger and older youth. It is important to note, however, that ETA specifically indicated that the Common Measures were not to supersede the existing statutory performance reporting requirements for WIA. Despite this, DOL has granted waivers to more than half of all states to permit implementation of and reporting on only the Common Measures rather than on the current fuller array of measures in WIA for youth, adults, and dislocated workers.[50]

The seven statutory WIA performance measures and three Common Measures for youth are used to evaluate youth outcomes after participants leave the Youth program. Each state is required to establish a "state adjusted level of performance" for each measure.[51] WIA itself is not detailed about the process of negotiation, however, DOL guidance indicates that states should negotiate performance level goals that keep in mind factors such as economic conditions, customers served, and workforce solutions that contribute to the regional economic competitiveness of their state and sub-state areas.[52] While ETA encourages states to serve "at-risk" populations—including the neediest youth[53]—and to account for the effect that at-risk populations might have on performance outcomes, states ultimately have the discretion to choose the populations (among eligible youth overall) it will serve and the adjustments that will be made on the basis of the populations served.

Stakeholders have asserted that performance measures do not adequately capture the gains made by the most at-risk youth, and may in fact lead programs to serve only the highest-functioning eligible youth to ensure that the programs meet their performance targets. As part of a 2008 report on disconnected youth, GAO documented that some local programs funded with Youth Activities dollars only accepted young people who tested at a specific grade level so that youth can more readily meet the goals of the program.[54] GAO further reported that DOL officials are aware that WIBs have implemented program contracts in a way that may unintentionally discourage programs from working with lower-skilled youth. For example, some contracts are issued for 12 months, which may be an inadequate timeframe to assist youth in meeting the outcomes. DOL told GAO that it has taken steps to conduct some training for WIBs to explain the importance of a longer-term investment in youth so that they can reach the outcomes expected by the program. GAO pointed out that DOL has not provided technical assistance more broadly on this issue. More recently, DOL reported that it will issue guidance on serving youth at varying skill levels, and plans to issue this guidance, along with other possible assistance to local WIBs.[55]

Stakeholders have proposed ways in which DOL and local boards can encourage programs to serve the most at-risk youth. GAO has suggested that the Common Measures may give local programs more flexibility to work with youth at different levels. The literacy or numeracy gains, one of the Common Measures, captures the share of youth who "increase one or more educational functional levels," and not necessarily the share of youth who reach a certain level of proficiency.[56] Nonetheless, GAO cautions that it may be too early to determine whether these new measures have resulted in reduced incentives for programs to select higher-performing youth.

Others have suggested that even the Common Measures do not necessarily encourage WIBs to serve higher-risk groups. Some have recommended that the performance levels be adjusted downward for states and local areas choosing to serve more challenging youth populations.[57] WIA's predecessor, JTPA, can provide insight into how adjustments may be made to account for local areas that serve the neediest youth, if this is in fact, a goal of WIA reauthorization. JTPA allowed for adjustments to national performance standards that were established by DOL for youth and other populations.[58] Governors adjusted the standards for service delivery areas (SDAs) based on economic and demographic factors. (Each state was divided by the governor into geographic areas referred to as SDAs for purposes of carrying out activities under JTPA.) The process of adjusting national performance standards to state and local areas was premised on the logic of "leveling the playing field" across areas with different local conditions and took one of two forms under JTPA—use of DOL adjustment models or use of an alternative approach approved by DOL.[59]

DOL provided adjustment models to states for the core performance measures for youth and other populations. The adjustment models were based on multiple regression analysis, which is a statistical technique for determining the relationship between outcomes (dependent variables) and explanatory factors (independent variables). In the context of JTPA (or any other program affected by locally varying populations and economic conditions), multiple regression allows analysts to estimate variations in an expected outcome (performance measure) across local areas (SDAs, in the case of JTPA) based on variations in characteristics of participants and local economic conditions. Each factor was assigned a weight (regression coefficient) that is used to adjust the differences among SDAs in explanatory factors. For example, multiple regression allows one to determine that, on average, a 10 percentage point increase in non-high school graduates participating in a JTPA program would lower the youth employment rate by 1.45 percentage points, all other characteristics being equal.[60] The adjustment models were thus used to determine the expected performance standard in any given SDA based on the mix of participants and economic conditions at the local level, with the goal of not penalizing those SDAs with harder-to-serve populations or more difficult economic conditions.

End Notes

[1] DOL expects the transfer to take place prior to the start of PY2010 (July 1, 2010). U.S. Department of Labor, Office of Job Corps, *Budget Justification of Appropriation Estimates for Committees on Appropriations, FY2010*, vol. III, p. OJC-16.

[2] The 108th, 109th, and 1 10th Congresses considered legislation to reauthorize WIA: H.R. 1261 and S. 1627 (108th), H.R. 27 and S. 1021 (109th), H.R. 3747 (1 10th) . For further information, see CRS Report RL32778, *The Workforce Investment Act of 1998 (WIA): Reauthorization of Job Training Programs in the 109th Congress*, by Blake Alan Naughton and Ann Lordeman; and CRS Report RS2 1484, *Workforce Investment Act of 1998 (WIA): Reauthorization of Title I Job Training Programs in the 108th Congress*, by Ann Lordeman.

[3] U.S. Congress, Senate Committee on Health, Education, Labor, and Pensions, Subcommittee on Employment and Workplace Safety, *Modernizing the Workforce Investment Act (WIA) of 1998 to Help Workers and Employers Meet the Changing Demands of a Global Market*, 111th Cong., 1st sess., July 16, 2009.

[4] U. S. Congress, House Committee on Education and Labor, *Ensuring Economic Opportunities for Young Americans,* 111th Cong., 1st session, October 1, 2009.

[5] For information on summer youth employment issues, see CRS Report R40830, *Vulnerable Youth: Federal Funding for Summer Job Training and Employment,* by Adrienne L. Fernandes.

[6] ARRA effectively authorizes programs funded by Youth Activities via the law to temporarily extend the age of eligibility from 21 to 24.

[7] These terms are defined in CRS Report R40929, *Vulnerable Youth: Employment and Job Training Programs* , by Adrienne L. Fernandes. Up to 5% of youth participants in a local area may be individuals who do not meet the income criteria, but have at least one barrier to employment, some of which are not identical to those listed above: (1) deficient in basic literacy skills; (2) a school dropout; (3) homeless or a runaway; (4) an offender; (5) one or more grade levels below the grade level appropriate to the individual's age; (6) pregnant or parenting; (7) possess one or more disabilities, including learning disabilities; or (8) face serious barriers to employment as identified by the local WIB (20 C.F.R. 664.220).

[8] U.S. General Accounting Office, *Workforce Investment Act: Youth Provisions Promote New Service Strategies, but Additional Guidance Would Enhance Program Development,* GAO-02-413, April 2002, pp. 20-21, http://www.gao.gov/new.items/d02413.pdf. (GAO is now now as the Government Accountability Office.) (Hereafter, Government Accountability Office, Workforce Investment Act: Youth Provisions Promote New Service Strategies, but Additional Guidance Would Enhance Program Development, April 2002.)

[9] U.S. Government Accountability Office, *Recovery Act: States' and Localities' Current and Planned Uses of Funds While Facing Fiscal Stresses,* GAO-09-829, July 2009, p. 61.

[10] Written Statement of Mary Sarris, Executive Director of the North Shore Workforce Investment Board, U.S. Congress, Senate Committee on Health, Education, Labor, and Pensions (HELP), Subcommittee on Employment and Workplace Safety, *Modernizing the Workforce Investment Act (WIA) of 1998 to Help Workers and Employers Meet the Changing Demands of a Global Market,* 111th Cong., 1st sess., July 16, 2009.

[11] U.S. Department of Labor, Employment and Training Administration, *LA 2005 Governor's Letter,* July 20, 2005, http://waivers.doleta.gov/lettersState_pdfview.cfm.

[12] Government Accountability Office, *Workforce Investment Act: Youth Provisions Promote New Service Strategies, but Additional Guidance Would Enhance Program Development,* April 2002. The eligibility criteria for in-school and out-of-school youth were under Section 263 of JTPA.

[13] Jobs For the Future, WIA Reauthorization Policy Principles and Recommendations First Edition—Youth Activities, last updated March 29, 2009. (Hereafter, Jobs for the Future, Reauthorization Policy Principles and Recommendations First Edition—Youth Activities); Linda Harris, Recommendations for WIA Reauthorization Legislation: Title I Provisions, Center for Law and Social Policy (CLASP), July 19, 2007, http://www.clasp.org/admin/site/publications/ files/0217.pdf (Hereafter, Linda Harris, Recommendations for WIA Reauthorization Legislation: Title I Provisions); National Youth Employment Coalition (NYEC), NYEC Recommendations for Reauthorization of the Workforce Investment Act, February 13, 2003, http://nyec.org/content/documents/NYEC_WIA_Position_Statement_Final.pdf (Hereafter, NYEC, NYEC Recommendations for Reauthorization of the Workforce Investment Act); and Sandra Kerka, WIA Reauthorization and Youth Programs, Ohio Learning Work Connection, 2004, http://cle.osu.edu/lwc-publications/youth-information-briefs/downloads/WIA-Reauthorization.pdf.

[14] See for example, U.S. General Accounting Office, *Workforce Investment Act: Labor Actions Can Help States Improve Quality of Performance Outcome Data and Delivery of Youth Services,* GAO-04-308, February 2004, pp. 17- 19. (GAO is now known as the Government Accountability Office.) (Hereafter, Government Accountability Office, *Workforce Investment Act: Labor Actions Can Help States Improve Quality of Performance Outcome Data and Delivery of Youth Services,* February 2004.)

[15] Jobs For the Future, WIA Reauthorization Policy Principles and Recommendations First Edition—Youth Activities, Linda Harris Recommendations for WIA Reauthorization Legislation: Title I Provisions.

[16] Jobs for the Future, Reauthorization Policy Principles and Recommendations First Edition—Youth Activities.

[17] For example, see U.S. Congress, House Committee on Education and the Workforce, H.Rept. 109-9, *Report to Accompany the Job Training Improvement Act of 2005,* 109th Cong., 1st sess., February 25, 2005.

[18] NYEC, NYEC Recommendations for Reauthorization of the Workforce Investment Act.

[19] Written Statement of Mary Sarris, Executive Director of the North Shore Workforce Investment Board, U.S. Congress, Senate Committee on Health, Education, Labor, and Pensions, Subcommittee on Employment and Workplace Safety, *Modernizing the Workforce Investment Act (WIA) of 1998 to Help Workers and Employers Meet the Changing Demands of a Global Market,* 111th Cong., 1st sess., July 16, 2009.

[20] U.S. Department of Labor, Employment and Training Administration, Training and Employment Guidance Letter No. 3-04 ("The Employment and Training Administration's (ETA's) new strategic vision to serve out-of-school and at- risk youth under the Workforce Investment Act (WIA)"), July 16, 2004; and U.S. Department of Labor, Employment and Training Administration, *Youth Services Section, WIA Planning Guidance Training,* no date.

[21] Social Policy Research Associates, The Workforce Investment Act After Five Years: Results from the National Evaluation of the Implementation of WIA, June 2004.

[22] For additional information about the transition to adulthood, see CRS Report RL33975, *Vulnerable Youth: Background and Policies*, by Adrienne L. Fernandes.

[23] CRS Report R40535, *Disconnected Youth: A Look at 16- to 24-Year Olds Who Are Not Working or In School*, by Adrienne L. Fernandes and Thomas Gabe, pp. 17-20.

[24] For further information about funding, see CRS Report R40929, *Vulnerable Youth: Employment and Job Training Programs* , by Adrienne L. Fernandes.

[25] U.S. Government Accountability Office, *Recovery Act: Funds Continue to Provide Fiscal Relief to States and Localities, While Accountability and Reporting Challenges Need to Be Fully Addressed*, GAO-09-1016, September 2009, http://www.gao.gov/new.items/d091016.pdf, pp. 62-79

[26] U.S. Department of Labor, Employment and Training Administration, Training and Employment Guidance Letter (TEGL) No. 3-99, ("Program Guidance for Implementation of Comprehensive Youth Services Under the Workforce Investment Act During the Summer of 2000"), January 31, 2000.

[27] U.S. Department of Labor, Employment and Training Administration, "Strategies to Transition Older Youth Into Workforce Activities After Summer 2009 (ARRA)," August 26, 2009, webinar on http://www.Workforce3One.org.

[28] U.S. Department of Labor, PY2007 *Workforce Investment Act Standardized Record Data (WIASRD) Data Book*, Table IV-1, http://www.doleta.gov/performance

[29] To receive "intensive" services (e.g., individual career planning and job training), an individual must have received core services and need intensive services to become employed or to obtain or retain employment that allows for self- sufficiency. To receive training services (e.g. occupational skills training), an individual must have received intensive services and need training services to become employed or to obtain or retain employment that allows for self- sufficiency.

[30] For further information about collaboration among federal workforce and education programs, see CRS Congressional Distribution memorandum, *Intersection of the Youth Workforce System and the Education System*, by Adrienne L. Fernandes and Rebecca R. Skinner, coordinators. Available upon request.

[31] The report found that in-school youth were most likely to receive services through—in this order—community organizations, secondary schools, colleges or universities, youth one-stop centers, adult one-stop centers, and other providers, such as local or state governments. Out-of-school youth were most likely to receive services through—in this order—community organizations, colleges or universities, secondary schools, adult one-stop centers, youth adult one- stop centers, and other providers, such as local or state governments. U.S. Government Accountability Office, *Workforce Investment Act: Labor Actions Can Help States Improve Quality of Performance Outcome Data and Delivery of Youth Services*, February 2004, pp. 17-19.

[32] Ibid, p. 23.

[33] Peter Edelman, Mark Greenberg, and Harry Holzer, Georgetown Center on Poverty, Inequality and Public Policy, *Youth Policy Proposals, Working Draft*, April 2009.

[34] U.S. Congress, Senate Committee on Health, Education, Labor, and Pensions, Subcommittee on Employment and Workplace Safety, Modernizing the Workforce Investment Act (WIA) of 1998 to Help Workers and Employers Meet the Changing Demands of a Global Market, hearing on WIA reauthorization, 111th Cong., 1st sess., July 16, 2009.

[35] For additional information, see Mathematica Policy Research for the U.S. Department of Education, *Schooling in the Workplace: Increasing the Scale and Quality of Work-Based Learning, Final Report*, January 2001, http://www.eric.ed.gov/ERICDocs/data/ericdocs2sql/content_storage

[36] For further information about youth councils and the local workforce plan, see CRS Report R40929, *Vulnerable Youth: Employment and Job Training Programs* , by Adrienne L. Fernandes.

[37] NYEC, NYEC Recommendations for Reauthorization of the Workforce Investment Act.

[38] Government Accountability Office, *Workforce Investment Act: Youth Provisions Promote New Service Strategies, but Additional Guidance Would Enhance Program Development*, April 2002, pp. 14-15.

[39] See, for example, U.S. Congress, House Committee on Education and the Workforce, H.Rept. 109-9, *Report to Accompany the Job Training Improvement Act of 2005*, 109th Cong., 1st sess., February 25, 2005. According to GAO's survey of local WIBs for its 2004 report, almost two-thirds of local WIBs reported that they would keep their youth council even if it became optional. Of those who reported that they would not keep their council, 73% would use a youth committee of the local WIB to perform the functions of a youth council. See Government Accountability Office, *Workforce Investment Act: Labor Actions Can Help States Improve Quality of Performance Outcome Data and Delivery of Youth Services*, February 2004, p. 20.

[40] Linda Harris, Recommendations for WIA Reauthorization Legislation: Title I Provisions.

[41] Ibid and statement of Harry Holzer, Georgetown Center on Poverty, Inequality and Public Policy at the April 15, 2009, WIA Listening Session on Youth, conducted by the Senate Committee on Health, Education, Labor, and Pensions (HELP).

[42] Jobs for the Future and John J. Heldrich Center for Workforce Development, *Evaluation of the Transition to Comprehensive Youth Services Under the Workforce Investment Act*, for the U.S. Department of Labor, Employment and Training Administration, 2002, http://www.heldrich.rutgers.edu/uploadedFiles/Publications/Youth_Council_Evaluation.pdf; and Richard Kazis, *Youth Councils and Comprehensive Youth Planning: A*

Report from Eight Communities, Jobs for the Future, Issue Brief, May 2001, http://www.eric.ed.gov
/ERICDocs/data/ ericdocs2sql/content_storage_01/0000019b/80/19/1d/6e.pdf.

[43] U.S. Government Accountability Office, *Workforce Investment Act: Youth Provisions Promote New Service Strategies, but Additional Guidance Would Enhance Program Development*, April 2002.

[44] Statement of Mala Thakur, National Youth Employment Coalition (NYEC), at the April 15, 2009, WIA Listening Session on Youth, conducted by the Senate Committee on Health, Education, Labor, and Pensions (HELP).

[45] U.S. Department of Labor, Employment and Training Administration, Training and Employment Guidance Letter (TEGL) No. 16-00, ("Availability of Funds to Support Planning Projects that Enhance Youth Connections and Access to the One-Stop System"), March 19, 2001.

[46] U.S. Government Accountability Office, *Youth Opportunity Grants: Lessons Can Be Learned from Program, but Labor Needs to Make Data Available*, GAO-06-53, December 2005.

[47] This is based on Congressional Research Service correspondence with the U.S. Department of Labor, Employment and Training Administration, September 2009.

[48] In their state plans, states must identify the expected (adjusted) level of performance for each of the core indicators for the first three program years of the plan, which covers five program years. In order to "ensure an optimal return on the investment of Federal funds in workforce investment activities," the Secretary and the governor of each state shall "reach agreement on the levels of performance" for all youth and other indicators identified in Section 136(b)(2)(A). This agreed-upon level then becomes the "state adjusted level of performance" that is incorporated into the plan. Section 136(b)(3)(A)(i) of WIA specifies that the state adjusted levels of performance must (1) be expressed in an "objective, quantifiable, and measurable form"; and (2) show the state's progress toward "continuously improving" performance.

[49] U.S. Department of Labor, Employment and Training Administration, Training and Employment Guidance Letter (TEGL) No. 18-04 ("Announcing the Soon-to-be Proposed Revisions to Existing Performance Reporting Requirements ... "), February 28, 2005.

[50] See U.S. Department of Labor, Employment and Training Administration, "Workforce Investment Act (WIA) Waiver Summary Report: WIA Inception—December 16, 2008," http://www.doleta.gov/waivers/pdf/ WIA_Waivers_Summary.pdf.

[51] Local areas must report to the state on these same core indicators. The local WIB must negotiate with the governor and reach agreement on the local levels of performance for each indicator.

[52] See, for example, U.S. Department of Labor, Employment and Training Administration, Training and Employment Guidance Letter (TEGL) No. 9-08, ("Negotiated Performance Goals of the Workforce Investment Act Title IB Programs and Wagner-Peyser Act Funded Activities for Program Year 2009"), June 29, 2009.

[53] DOL advises that states should be aware of ETA's strategic vision of serving the neediest youth, including out-of-school youth, youth in foster care, youth in the juvenile justice system, children of incarcerated parents, migrant youth, youth with disabilities, and Native American youth. See TEGL 9-08 and TEGL 3-04.

[54] U.S. Government Accountability Office, *Disconnected Youth: Federal Action Could Address Some of the Challenges Faced by Local Programs That Reconnect Youth to Education and Employment*, GAO-08-3 13, February 2008, pp. pp. 3 1-33.

[55] This is based on Congressional Research Service correspondence with the U.S. Department of Labor, Employment and Training Administration, September 2009.

[56] See U.S. Department of Labor, Employment and Training Administration, "Workforce Investment Act (WIA) Waiver Summary Report: WIA Inception—December 16, 2008," http://www.doleta.gov/waivers/pdf/ WIA_Waivers_Summary.pdf.

[57] Center for Law and Social Policy and National Youth Employment Coalition, Recommendations to USDOL on Guidance to States on Implementing Youth Activities in the Recovery Act, February 25, 2009.

[58] The performance measures used for youth fluctuated over time, but generally youth were subject to three to seven measures each program year.

[59] As noted in a DOL guide on JTPA, "performance standards are adjusted to 'level the playing field' by making the standards neutral with respect to who is served and to local economic conditions. For example, an SDA serving a hardto-serve population would be given a lower standard than an SDA serving a less hard-to-serve population. Although set at different levels, meeting those two standards would require the same level of SDA effort." See Social Policy Research Associates, *Guide to JTPA Performance Standards for Program Years 1998 and 1999*, February 8, 1999, pp. III-1. Despite the fact that JTPA allowed states to develop their own adjustment models, states had to follow strict criteria from DOL. In addition, developing an adjustment model requires a degree of expertise in statistical analysis. For these reasons, there is some question of whether or not states were actually discouraged from developing their own models. See Carolyn J. Heinrich and Burt S. Barnow, *One Standard Fits All? The Pros and Cons of Performance Standard Adjustments*, La Follette School of Public Affairs, Working Paper 2008-023, Madison, WI, November 18, 2008.

[60] This example is from the PY1998 and PY1999 national model. Social Policy Research Associates, *Guide to JTPA Performance Standards for Program Years 1998 and 1999*, February 8, 1999, Appendix A.

In: Vulnerable Youth and Employment Issues
Editor: Christopher E. Perry

ISBN: 978-1-61122-020-9
© 2011 Nova Science Publishers, Inc.

Chapter 3

VULNERABLE YOUTH: FEDERAL FUNDING FOR SUMMER JOB TRAINING AND EMPLOYMENT

Adrienne L. Fernandes

SUMMARY

For decades, the federal government has played a role in helping vulnerable young people secure employment and achieve academic success through job training and employment programs, including summer youth employment opportunities. The enactment of the Workforce Investment Act (WIA, P.L. 105-220) in 1998 marked the first time since 1964 that states and localities did not receive funding specifically designated for summer employment programs for vulnerable youth. Although WIA does not authorize a stand-alone summer program, the law requires that local areas funded under its Youth Activities (Youth) program provide summer employment opportunities as one of 10 elements available to eligible low-income youth with barriers to employment. Together, these elements are intended to provide a comprehensive year-round job training and employment program for youth. Approximately one-quarter of youth in the program participate in summer employment activities, which are required to be directly linked to academic and occupational learning. Funding authorization for WIA expired in FY2003, but Congress has continued to appropriate funds for WIA, including the Youth program.

The current economic downturn has increased focus on the role of the summer employment element, particularly given recent evidence that summer youth employment is at a 60-year low. On February 17, 2009, President Obama signed into law the American Recovery and Reinvestment Act of 2009 (P.L. 111-5, ARRA, or Recovery Act). One of the stated purposes of ARRA is to preserve existing jobs and create new jobs. To this end, the law appropriated $1.2 billion for grants for the WIA Youth program. In the accompanying conference report, Congress specified that funds should be used for both summer youth employment and year-round employment opportunities, particularly for youth up to age 24. ARRA additionally established a role for the Inspectors General of various federal agencies and the U.S. Government Accountability Office (GAO) in overseeing use of ARRA funding.

In the summer of 2009, more than 329,000 youth participated in summer employment opportunities funded under ARRA. In its guidance on funding provided for the Youth Activities program, the Department of Labor (DOL) has emphasized that local areas have flexibility in carrying out certain aspects of the summer employment component as funded under ARRA. For example, local areas can determine whether follow-up will be required for youth served with ARRA funds during the summer months only. This is compared to WIA's normal requirement that all youth receive follow-up services. As part of its ARRA oversight efforts, GAO is conducting bimonthly reviews on the use of funds for nine federal programs by selected states, including the WIA Youth program. According to GAO, localities in these states have used Youth Activities funds to expand summer employment opportunities for youth, including in the public sector and private sector, and in nonprofit organizations.

This chapter provides an overview of current efforts to secure job training and employment for youth during the summer months, and addresses issues related to these efforts. For example, DOL has issued formal guidance to provide direction to states about carrying out summer youth employment under ARRA. Some of this guidance is different from previous guidance provided under WIA, in that it is tailored to the requirements of the Recovery Act. Further, with increased focus on the summer jobs component, policymakers may consider, as part of any efforts to reauthorize WIA, whether the law should place greater emphasis on summer employment. Past evaluations of federally funded programs have shown mixed results in the achievement of goals, although these programs are not necessarily comparable to the summer youth opportunities currently offered by states and localities.

INTRODUCTION

The federal government has long played a role in helping vulnerable young people secure employment and achieve academic success through job training and employment programs, including summer youth employment opportunities. These programs have sought to increase youth employment, educational attainment, and other positive outcomes. In some years, hundreds of thousands of youth have participated in the programs.

The enactment of the Workforce Investment Act (WIA, P.L. 105-220) in 1998 marked the first time since 1964 that states and localities did not receive funding for summer employment programs for vulnerable youth. However, the law requires that local areas funded under its Youth Activities (Youth) program provide summer employment opportunities as one of 10 elements available to low-income youth with barriers to employment. The current economic downturn has increased focus on the summer employment component, especially given recent evidence that employment for youth during the summer is at a 60-year low. In February 2009, President Obama signed into law the American Recovery and Reinvestment Act of 2009 (P.L. 111-5, ARRA, Recovery Act). One of the stated purposes of ARRA is to preserve existing jobs and create new jobs. To this end, the law appropriated $1.2 billion for the Youth program. The law emphasized that funds should be spent on summer youth employment opportunities, as well as year-round employment activities for older youth.

This chapter provides an overview of current efforts to employ youth during the summer months, particularly under the Recovery Act, and the issues surrounding these efforts.

Appendix A provides descriptions of terms applicable to the WIA Youth program and Appendix B discusses evaluations of past stand-alone summer youth programs that were federally funded.

BACKGROUND

History

Since 1964, the federal government has funded job training and employment programs for youth, including programs specifically targeted at youth during the summer months. The purpose of these summer programs was often both to employ youth and to assist them in maintaining the academic gains they made during the previous school year. Generally, these young people were eligible to participate if they were economically disadvantaged and had a barrier to securing employment or completing their education. Four laws that preceded WIA provided funding specifically for summer youth employment programs (see **Appendix B** for a summary of research on these programs). The enactment of WIA in 1998 marked the first time in decades that states and localities did not receive funding for stand-alone summer employment programs for vulnerable youth. However, all local areas must provide summer employment opportunities as part of their WIA Youth programs.

Summer Youth Employment Declining

The current economic recession has focused attention on the role of the federal and state governments in supporting workers who have been laid off or are at risk of being laid off. Youth are particularly vulnerable to problems with securing and retaining jobs during downturns in the economy. During the summer, when teens are most likely to have jobs, the rate of employment has decreased most steeply. In June 2000, nearly half (46.7%) of all teens were employed, compared to 29.3% in June 2009.[1] The June 2009 employment rate is the lowest it has been during the post-World War II period.[2] Young men have experienced the greatest losses in summer employment. Among males ages 16 through 19, just over one-quarter (27.6%) were employed in June 2009, compared to 46.1% in June 2000.[3] The declining rate of teen employment overall appears to be attributable to rising levels of joblessness and not to a declining interest in employment among teens.[4] According to the research literature, possible consequences of reduced work among teens are reduced employment, earnings, and labor productivity in the future, and less output in the economy.[5]

Similarly, the employment rates of young adults ages 20 through 24 have declined steadily.[6] Among males ages 20 through 24, the average employment-to-population ratio was 65.1% from January through June 2009, which represents about a 12% decrease from the same period in 2000. The 2009 employment-to-population ratio is the lowest it has been in approximately 60 years.

WIA YOUTH ACTIVITIES PROGRAM

The Youth Activities program is authorized by WIA[7] and is the primary source of federal funding for youth employment and job training activities, including summer employment opportunities, targeted to vulnerable youth.[8] A youth is eligible for Youth Activities if he or she is age 14 through 21,[9] is a low-income individual, and has one or more of the following barriers: he or she is deficient in basic literacy skills; a school dropout; homeless, a runaway, or a foster child; pregnant or parenting; or an offender; *or* in need of additional assistance to complete an educational program or to secure and hold employment.[10] At least 30% of all Youth Activities funds must be used for activities for out-of-school youth, *or* youth who have dropped out or have received a high school diploma or its equivalent but are basic-skills deficient, unemployed, or underemployed.[11]

The purpose of the Youth Activities program is to facilitate job training, employment, and educational attainment for select youth. The Youth Activities formula grant is distributed by the Department of Labor (DOL) to state workforce investment boards (WIBs), based on the unemployment and poverty status of youth in each state.[12] State WIBs coordinate workforce services for a state. As part of their oversight of these services, the state WIB creates a five-year state plan that addresses several items related to employment and training needs and activities, as well as performance and accountability.

State WIBs distribute Youth Activities funds to local WIBs, which oversee workforce services in a particular area of a state. Among other activities, each local board must establish what is known as a "youth council," comprised of representatives that assist the WIB in awarding grants or contracts to providers that carry out youth workforce activities. WIA is silent on the types of entities that may be contracted to provide services for youth. [13] However, local WIBs tend to award grants or contracts to a number of entities, including secondary schools, colleges or universities, and community organizations to carry out a local youth program for each local area overseen by a WIB.

Workforce programs carried out by local WIBs must provide 10 activities or "elements" to youth. The elements pertain to summer employment, educational achievement, employment services, leadership development activities, additional support for youth services, and follow-up services for 12 months.[14] The 10 program elements are summarized in **Table A-2** of **Appendix A**. Local WIBs have the option of also providing "other elements and strategies as appropriate to the needs and goals of the participants."[15]

Separately, a one-stop system is established by a local WIB to coordinate employment and training services for adult job seekers, dislocated workers, and youth.[16] Approximately 20 federal programs must provide services through the one-stop system, either by co-location, electronic linkages, or referrals. The local youth program is a required partner, and must use a portion of its funds to create and maintain the one-stop delivery system. The local program enters into a memorandum of understanding with the local WIB relating to the operation of the one-stop, among other requirements.[17]

Funding

Congress has appropriated funding for Youth Activities since FY2000, the first year WIA was implemented. Authorization for funding WIA programs expired with the end of FY2003; however, Congress has continued to appropriate funds for the programs since this time.

As shown in **Table 1**, funding for Youth Activities has ranged from about $924 million to $1.1 billion in each of FY2000 through FY200 10, except in FY2009. The total appropriation for FY2009 was $2.1 billion, including $924.1 million plus $1.2 billion appropriated under the Recovery Act. In the accompanying conference report to ARRA, Congress specified that funds should be used for summer youth employment and to expand year-round employment opportunities for youth up to age 24 (from age 21, as generally required under WIA).

Funding under ARRA

Of $1.2 billion that Congress appropriated for the WIA Youth program under ARRA, $1.1 88 billion was available for youth programming and $12 million was available for administrative purposes. According to DOL, of the $1.1 88 billion, over $821 million has been expended as of March 2010.[18] All funds have been obligated. States are not required to report costs related to summer youth employment, and therefore DOL does not track the amount expended for summer youth employment opportunities or the nine other activities that are to be provided through the Youth Activities program.

Table 1. Final Funding for DOL Job Training Programs, FY2000-FY2009
(Nominal Dollars) (Dollars in Thousands)

Fiscal Year	Youth Activities
FY2000	$1,000,965
FY2001	1,127,965
FY2002	1,127,965
FY2003	994,459
FY2004	995,059
FY2005	986,288
FY2006	940,500
FY2007	940,500
FY2008	924,069
FY2009	2,124,069 (924,069 + 1,200,000 under ARRA)
FY2010	924,069

Source: Congressional Research Service presentation of U.S. Department of Labor, Employment and Training Administration, *State Statutory Formula Funding*, available at http://www.doleta. gov/budget/statfund.cfm; and U.S. Congress, House Committee on Appropriations, *Departments of Transportation and Housing and Development, and Related Agencies Appropriations Act, 2010*, report to accompany H.R. 3288/P.L. 111-117, 111th Cong., [1st] sess., December 8, 2009, H.Rept. 111-366.

Note: The program year for Youth Activities is July 1 through June 30, although funds may be made available on April 1, pursuant to Section 1 89(g)(1)(B) of the Workforce Investment Act. Funds for the program are available in the program year in which the funds are appropriated and for two subsequent program years. ARRA funds were appropriated in PY2008; these funds are available for the balance of PY2008 and all of PY2009 and PY20 10, which extends through June 30, 2011.

Funds made available for the WIA Youth program under ARRA are available through PY20 10 (June 30, 2011).[19] For the purposes of the summer youth component, youth may participate in summer activities from May 1 through September 30,[20] although funding in 2011 ends in June of that year. DOL has stated that it is the intent of both Congress and the department to use a majority of the funds within the first year after they were made available.[21]

Summer Youth Employment Opportunities

Summer 2000 marked the first time since 1964 that a stand-alone summer youth employment program was not authorized or funded. Unlike previous federal legislation, WIA sought to provide a comprehensive job training and employment system for youth throughout an entire year by addressing their employment, education, and related needs, such as social supports.[22] Specifically, local WIBs must provide "summer employment opportunities that are directly linked to academic and occupational learning."[23] According to the WIA regulations, the summer youth element is not intended to be a stand-alone program, and local programs are encouraged to integrate a youth's participation in summer youth opportunities within an overall strategy that meets the youth's employment and training needs.[24] Youth who participate in summer activities are to receive a minimum of 12 months of follow-up, as with any other youth who participates in the local program.[25] Local WIBs may determine how much of the available youth funds will be used for summer and for year-round youth activities.

In 2000, DOL's Employment and Training Administration (ETA) issued a Training and Employment Guidance Letter (TEGL) to the state and local workforce investment communities about implementing the summer youth employment element for the first time.[26] ETA advised that local areas could choose different approaches for providing summer youth employment opportunities. Summer employment participants could be transitioned into year-round services to assist youth in attaining positive academic and employment outcomes. Local areas could alternatively provide follow-up activities for youth who do not continue with year-round activities. Such follow-up activities could include job shadowing, a "Youth Day" career exploration activity organized at a one-stop center, periodic telephone calls to inform youth of ongoing activities such as job fairs, and mentoring and tutoring by adults. ETA advised that youth who were determined to be deficient in basic skills should continue to be served until they become proficient. ETA went on to say that local workforce areas and schools should collaborate on summer programming efforts to ensure that youth achieve these skills. Further, because local areas anticipated decreases in funding for summer youth employment opportunities, ETA suggested that local WIBs leverage resources to adequately carry out the summer program with private sector and other funding sources. Among other resources, ETA directed state and local WIBs to educate local business leaders about the use of the Work Opportunity Tax Credit (WOTC) in order to encourage others in the business community to hire youth with barriers to employment.[27]

A 2004 report on the implementation of WIA found that local areas appeared to use three approaches to carry out summer opportunities: (1) many local areas maintain a fairly traditional summer youth program, although on a smaller scale than in the past, with a new emphasis on academic and occupational learning, such as competency-based instruction provided at the work site; (2) a smaller number of local areas substantially revamped their summer program by linking summer and year-round activities that are similar; and (3) several local areas decided to supplement their WIA summer opportunities with non-WIA funding to compensate for the loss of a large-scale program.[28]

Participants in Summer Youth Activities

The data on participation in WIA are based on the concept of program "exiters." An exiter is a participant who had received a service funded by WIA but had not received the service for 90 consecutive calendar days prior to data collection, and is not scheduled to receive future services. Thus, the date on which an individual has finished his or her participation in WIA determines the program year for which data are generated on the exiter. The most recent data on youth participants (i.e., exiters) are for April 1, 2007, through March 31, 2008.[29] Over 108,000 youth ages 14 through 21 exited the program, of whom 24.1% participated in summer employment opportunities in the summer of 2007.[30] Youth who participated in Youth Activities during this year tended to be female (57.8%), African American (34.8%) or Hispanic (29.4%), and ages 16 to 17 (48.6%). The most common barrier was that youth were deficient in basic skills (57.1%).

Through March 2010, 375,607 youth participated in WIA Youth program activities funded by ARRA, of whom 329,538 (87.7%) participated in summer employment opportunities.[31]

SUMMER EMPLOYMENT OPPORTUNITIES FUNDED BY ARRA

Congress encourages that funds appropriated under ARRA be made available specifically for summer youth employment opportunities, as well as year-round activities for older youth. The law's accompanying conference report (H.Rept. 111-16) states

> The conferees are particularly interested in [WIA Youth] funds being used to create summer employment opportunities for youth and language applying the work readiness performance indicator to such summer jobs is included as an appropriate measure for those activities. Year-round youth activities are also envisioned and the age of eligibility for youth services provided with the additional funds is extended through age 24 to allow local programs to reach young adults who have become disconnected from both education and the labor market.[32]

The conference report references an existing WIA Youth Activities' measure—the work readiness indicator, which is part of the basic skills performance indicator—for purposes of evaluating performance of the summer youth component. The work readiness indicator measures the number of work readiness skills goals attained by youth divided by the number of work readiness skills goals set overall.[33]

This next section of the report discusses DOL guidance for implementing the summer youth employment component, as funded by ARRA. This discussion is followed by an overview of efforts to monitor the implementation and performance of the program by both DOL and the Government Accountability Office (GAO).[34]

Guidance on Implementation of ARRA

On March 18, 2009, ETA issued a TEGL on implementation of WIA funds under ARRA.[35] The TEGL provides specific instructions on the WIA Youth program. Although Youth Activities funds appropriated under the Recovery Act are available for any of the 10 program elements, the letter emphasizes that the funds should be targeted to summer employment opportunities, particularly during the summer of 2009, as well as activities to serve youth who are not working or in school. The TEGL also provides guidance to local WIBs on implementing summer youth employment models. Local WIBs are advised to use http://www.workforce3one.org, DOL's interactive knowledge sharing and learning platform, for information about using ARRA funds. Among other resources, the website includes tools and resources dealing with worksite agreements, methodologies for measuring work readiness, training materials for staff and workforce supervisors, and past technical assistance materials developed under the Job Training Partnership Act (JTPA) summer employment program. (JTPA directly preceded WIA and funded a standalone summer program.) The TEGL provides examples of summer employment experiences that involve "green" jobs (defined as those involving solar, geothermal, wind power design, and the use of environmentally friendly building materials); registered apprenticeship programs, which provide hands-on training and experience needed in a potential career field; and integration of work-based and classroom-based learning opportunities.

According to the TEGL, local boards that carry out summer youth employment opportunities must ensure they include "work experience," as defined in regulation. "Work experience" refers to planned, structured learning experiences that take place at a worksite for a limited period of time, and experiences designed to enable youth to gain exposure to the working world and its requirements, including service learning, paid or unpaid community service, internships and job shadowing, and integration of basic academic skills into work activities, among other activities.[36] (**Table A-3** in **Appendix A** includes a more detailed definition of the term.)

All states and local areas are advised to ensure that worksites participating in the summer employment program introduce and reinforce the "rigors, demands, rewards, and sanctions associated with holding a job ... [w]ork experience provided to summer employment participants should be structured to impart measurable communication, interpersonal, decision-making, and learning skills." DOL goes on to state that work experience arrangements for youth should not unfavorably impact current employees or existing contracts for services or collective bargaining agreements. State and local areas should also consider summer employment activities in the public sector and private sector, including nonprofit entities.

Differences between Implementation under WIA and ARRA

The TEGL emphasizes that local areas have flexibility in carrying out certain aspects of summer employment models. First, local areas can determine whether follow-up will be required for youth served with ARRA funds during the summer months only. Under current law, local programs must provide follow-up for youth who participate in one or more of the 10 program elements, and this follow-up must be for at least 12 months.[37] Second, local areas have flexibility under ARRA in determining the type of assessments and individual service strategies (ISS) used for youth served during the summer months only. Specifically, local areas must conduct *some* level of assessment and development of ISS. This is in contrast to the WIA requirement that local programs provide a *full* objective assessment, which includes an assessment of basic skills, and comprehensive ISS.[38] Third, local programs that use Recovery Act dollars for summer youth employment opportunities *may* determine whether "it is appropriate" that academic learning be directly linked to these activities. As discussed above, summer youth employment opportunities as enacted under WIA refers to activities that are to be "directly linked to academic and occupational learning."[39]

State Plan

Each state submits a five-year state plan that describes the workforce development activities to be undertaken by the state and how the state will implement key requirements of WIA. State plans include a section to address strategies for serving youth. As set forth in the TEGL, DOL required that all states submit a modification to their state plan by June 30, 2009, because of changes to WIA as a result of the Recovery Act, and due to the economic downturn's effect on states' workforces and economies.[40]

The state plan was to address specific questions related to youth services provided with ARRA funds, including

> (1) Describe the anticipated program design for the WIA Youth funds provided under the Recovery Act. Include in this description a program design for both younger, in-school and older or out-of-school youth (including the 22-24 year olds that can be served with Recovery Act funds). (2) Will the state use the Recovery Act funds to fund only 2009 summer youth activities or some combination of activities in 2009 and 2010? If using the funds over two summers, what percentage of funds does the state anticipate using the first summer? (3) If using the funds for summer employment opportunities, describe how the state will deliver summer employment opportunities. (4) Describe any policies or strategies the state is implementing to ensure that local areas implement activities that support out-of-school youth during summer and/or non-summer months, such as supportive services, needs-based payments, or day-care.

Use of Waivers

Section 1 89(i)(4) of WIA permits DOL to grant waivers to states or local areas pursuant to a request submitted by the state. Waivers may be granted for any of the statutory or regulatory requirements, except those relating to wage and labor standards.[41] Since WIA was enacted, DOL has issued waivers for youth-related matters.[42]

The March 2009 TEGL advises states and local boards about two waivers for expedited and emergency procurement procedures for carrying out activities funded by ARRA.[43] These waivers were to be submitted with the state plan (see above). First, states were authorized to seek a waiver for procurement requirements for youth summer employment providers. Under WIA, providers of youth services must be awarded a grant or contract on a competitive basis. Alternatively, states could have applied for a waiver to conduct an expedited, limited competition to select service providers. The waiver applied only to ARRA funding used for the summer employment program element in the summer of 2009. Second, states were eligible to seek a waiver requesting that ETA waive the youth performance measures for older youth (ages 18 through 24) served with ARRA beyond the summer months who participated only in work experience. The waiver would have permitted states to use the work readiness indicator as the only indicator, and the waiver would be applicable for six months following the summer period, to March 2010. When submitting these waiver requests, states were to provide detailed justifications and assurances.

Performance

Work Readiness Performance Measure

As enacted, WIA sets forth state and local performance measures as part of the accountability system to assess the effectiveness of state and local areas in continuously improving workforce investment activities.[44] The measures for youth ages 14 through 18 are different than those for youth ages 19 through 21 in the program. The measures for younger youth focus on basic skill attainment, attainment of a high school diploma or its equivalency, and retention in an academic or employment placement. The older youth outcomes focus on employment; specifically, entry into employment, retention, change in earnings, and academic or employment placement.

ARRA directs DOL to measure the performance of local programs that carry out summer employment opportunities through the work readiness indicator, which is one part of the basic skills performance indicator for younger youth. In a May 2009 TEGL on performance indicators for WIA programs funded by ARRA, DOL advises that states and/or local areas were to establish a methodology for determining work readiness skills upon beginning and completing the summer experience, and should choose from a variety of assessment tools, including worksite supervisor evaluations, work readiness skills checklists administered by program staff, portfolio assessments, and other relevant forms of assessing work readiness skills.[45]

Oversight

DOL Oversight

States currently submit data on the demographics and outcomes of youth who participate in local programs funded by Youth Activities on an annual basis. DOL is now requiring states to submit supplemental reports on a monthly basis—with aggregate counts of youth who participate in activities funded by the Recovery Act, including the characteristics of participants who participate in summer employment (i.e., gender, race, education level, school status, age), the number of participants in summer employment, services received, attainment of a work readiness skill, and completion of summer youth employment.[46] According to DOL, the monthly reports will assist the department in analyzing the level of program participation and in gaining insight into the activities that states and local areas are offering to participants, particularly because there is only one outcome available to measure program impact.[47] Youth who participate in summer employment only are not be reported in the regular WIA Youth reports that are compiled to create a profile of youth who have finished the program, as discussed above.

In addition, recipients of ARRA dollars must submit detailed information on the use of the funds every quarter, beginning with the quarter ending September 30, 2009, including information on jobs created and retained.[48] This includes jobs created and retained by the WIA Youth program with ARRA dollars both during the summer and outside the summer months. Further, estimates of jobs created and retained are to include all paid work opportunities and exclude academic opportunities.

DOL contracted with Mathematica Policy Research, Inc., a social policy research organization that is currently conducting an evaluation of the WIA Youth program overall, to examine how 20 communities carried out ARRA-funded summer employment activities in summer 2009. Mathematica used state performance data submitted by states to DOL through December 31, 2009, and conducted interviews with stakeholders during visits to the 20 communities. Overall, Mathematica found that the initiative was "implemented successfully without any major problems," but that localities experienced some challenges, including the process of determining eligibility, recruiting older youth, recruiting private sector employers, understanding what constitutes "green jobs," and matching youth to employers, among other issues.[49] DOL has also contracted with Brandeis University to conduct similar research, but with a focus on four communities: Chicago, Detroit, Indianapolis, and Phoenix. Results are forthcoming.[50]

In late 2009, DOL convened two national summits to facilitate sharing of lessons learned from local practitioners who ran summer employment programs with ARRA funds.[51] The summits focused on taking the experience of the summer program and applying it to future programming, transitioning older youth and out-of-school youth, and green jobs and other emerging industries such as health care. The summits also touched on the skills that employers want from youth, how youth are training for their jobs, how to evaluate whether a youth is prepared to work, and case management for youth, among other topics.

At the summits, DOL reported that 63% of youth met the work readiness attainment rate established by their local programs.[52] DOL cautioned that these rates are preliminary and may increase as more data become available from states. According to DOL, summer youth activities were successfully implemented in many locations, but local program officials, employers, and youth believe that measuring actual outcomes has "proven challenging and may reveal little about what the summer activities achieved."

As part of its guidance to states on PY20 10 WIA Youth program funding, DOL stated that it will soon provide additional guidance on the work readiness indicator, in response to concerns raised by the Government Accountability Office about how the performance measure has been used to measure gains made by youth participating in the program as funded under ARRA (see below).[53] In addition, the guidance encourages states and local areas to continue to focus on summer employment opportunities (as well as paid and unpaid work experiences) during PY20 10 with the use of regular WIA Youth funds.

Finally, ARRA requires the Inspector General (IG) of each agency to take on oversight responsibilities. The DOL IG has issued an outline for how the office is monitoring ARRA funding received by the department, including WIA Youth Activities funds used for summer employment activities.[54] Specifically, the IG reports that it is looking into whether DOL has provided sufficient guidance and technical assistance to ensure that funds were mainly used to create paid work experiences for youth participants in the summer of 2009, and to determine whether state and local area workforce plans include paid summer and year-around opportunities.

GAO Oversight

In addition to oversight by agencies that administer ARRA funds, the law directs GAO to conduct bimonthly reviews on the use of funds by selected states and localities. GAO has begun oversight efforts, and is focusing on 16 states and the District of Columbia.[55] These jurisdictions represent about 65% of the U.S. population and are estimated to receive about two-thirds of the federal assistance available through ARRA. As part of its work in overseeing use of ARRA funds, GAO has issued a series of reports on the approaches taken by the selected states and the District of Columbia to ensure accountability for the ARRA funds they receive and to evaluate the impact of these funds. The reports focus on nine federal programs that are estimated to account for approximately 87% of ARRA outlays in FY2009 for programs administered by states and localities. One of the nine programs is WIA Youth Activities, which accounts for 1% of all ARRA dollars appropriated to these programs.

Implementation

For the purposes of its oversight of the Youth program, GAO is examining how the program is carried out in 16 states.[56] As part of its assessment, in September 2009,[57] GAO found that states were generally successful in increasing the number of youth who participated in summer activities and meeting their targets. Worksites for ARRA-funded summer youth activities included public sector, private sector, and nonprofit organizations at local government offices, public parks, recreation centers, camps, public schools, and community colleges. For example, in Chicago, the Museum of Science and Industry enrolled youth as peer educators who facilitated children's science activities at sites throughout the city, such as libraries and schools. In addition, some youth also received academic and occupational skills training, such as academic projects overseen by certified teachers, GED training courses, and a summer learning program that featured classes and workshops to study visual arts.[58] Separately, local areas reported to GAO that they used several approaches to paying youth, such as direct deposit, prepaid debit cards, or paper checks. In at least one jurisdiction, Detroit, GAO observed that youth waited in long lines to get their paychecks.

In a follow-up report, issued in March 2010, GAO reported that of the youth in the 16 states that were included in the assessment, on average, 82% completed their summer work experience without dropping out prior to the scheduled end date of the work experience in the summer of 2009.[59] According to GAO, this is the same share of youth nationwide who completed their summer work experience over the same period.

Challenges with Implementation

According to GAO, challenges reported by states and local officials in implementing summer youth employment opportunities included (1) tight time frames for implementing the program, (2) lack of staffing capacity to meet expanding needs, (3) difficulty in determining and documenting youth eligibility, (4) difficulty in recruiting youth, (5) lack of guidance about what constitutes "green" jobs, and (6) challenges with implementing the work readiness indicator.

States and local areas had about four months to begin their summer employment activities. Officials reported that such a process would normally begin many months earlier. Some local areas reported that they lacked recent experience operating this kind of program, and had to quickly decide how to structure the program and recruit worksites and participants.

As discussed below, until FY2000, federal funds supported stand-alone summer programs. With the enactment of WIA, many states and local areas had greatly reduced their summer employment and training activities. Even those areas that had maintained formal summer programs had to act quickly to expand these programs. Another concern raised by officials was that states had been downsizing or did not have the flexibility to hire additional staff due to hiring freezes and budget cuts.

Local areas additionally reported that youth had challenges with providing the documents required to prove WIA program eligibility, and that the income eligibility requirements for the program may exclude some needy youth (see **Table A-1** for a definition of low-income as it pertains to eligibility for the program). Officials in Philadelphia reported that some youth applicants whose parents had recently lost their jobs were not eligible because eligibility was based on income earned during the period preceding the job loss.[60] In seven states, officials mentioned that youth and their parents had challenges in providing the proper documentation in a timely manner.[61] Youth often had to come back to the workforce office to provide the documentation needed to be eligible. Documenting eligibility was especially challenging for youth ages 18 through 24 because many did not have basic documents, such as a birth certificate or proof of household income. Recruiting youth was also reported as a challenge. Local officials used various forms of advertisement and increased wages to attract youth to the program.

While DOL has encouraged states and local areas to provide opportunities for "green" jobs, some officials reported that they were not always clear about what constituted such a job. The methods for defining green jobs varied across states, and in some cases, it was unclear whether youth working in jobs classified as green jobs were actually working toward green educational or career pathways. For example, in Georgia, an organic food company was considered a green employer, but the youth was performing clerical duties.[62] To address this issue, GAO recommended that DOL provide additional guidance about the nature of these jobs and the strategies that could be used to prepare youth for careers in green industries.[63] DOL responded that it is taking steps to better understand and define green jobs, such as holding technical assistance forums that will focus on ways to prepare youth for green industries, among other efforts.

Finally, GAO cited concerns about the work readiness indicator. In its September 2009 report, GAO found that states and localities are using different strategies for measuring work readiness, and therefore DOL will face challenges evaluating the program on a national level. GAO reported that of 10 states reviewed, only Illinois established a uniform approach for measuring work readiness gains. The other nine states used measurements that varied across local areas and sometimes from contractor to contractor. For example, in Columbus, OH, officials used a work readiness assessment tool with questions that addressed collaboration in the workplace, problem solving, and characteristics of good leadership.[64] Youth were also required to do an extensive self evaluation across these dimensions. In nearby Dayton, OH, officials gave youth a 20-question true-false survey that included questions such as "I understand the importance of demonstrating a positive attitude in the workplace." Other areas did not employ pre-tests to establish a benchmark to which youth could be compared later.

GAO went on to recommend that DOL provide additional guidance on how to measure work readiness of youth, with a goal of improving the comparability and rigor of the measure.[65] DOL responded that the measure may not be as meaningful because of the differences in how states and localities have evaluated progress made by youth. The department is looking to refine the indicator and determine a more effective way to measure it.

Oversight by States and Localities

The states reviewed by GAO reported that they planned to implement (or were already implementing) procedures to monitor summer youth employment opportunities carried out by local WIBs. Such activities included financial auditing; site visits; assessments to identify local areas that may have challenges with implementation due to certain factors, such as having a larger program; periodic meetings with local program directors; and reviews of files concerning eligibility, contracts, and other topics. The jurisdictions also reported that they had the capacity to track and report on ARRA-funded expenditures for WIA Youth Activities separately from those not funded by the act. Further, states and local areas reported increasing their staff to meet the demands of monitoring the expanded summer youth activities.

PENDING LEGISLATION

Two bills, one that has passed the House and another that may soon be voted on by the House, would provide additional funding for summer employment opportunities.

The Jobs for Main Street Act (H.R. 2847)—part of the Commerce-Justice-Science FY20 10 appropriations bill[66]—passed the House on December 16, 2009, and would appropriate $500 million in WIA Youth program dollars that are to be used exclusively for summer employment opportunities. The conference report specifies that the program funds are to be "solely" for summer employment programs, and that the work readiness indicator, as specified above, is to be used to measure the effectiveness of the summer youth component. Further, the bill states that for purposes of meeting the low-income eligibility standard of WIA, youth qualify if they meet the eligibility requirements for free meals under the National School Lunch Act during the most recent school year.

Funding for the Youth Activities program, including summer youth employment, is also part of the American Jobs and Closing Tax Loopholes Act of 2010 (H.R. 4213), which passed the House on May 27, 2010, as an amendment to the Senate-passed version of the bill.[67] The bill would appropriate $1 billion to the Youth Activities program. Among other requirements, H.R. 4213 stipulates that the work readiness indicator would be the only measure of performance used to assess the effectiveness of summer employment for youth provided with these funds.

ISSUES FOR CONGRESS

The increased focus on summer jobs for youth raises several issues related to its implementation, in addition to those highlighted by both DOL and GAO, such as implementation of the work readiness indicator. First, DOL has issued formal guidance to provide direction to states about carrying out summer youth employment. Some of this guidance is different from previous guidance provided under WIA. Second, while ARRA and guidance by DOL focus on the summer youth provisions, they also emphasize that older out-of-school youth should also have opportunities to participate in activities funded under ARRA. The extent to which states and localities will be serving these youth is not clear. Third, with increased focus on the summer jobs program, policymakers may consider, as part of any efforts to reauthorize WIA, whether the law should place greater emphasis on summer employment.

Modifications to WIA Youth Requirements under ARRA

Congress may wish to consider whether certain program elements that are required in WIA should be modified when implemented under ARRA. As discussed previously, the March 18, 2009, TEGL appears to change three requirements under WIA that apply to the Youth program.[68] These requirements were not altered by ARRA or the accompanying conference report; however, through the TEGL, DOL has provided guidance on carrying out the requirements differently for ARRA-funded activities. First, as noted above, local programs are required by WIA to provide 12 months of follow-up for youth who participate in one or more of the 10 program elements. However, the TEGL advises that follow-up is optional for those youth who participate only in summer employment activities. The TEGL goes on to say that summer employment programs generally extend six to eight weeks, and local areas should provide follow-up services only when deemed appropriate.

Second, the TEGL enables local areas to determine the types of assessments summer youth participants are required to undergo. This is in contrast to the WIA requirement that local programs provide a full objective assessment, which includes an assessment of basic skills, and a comprehensive ISS as specified in regulations. Third, local programs that use Recovery Act dollars for summer youth employment opportunities *may* determine whether "it is appropriate" that academic learning be directly linked to these opportunities. This is another major distinction between implementation of WIA and ARRA, as noted only in the TEGL (and not in ARRA or the accompanying conference report). As discussed above, WIA requires these linkages to be in place.

DOL may have introduced these modifications to carry out one of the purposes of the Recovery Act—to create new jobs—and to do so quickly. These changes may give flexibility to local programs that want to concentrate on creating summer employment opportunities for youth, rather than follow-up or other activities that do not directly involve actual employment. In addition, these changes presumably are being examined as part of a state's plan and general oversight by DOL. On the other hand, DOL may have considered allowing these elements to be optional for jurisdictions that seek a waiver, in order to more closely monitor any deviations from current law that were not explicitly authorized under ARRA.

In-School and Out-of-School Youth

An ongoing discussion among advocates and stakeholders is the extent to which the WIA program should serve out-of-school youth versus in-school youth. WIA requires that at least 30% of all Youth Activities funds must be used for activities for out-of-school youth, *or* youth who have dropped out or have received a high school diploma or its equivalent but are basic-skills deficient, unemployed, or underemployed. This requirement applies to ARRA. Yet ARRA potentially introduces a complication because of its emphasis on both summer employment opportunities—that tend to target younger, in-school youth—and year-round activities for older youth.

The March 2009 TEGL appears to address both directives from Congress about summer employment and serving older youth. The TEGL also states that funds should be targeted to summer youth employment, particularly during the summer of 2009. Based on preliminary information from GAO, some states appear to be using at least half or all of their ARRA funds for summer employment in 2009. At least four of 16 states reported that local WIBs were required to have spent 50% to 70% of their ARRA Youth dollars by September or October 2009. Further, according to DOL, about 37% were not in school as of March 2010 (recent data are not available on younger and older youth).[69] These preliminary data raise questions about the extent to which these youth have been served.

Nonetheless, older youth could be engaged in ARRA-funded activities after the summer, although data do not appear to be available on the share of younger and older youth engaged in such activities. The March 2009 TEGL advises that states and local areas develop strategies to serve youth in the post-summer months. For older and out-of-school youth who did not return to school in the fall, state and local areas were advised in the TEGL to consider "work experiences and other appropriate activities beyond the summer months including training opportunities and reconnecting to academic opportunities." ETA suggests the type of services that can be made available to these youth, such as short-term subsidized work experience and co-enrolling them in adult training services. In addition, the TEGL suggests that states could have sought a waiver, as part of their state plan submission, to use the work readiness indicator to evaluate older youth ages 18 through 24 served under WIA for up to six months beyond the summer of 2009.

Should WIA Include a Stand-Alone Summer Employment Program?

Authorization for funding WIA programs expired with the end of FY2003. Congress has continued to appropriate funds for the programs through annual appropriation laws, and in some years has considered proposals to reauthorize the law. With increased focus on the summer jobs program, policymakers may consider, as part of any efforts to reauthorize WIA, whether the law should place greater emphasis on summer employment, as predecessor legislation did.

For decades, the federal government played a role in helping young people secure employment and achieve academic success through employment programs, including those with a summer youth employment focus. Generally, these young people were eligible for the programs because they were economically disadvantaged and had a barrier to securing employment or completing their education. The enactment of WIA in 1998 marked the first time since 1964 that states and localities did not receive funding for stand-alone summer employment programs for vulnerable youth. However, as noted above, all local areas must provide summer employment opportunities as part of their WIA Youth programs.

Four laws that preceded WIA provided funding specifically for summer youth employment activities:[70]

- Economic Opportunity Act of 1964 (EOA, P.L. 88-452): The act established the Neighborhood Youth Corps (NYC), which included programs for in-school and out-of-school youth. The NYC summer program for in-school youth was primarily intended to help high school age, low-income youth remain in school by providing them with summer employment.
- Comprehensive Employment and Training Act (CETA, P.L. 93-203): Enacted in 1973, CETA authorized the Summer Program for Economically Disadvantaged Youth (SPEDY). Similar to NYC, its primary purpose became one of providing work experience to economically disadvantaged youth ages 14 to 21 during the summer to enhance their future employability.
- Youth Employment and Demonstrations Project Act (YEDPA, P.L. 9 5-93): YEDPA extended funding for SPEDY and established new employment, training, and demonstration programs for youth. Summer employment was not a primary focus of the law, although summer employment was a component of one of the demonstration programs, the Youth Incentive Entitlement Pilot Program (YIEPP). Youth ages 16 to 19 who lived in 17 pilot sites were eligible for jobs through the program.
- Job Training Partnership Act (JTPA, P.L. 97-300): JTPA was enacted in 1982 and repealed CETA. JTPA's Summer Youth Employment and Training Program (SYETP) provided summer employment to disadvantaged youth. SYETP was similar to its predecessor, and provided employment and training activities during the summer months to low-income youth ages 14 through 21 to strengthen basic educational skills, encourage school completion, provide work exposure, and enhance citizenship skills. A separate demonstration program authorized under JTPA—the Summer Training and Employment Program (STEP)—included work experience, basic skills remediation, and life skills for youth ages 14 and 15.

CRS conducted a review of the social science literature for studies of the summer jobs programs established by these four laws to better understand how they operated, and whether any findings could be applied to current efforts to expand employment for youth during the summer. The search yielded a small number of studies that examined how the programs were implemented and evaluated program effectiveness.[71] Notably, some of the studies examined the effectiveness of summer programs in the context of larger employment programs of which they were a part. **Appendix B** provides a detailed summary of findings.

Overall, the studies show mixed results about both program implementation and effectiveness. A few of the studies examined implementation of two of the programs, and showed that these programs were carried out unevenly at some sites. For example, based on an assessment of the NYC program as it operated in the District of Columbia and surrounding areas, GAO found that the program did not enroll youth most at-risk of dropping out, as intended. However, it generally provided youth with useful work experience and adequate supervision. In a separate study, GAO found that at some SPEDY worksites, the program did not provide youth with meaningful work tasks and training to enhance their future employability. GAO concluded that DOL did not adequately monitor the program.

The studies also examined program effectiveness. The studies assessed whether the programs met goals generally related to education and employment, such as improving rates of dropout and future employment. Most programs appear to have met some of their goals, but with mixed results because they benefited select groups of youth and/or led to positive outcomes only for a short period of time. Evaluations of the NYC's in-school and summer youth programs, which used random assignment, found that they generally did not reduce the likelihood that an eligible youth would drop out, although certain youth, including black males and Indian youth, were more likely to graduate from high school than their counterparts in the control group. An evaluation of NYC's successor, SPEDY, found no differences in full-time employment between the treatment (enrolled in the program) and control groups, but did find that youth in the program were more likely to be employed part-time; these findings should be interpreted with caution, given challenges with implementing the random design of the program.

Programs that were carried out in the late 1970s and 1980s showed similarly inconsistent results, although the YIEPP study appeared to be most promising. YIEPP was funded from 1978 through 1981 and the evaluation showed that the in-school and summer components of the program led to positive effects for black youth in terms of employment and wages; however, the program did not improve success in school. Unlike random assignment evaluations, the YIEPP study compared communities that received YIEPP funds to those that did not. Finally, an evaluation of STEP, a short-term pilot program in the 1980s, found that this program resulted in short-term benefits, such as mitigating learning losses that typically occur during summer months for youth. Over the long term, the study found that the earlier results did not persist for many youth.

These studies are not sufficient for drawing conclusions about the effectiveness of summer jobs in general for a few reasons. First, the research literature does not provide enough information to determine the extent to which the programs are comparable. The summer programs appear to have been implemented somewhat differently, and in some cases were evaluated using distinct methodologies. Differences between the programs seem to be that they were carried out over varying periods; involved different types of grantees; used distinct eligibility criteria, particularly for YIEPP; and may have had inconsistent oversight by DOL and other entities with oversight capacity. Based on the evaluations, some of the programs also appeared to have had greater difficulty in implementing the program and targeting the most at-risk youth.

Second, the evaluations beg the question of whether the programs met other goals that were not necessarily measured, but may have been of interest to policymakers. For example, all of the programs seemed to meet a possible policy goal of providing employment opportunities to youth who would otherwise be idle during the summer months (although at least one program, the NYC, did not provide meaningful work opportunities at many sites). Tens of thousands to 1 million youth participated in the programs each summer. One of the studies found that two-thirds of youth in communities with YIEPP grants participated in the program. The programs may have additionally enriched youth in other ways that were not measured by the studies by providing, for example, opportunities for youth to participate in cultural events and to gain soft skills for work, such as arriving on time and interacting appropriately with co-workers.

Finally, the ARRA summer jobs component may be subject to more distinct, and possibly more rigorous, oversight than previous summer programs. As discussed above, ETA, the DOL IG's Office, and GAO are monitoring the program. In addition, ETA has contracted with Mathematica to better understand the how the Youth Activities program overall, including summer employment opportunities, is carried out. This oversight may provide information about the extent to which recent summer employment activities have been implemented successfully, and whether they have helped to alleviate youth unemployment, at least temporarily, among other possibilities.

APPENDIX A. WORKFORCE INVESTMENT ACT YOUTH ACTIVITIES PROGRAM

Table A-1. Definitions of Select Terms Used in WIA Youth Programs

Deficient in basic literacy skills may be defined at the state or local level. The definition must include criteria to determine that an individual (1) computes or solves problems, reads, writes, or speaks English at or below the 8th grade level on a generally accepted standardized test or received a comparable score on a criterion-referenced test, or (2) is unable to compute or solve problems, read, write, or speak English at a level necessary to function on the job, in the individual's family, or in society. If the definition is established at the state level, the policy must be included in the state plan (20 CFR 664.205).
Ever in foster care refers to a person who is in foster care or has been in the foster care system (as defined in PY2007 WIASRD Data Book, Appendix B).
Follow-up refers to services that may include (1) the leadership development and supportive service activities defined in regulation; (2) regular contact with a youth participant's employer, including assistance in addressing work-related problems that arise; (3) assistance in securing better paying jobs, career development, and further education; (4) work-related peer support groups; (5) adult mentoring; and (6) tracking the progress of youth in employment after training (20 CFR 664.450).
Individual with a disability means an individual with any disability as defined in Section 3 of the Americans with Disabilities Act of 1990. The act defines "disability" with respect to an individual as (1) a physical or mental impairment that substantially limits one or more major life activities of such individual; (2) a record of such an impairment; or (3) being regarded as having such an impairment. "Being regarded as having such an impairment" refers to whether the individual establishes that he or she has been subjected to an action prohibited under the Americans with Disabilities Act because of an actual or perceived physical or mental impairment whether or not the impairment limits or is perceived to limit a major life activity.
Low-income individual means an individual who (1) receives, or is a member of a family that receives, cash payments through a federal, state, or local income-based public assistance program; (2) received an income, or is a member of a family that received a total family income (excluding unemployment compensation and certain other payments), for the six-month period prior to applying for youth employment and training activities, that, in relation to family size, did not exceed the higher of the poverty line, for an equivalent period, or 70% of the lower living standard income level, for an equivalent period; (3) is a member of a household that receives food stamps, now renamed SNAP (or has been determined to be eligible for food stamps within the six-month period prior to applying for youth employment and training activities); (4) qualifies as a homeless individual, as defined by the McKinney-Vento Homeless Assistance Act; or (5) is a foster child, on behalf of whom state or local government payments are made. In cases permitted by DOL in regulations, an individual with a disability whose own income meets the standards specified in the first two criteria but who is a member of a family whose income does not meet such requirements may qualify (WIA Section (101)(25)).

Table A-1. (Continued)

Out-of-school youth means a youth eligible for services under Youth Activities who is a school dropout, or an eligible youth who has received a secondary school diploma or its equivalent but is basic-skills deficient, unemployed, or underemployed (WIA Section (101)(33) and 20 CFR 664.300).
Offender means any adult or juvenile who (1) is or has been subject to any stage of the criminal justice process, for whom services under this act may be beneficial; or (2) requires assistance in overcoming artificial barriers to employment resulting from a record of arrest or conviction (WIA Section (101)(27)).
Pregnant or parenting youth is an individual who is under 22 years of age and pregnant, or a youth (male or female) who is providing custodial care for one or more dependents under age 18 (as defined in PY2007 WIASRD Data Book, Appendix B).
Requires additional assistance refers to an individual who needs help in completing an educational program or securing and holding employment. The term may be defined at the state or local level. If the definition is established at the state level, the policy must be included in the state plan (20 CFR 664.210).
School dropout refers to an individual who is no longer attending any school and who has not received a high school diploma or its equivalent. A youth's dropout status is determined at the time he or she registers for youth activities. An individual who is not in school at the time of registration and is subsequently placed in an alternative school may be considered an out-of-school youth.
Underemployed refers to an individual who is working part-time but desires full-time employment, or who is working in employment not commensurate with the individual's demonstrated level of educational and/or skill achievement. (20 CFR 668.150. The definition is in a section of the WIA Regulations that pertains to WIA Indian programs; presumably, the definition would be applicable to any reference to "underemployed" in WIA, including its reference in the WIA Youth Activities program.)
Unemployed refers to an individual who is without a job and who wants and is available for work. The determination of whether an individual is without a job shall be made in accordance with the criteria used by the Bureau of Labor Statistics of the Department of Labor in defining individuals as unemployed (WIA Section 101(47)).

Source: Congressional Research Service, based on Sec. 101 of the Workforce Investment Act, accompanying regulations (20 CFR Part 652 and Parts 660 through 671), and U.S. Department of Labor, Employment and Training Administration, *PY2007 WIASRD Data Book*, Appendix B.

Table A-2. Elements of Youth Programs Funded by WIA Youth Activities

Educational achievement
• Tutoring, study skills training, and instruction leading to completion of secondary school, including dropout prevention strategies. • Alternative secondary school services, as appropriate.
Summer employment opportunities
• Summer employment opportunities that are directly linked to academic and occupational learning.
Employment services
• As appropriate, paid and unpaid work experiences, including internships and job shadowing. • Occupational skill training, as appropriate.

Table A-2. (Continued)

Leadership development activities
• Leadership development opportunities, which may include, but are not limited to, community service and peer-centered activities encouraging responsibility and other positive social behaviors during non-school hours, as appropriate; community and service learning projects; organizational and team work training, including team leadership training; and citizenship training, including life skills training such as parenting, work behavior training, and budgeting of resources, among other activities.
Additional support for youth services
• Supportive services. • Adult mentoring for the period of participation and a subsequent period, for a total of not less than 12 months. • Comprehensive guidance and counseling, which may include drug and alcohol abuse counseling and referral, as appropriate.
Follow-up services
• Follow-up services for not less than 12 months after the completion of participation, as appropriate. Follow-up services for youth include regular contact with a youth participant's employer, including assistance in addressing work-related problems that arise; assistance in securing better jobs, career development, and further education; work-related peer groups; adult mentoring; and tracking the progress of youth in employment after training.

Source: Congressional Research Service, based on Sec. 1 29(c)(2), Title I of the Workforce Investment Act and U.S. Department of Labor, Employment and Training Administration, *PY2007 WIASRD Data Book*, Appendix B.

Table A-3. "Work Experiences" for Youth, for Purposes of WIA Youth Activities

Work experiences are planned, structured learning experiences that take place in a workplace for a limited period of time. As provided in WIA Section 129(c)(2)(D) and Section 664.470, work experiences may be paid or unpaid.
Work experience workplaces may be in the private, for-profit sector; the nonprofit sector; or the public sector.
Work experiences are designed to enable youth to gain exposure to the working world and its requirements. Work experiences are appropriate and desirable activities for many youth throughout the year. Work experiences should help youth acquire the personal attributes, knowledge, and skills needed to obtain a job and advance in employment. The purpose is to provide the youth participant with opportunities for career exploration and skill development, and is not to benefit the employer, although the employer may, in fact, benefit from the activities performed by the youth. Work experiences may be subsidized or unsubsidized and may include the following elements:
(1) instruction in employability skills or generic workplace skills, such as those identified by the Secretary's Commission on Achieving Necessary Skills (SCANS);
(2) exposure to various aspects of an industry;
(3) progressively more complex tasks;
(4) internships and job shadowing;
(5) the integration of basic academic skills into work activities;
(6) supported work, work adjustment, and other transition activities;
(7) entrepreneurship;
(8) service learning;

Table A-3. (Continued)

(9) paid and unpaid community service; and
(10) other elements designed to achieve the goals of work experiences.
In most cases, on-the-job training is not an appropriate work experiences activity for youth participants under age 18. Local program operators may choose, however, to use this service strategy for eligible youth when it is appropriate based on the needs identified by the objective assessment of an individual youth participant.

Source: Congressional Research Service, based on 20 CFR 664.460.

APPENDIX B. DETAILED FINDINGS FROM STUDIES OF SELECT FEDERALLY FUNDED SUMMER JOB PROGRAMS

Summer Youth Activities Funded by EOA

The Economic Opportunity Act of 1964 authorized DOL to formulate and carry out programs to provide (1) part-time employment, on-the-job training, and useful work experience for low- income youth of high school age who need the earnings to permit them to resume or maintain attendance in school; and (2) useful work and training designed to assist unemployed, underemployed, or low-income persons ages 16 and older with developing occupational potential and obtaining employment.[72] Based on this authority, DOL established the Neighborhood Youth Corps (NYC). The in-school and summer components of the program were intended to achieve the first objective. These components emphasized job training and work experience, as well as services tailored to each youth, such as remedial education, tutoring, cultural enrichment activities, and personal and vocational counseling. NYC was operated by public or private nonprofit agencies. The program was carried out until 1973, when it was succeeded by a similar program. For FY1 970 and FY1 971 (the latest data available), DOL allocated approximately $471.3 million for the summer youth component.[73] Approximately 1 million youth participated in the program during this two-year period.

In the mid-1960s, the University of Wisconsin evaluated the NYC's in-school and summer components, using a sample of youth participants.[74] The evaluation of the program focused on educational outcomes. The evaluation found that the program had no statistically significant effect on the probability of an enrollee's graduation from high school or on the number of high school grades completed. However, the program improved the probability that black males and Indian youth generally would graduate from high school, compared to their counterparts in the control group. Male participants who graduated from high school were more likely to go on to a post-secondary educational placement. Further, while participation in the program yielded additional monetary benefits for participants who entered the labor market after leaving high school, particularly for black youth, this difference was likely due to their immediate participation in the labor market, compared to their control-group peers who had a lag in entry.

In a series of studies of the in-school and summer NYC components, as they operated in the late 1 960s and early 1 970s, GAO found somewhat similar results to those of the University of Wisconsin study. Overall, GAO found that participation in the program had no significant effect on whether a youth from a low-income family continued in school. GAO attributed the lack of effectiveness to "too simplistic an approach to bring about any dramatic results, given the complexity of the dropout problem and the variety of social and personal factors causing students to drop out."[75] Also, according to GAO, the program did not appear to adequately evaluate whether youth were at risk of dropping out.

In a separate report specifically focused on the implementation of the summer youth component in the District of Columbia metropolitan area, GAO found that even after DOL planned to better assess the dropout potential of eligible youth, many enrollees did not exhibit the characteristics of youth who might drop out.[76] This study also showed that the program did not have a significant effect on whether a youth from a low-income family would drop out, and that remedial education was not sufficiently integrated into the program. Nonetheless, GAO determined that at most, but not all, of the worksites visited in the District of Columbia and surrounding area, participants appeared to have been provided with useful work experience and adequate supervision.

Select Research on Summer Youth Activities Funded by CETA[77]

The primary purpose of the Summer Program for Economically Disadvantaged Youth (SPEDY), as authorized by the Comprehensive Employment and Training Act (CETA), was to provide work experiences to economically disadvantaged youth ages 14 to 21 during the summer to enhance their future employability. The program was aimed at school dropouts, potential dropouts, and in- school youth with barriers to work. Youth worked in the public and private sectors. DOL operated the program until 1983, when it was replaced by a summer program authorized under JTPA. In FY1981 (the latest data readily available), SPEDY served approximately 774,000 youth (though it served as many as 1 million youth in previous years).[78]

Process and outcome evaluations of the program were conducted by GAO and a research organization contracted by DOL. Reports by GAO in the 1970s identified problems with the operation and management of the program. The earliest of the GAO's reports found that youth were not given enough work; were certified present at jobs when they were absent; were paid late, incorrectly, or not at all; and were given few meaningful work opportunities. These reports also concluded that DOL inadequately monitored the program. A GAO report from 1979, based on visits to 230 SPEDY worksites, corroborated these previous findings.[79] Further, the report found that youth were not provided with meaningful work tasks and training to develop their skills and enhance future employability. GAO established criteria for determining work experiences that were meaningful[80] and reported that about half of the sites visited met its minimum standard for such experiences—they provided enough useful work, developed good work habits, and had good supervision. Notably, even these sites did not necessarily provide continuously useful work, as some youth were idle or were not adequately supervised.

Examples of problems raised by GAO included lack of equipment for youth to perform work, a failure of planned programs to materialize, too many participants for the type of work available, emphasis on recreational activities over vocational and related activities, lack of consequences for youth arriving to work late or leaving early, and lack of adequate attendance records. GAO concluded that these problems resulted from poor oversight by DOL and grantees. According to GAO, although DOL promulgated regulations to increase emphasis on monitoring of SPEDY sites and to ensure meaningful work, few grantees effectively evaluated and monitored proposed and ongoing activities. Further, DOL did not ensure that the requirements were met, nor did they allocate program funds on the basis of need or past performance in meeting program goals. GAO also concluded that grantees did not make a strong effort to recruit the most at-risk youth, including school dropouts.

In a separate report on the program effects of youth participants at eight SPEDY sites, researchers that contracted with DOL evaluated select aspects of the program.[81] The evaluation found that there was no significant difference between participants and the control group in the rate of full- time employment, although there was a relatively large and statistically significant difference in part-time employment. In addition, the program did not appear to have a significant impact on the likelihood of contact with the criminal justice system. Notably, the evaluation attempted to randomly assign youth to treatment and control groups, but had difficulty doing so;[82] therefore, these findings should be interpreted with caution.

Select Research on the Summer Employment Activities Funded by YEDPA

The Youth Employment Demonstration Program Act (YEDPA) extended funding for SPEDY and established new employment, training, and demonstration programs for youth. Summer employment was not a primary focus of the law, although summer employment was a component of one of the demonstration programs, the Youth Incentive Entitlement Pilot Program (YIEPP). YIEPP targeted low-income youth ages 16 to 19 who had not yet graduated from high school. All eligible youth who lived in one of 17 communities that received funding were eligible to participate. Youth were guaranteed jobs part-time during the school year and full-time during the summer months, and did not receive skills training, job search assistance, or other types of assistance. To continue their participation in the program, youth were required to enroll in school or in an approved alternative education program and to make satisfactory progress toward a high school diploma. The program extended from 1978 through 1981. More than 70,000 youth participated.

An evaluation of both the in-school and summer components of the program shows that it had positive effects overall.[83] The study examined the program's effects on black youth only, due to the relatively small number of Hispanic and white youth and implementation challenges at some of the pilot sites with these students. Youth were not randomly assigned to participate in the program, given that any youth in the pilot community could participate. Instead, each pilot site was matched to a comparison site that did not receive YIEPP funding but was comparable in terms of its size and demographics.[84] The evaluation found that the program significantly lowered the unemployment rate for black youth to nearly the same rate as that of whites in the communities. Youth were also more likely to experience increases in earnings as a result of the program, due largely to the enhanced employment rates, as well as modest increases in hours and wages. Further, the evaluation found that two-thirds of eligible youth participated in the program, suggesting, in part, that youth were willing to work at the minimum wage, but that in the absence of such a program, employers may not hire as many youth at the minimum wage who wish to work. In the follow-up semester after the program, earnings were estimated to be 39% above weekly earnings in the absence of the program, or an annual increase of approximately $545; researchers did not evaluate whether these earnings persisted. The evaluation also showed that YIEPP was unable to improve school enrollment and success.[85]

Select Research on Summer Youth Activities Funded by JTPA

The Job Training Partnership Act (JTPA) authorized the Summer Youth Employment and Training Program (SYETP), which provided employment and training activities during the summer months to low-income youth ages 14 through 21 to strengthen basic educational skills, encourage school completion, provide work exposure, and enhance citizenship skills. In the summer of 1997, about 530,000 youth participated in the program.[86] Separately, a demonstration program, STEP, provided summer jobs, remedial academic education, and sex education to disadvantaged youth ages 14 and 15 at risk of dropping out.[87] Youth were paid for their participation in work and remedial education.

The research on SYETP appears to be limited.[88] CRS identified a study, from 1984, which showed that the program was successful in increasing the total summer job opportunities available to disadvantaged minority youth.[89] The study additionally showed that for every three SYTEP jobs provided, two youth were employed who otherwise would not have worked that summer. A process evaluation of SYTEP by GAO found that the program intended to increase efforts to provide remedial education to youth in the program, but that this would likely reduce the number of youth served (based on the literature, it is unclear whether this happened).[90] Finally, an additional study, discussed below, involved youth who were assigned to SYETP as control group participants for the Summer Training and Employment Program (STEP) program, a five-year pilot program funded by JTPA and carried out in tandem with SYETP.

An evaluation of STEP involved random assignment of eligible youth into a treatment group (participation in STEP) and a control group (participation in SYETP) at five sites. The evaluation found that STEP significantly increased short-term benefits in outcomes related to education and knowledge about contraception. In the first summer of STEP, the learning losses that typically occur during the summer for low-income youth were mitigated. Youth in the program also outscored their counterparts in the control group in both reading and math. In addition, the program had impacts on youth's knowledge of contraceptive information, and some participants—those in the first cohort of the study—who were sexually active were more likely to report using contraception than youth in the control group. Over the long-term, the study found that the program *did not* have an impact on most outcomes considered. Approximately two years after the program ended, participants were just as likely as SYTEP participants to drop out; those remaining in school performed similarly on standardized tests, and treatment youth had completed approximately the same number of grades and graduation credits as their counterparts. Other outcomes related to fertility show mixed results, in that the program was successful for some groups and in some locations; the evaluation concluded that the program probably did not affect sexual behavior.

End Notes

[1] U.S. Department of Labor, Bureau of Labor Statistics, *The Employment Situation*, http://www.bls.gov/schedule/archives/empsit_nr.htm.

[2] Andrew Sum, Joseph McLaughlin, and Sheila Palma, *The Collapse of the Nation's Male Teen and Young Adult Labor Market, 2000-2009: The Lost Generation of Young Male Workers*, Center for Labor Market Studies, Northeastern University, prepared for C.S. Mott Foundation, July 2009, http://www.nyec.org/content/documents/ThecollapseoftheNation'sMaleTeenandYoungAdult.pdf. (Hereafter, Sum, McLaughlin, and Palma, *The Collapse of the Nation's Male Teen and Young Adult Labor Market, 2000-2009*.)

[3] Ibid.

[4] Andrew Sum et al., *The Historically Low Summer and Year Round Teen Employment Rate: The Case for an Immediate National Public Policy Response to Create Jobs for the Nation's Youth*, Center for Labor Market Studies, Northeastern University, September 15, 2008, http://www.nyec.org/content/documents/The_Historically_Low_Summer_2008_Teen_Employment_Rate.pdf. (Hereafter, Sum et al., *The Historically Low Summer and Year Round Teen Employment Rate*.)

[5] Ibid.

[6] Sum, McLaughlin, and Palma, *The Collapse of the Nation's Male Teen and Young Adult Labor Market, 2000-2009*.

[7] Title I, Chapter 4 of the Workforce Investment Act.

[8] Older youth (ages 18 through 21) may also receive services through programs funded by Adult Activities or Dislocated Worker Activities, separate grant programs for adults. These youth can either be enrolled in one of these programs or they can be co-enrolled in one of the programs and Youth Activities as long as they receive services under both funding streams. For an overview of these other programs, see CRS Report RL33687, *The Workforce Investment Act (WIA): Program-by-Program Overview and Funding of Title I Training Programs*, by David H. Bradley.

[9] ARRA extends the age of eligibility to 24 for activities funded pursuant to the law.

[10] These terms are defined under Appendix A. Up to 5% of youth participants in a local area may be individuals who do not meet the income criteria, but have at least one barrier to employment, some of which are not identical to those listed above: (1) deficient in basic literacy skills; (2) a school dropout; (3) homeless or runaway; (4) an offender; (5) one or more grade levels below the grade level appropriate to the individual's age; (6) pregnant or parenting; (7) possess one or more disabilities, including learning disabilities; or (8) face serious barriers to employment as identified by the local workforce investment board (WIB) (20 CFR 664.220).

[11] Section 101(33) of the Workforce Investment Act.

[12] Under current law, of the funds appropriated for Youth Activities, not more than 0.25% is reserved for outlying areas and not more than 1.5% is reserved for Youth Activities for Native Americans. The remainder of funds are allocated to states by a formula based one-third on the relative number of unemployed individuals residing in areas of substantial unemployment (an unemployment rate of at least 6.5%), one-third on the relative "excess" number of unemployed individuals (an unemployment rate more than 4.5%), and one-third on the relative number of low-income youth.

[13] The state WIB identifies the criteria to be used by local boards in awarding grants for youth activities, including criteria that the governor and local WIBs will use to identify effective and ineffective youth activities and providers of such activities (Section 1 12(a)(18) of the Workforce Investment Act).

[14] Local programs that receive Youth Activities funding need not provide all 10 program elements if certain services are already accessible for all eligible youth in the area; however, these other services must be closely coordinated with the local programs. Department of Labor, Employment and Training Administration, Training and Employment Guidance Letter (TEGL) No. 9-00, ("Workforce Investment Act of 1998, Section 129—Competitive and Noncompetitive Procedures for Providing Youth Activities Under Title I"), January 23, 2001, http://wdr.doleta.gov/ directives/corr_doc.cfm?DOCN= 1253; and Department of Labor, Employment and Training Administration, Training and Employment Guidance Letter (TEGL) No. 18-00 ("Program Guidance for Implementation of Comprehensive Youth Services Under the Workforce Investment Act"), April 23, 2001, http://wdr.doleta.gov/directives/corr_doc.cfm? DOCN= 1286.

[15] 20 CFR 664.600(b).

[16] A small number of one-stop centers have been established exclusively for youth. See U.S. General Accounting Office, *Workforce Investment Act: Labor Actions Can Help States Improve Quality of Performance Outcome Data and Delivery of Youth Services*, GAO-04-308, February 2004. (GAO is now known as the Government Accountability Office.)

[17] Department of Labor, Employment and Training Administration, TEGL No. 16-00 ("Availability of Funds to Support Planning Projects that Enhance Youth Connections and Access to the One-Stop System"), March 19, 2001, http://wdr.doleta.gov/directives

[18] Congressional Research Service correspondence with the Department of Labor, Employment and Training Administration, March 2010.

[19] The program year for Youth Activities is July 1 through June 30.

[20] Department of Labor, Employment and Training Administration, Training and Employment Guidance Letter (TEGL) No. 14-08 ("Program Guidance for Implementation of the Workforce Investment Act and Wagner-Peyser Act Funding in the American Recovery and Reinvestment Act of 2009 and State Planning Requirements for Program Year 2009"), March 18, 2009, p. 23, http://wdr.doleta.gov/directives. (Hereafter, Department of Labor, Employment and Training Administration, TEGL No. 14-08.)

[21] Ibid, p. 9.

[22] Department of Labor, Employment and Training Administration, Training and Employment Guidance Letter (TEGL) No. 3-99 ("Program Guidance for Implementation of Comprehensive Youth Services Under the Workforce Investment Act During the Summer of 2000"), January 31, 2000, http://wdr.doleta.gov/directives. (Hereafter, Department of Labor, Employment and Training Administration, TEGL No. 3-99, January 31, 2000.)

[23] Section 129(c)(2)(C) of the Workforce Investment Act.

[24] 20 CFR 664.600.

[25] Section 129(c)(2)(I) of the Workforce Investment Act and 20 CFR 664.450. The types of services provided and the duration of services must be determined based on the needs of the individual. The scope of these follow-up services may be less intensive for youth who have only participated in summer youth employment opportunities.

[26] Department of Labor, Employment and Training Administration, TEGL No. 3-99, January 31, 2000.

[27] For additional information, see CRS Report RL3 0089, *The Work Opportunity Tax Credit (WOTC)*, by Linda Levine.

[28] Social Policy Research Associates, *The Workforce Investment Act After Five Years: Results from the National Evaluation of the Implementation of WIA*, prepared for U.S. Department of Labor, June 2004, pp. VIII-9 and VIII-10, http://www.doleta.gov/reports/searcheta/occ/papers/SPR-WIA_Final_Report.pdf.

[29] Although inconsistent with the program year (July 1—June 30), these data are the most recent available. Department of Labor, Employment and Training Administration, *PY2007 WIASRD Data Book*, December 17, 2008, http://www.doleta.gov/performance

[30] Participation in summer youth activities appears to be declining over time. For example, more than one-third of youth (37.7%) participated in these activities in PY2004, compared to 33.2% in PY2005 and 27.9% in PY2006.

[31] U.S. Department of Labor, Employment and Training Administration, "American Recovery and Reinvestment Act of 2009, Monthly Participation Reports, as of March 2010," http://www.doleta.gov/Recovery/MonthlyReports/ 201003.cfm.

[32] ARRA extends the age of eligibility through 24 for activities funded pursuant to the law.

[33] The Workforce Investment Act of 1998, Department of Labor, Employment and Training Administration, Training and Employment Guidance Letter (TEGL) No. 7-99 ("Core and Customer Satisfaction Performance Measures for the Workforce Investment System"), March 3, 2000, http://wdr.doleta.gov/directives and Department of Labor, Employment and Training Administration, Training and Employment Guidance Letter (TEGL) No 17-05 ("Common Measures Policy for the Employment and Training Administration's (ETA) Performance Accountability System and Related Performance Issues," Attachment D), February 17, 2006, http://wdr.doleta.gov/ directives/corr_doc.cfm?DOCN=2195.

[34] For an overview of oversight activities required by ARRA, see CRS Report R40572, *General Oversight Provisions in the American Recovery and Reinvestment Act of 2009 (ARRA): Requirements and Related Issues*, by Clinton T. Brass.

[35] Department of Labor, Employment and Training Administration, TEGL No. 14-08.

[36] 20 CFR 664.460.

[37] 20 CFR 664.450.

[38] Local areas must "provide an objective assessment of the academic levels, skill levels, and service needs of each participant, which assessment shall include a review of basic skills, occupational skills, prior work experience, employability, interests, aptitudes (including interests and aptitudes for nontraditional jobs), supportive service needs, and developmental needs of such participant, except that a new assessment of a participant is not required if the provider carrying out such a program determines it is appropriate to use a recent assessment of the participant conducted pursuant to another education or training program." In addition, local areas must, "develop service strategies for each participant that shall identify an employment goal (including, in appropriate circumstances, nontraditional employment), appropriate achievement objectives, and appropriate services for the participant taking into account the assessment conducted [as required under this section]" Section 129(c)(1)(A) of the Workforce Investment Act.

[39] Section 129(c)(2)(C) of the Workforce Investment Act.

[40] In anticipation of WIA reauthorization, ETA originally required states to submit a state plan for the first two years of the five-year planning cycle, or PY2005 and PY2006. However, due to uncertainty about WIA

reauthorization, ETA directed states to submit a modification request to extend the life of the state plan for two additional years, PY2007 and PY2008. In the March 2009 TEGL, ETA requested all states to submit by April 15, 2009, a request to extend the current plan into PY2009. In addition, states were also asked to separately submit, by June 30, 2009, a state plan modification describing strategies to respond to the economic downturn and to implement the Recovery Act.

[41] The law specifies that the wage and labor standards include non-displacement protections, worker rights, participation and protection of workers and participants, grievance procedures and judicial review, nondiscrimination, allocation of funds to local areas, eligibility of providers or participants, the establishment and functions of local areas and local boards, and procedures for review and approval of plans.

[42] Department of Labor, Employment and Training Administration, "Workforce Investment Act Waiver Summary Report," available at http://www.doleta.gov/waivers/pdf/WIA_Waivers_Summary.pdf.

[43] Such waivers would need to be included as part of the state's submission of its state plan. As mentioned above, states were required to submit a new state plan given the current economic downturn and the availability of funds under ARRA.

[44] Section 136 of the Workforce Investment Act describes the "performance accountability system" for WIA. For each of the core indicators, each state is required to establish a "state adjusted level of performance." That is, the "measures" are identified in WIA Section 136, but the "levels" are determined by negotiation between states and DOL. Measures are reported as part of the Workforce Investment Act Standardized Record Data (WIASRD), which also collects demographic and other information about youth, adult, and dislocated workers who exit the program.

[45] Department of Labor, Employment and Training Administration, Training and Employment Guidance Letter (TEGL) No. 24-08 ("Workforce Investment Act and Wagner-Peyser Act Performance Accountability Reporting for the American Recovery and Reinvestment Act of 2009"), May 21, 2009, http://wdr.doleta.gov/directives DOCN=2760. (Hereafter, Department of Labor, Employment and Training Administration, TEGL No. 24-08, May 21, 2009.)

[46] This date was provided in U.S. Government Accountability Office, *Recovery Act: States' and Localities' Current and Planned Uses of Funds While Facing Fiscal Stresses*, GAO-09-829, July 2009, pp. 53-63, http://www.gao.gov/ new.items/d09829.pdf. (Hereafter, U.S. Government Accountability Office, *Recovery Act: States' and Localities' Current and Planned Uses of Funds While Facing Fiscal Stresses*, July 2009.)

[47] Department of Labor, Employment and Training Administration, Training and Employment Guidance Letter No. 24- 08, May 21, 2009.

[48] U.S. Government Accountability Office, *Recovery Act: Funds Continue to Provide Fiscal Relief to States and Localities, While Accountability and Reporting Challenges Need to Be Fully Addressed*, September 2009.

[49] Jeanne Bellotti et al., *Reinvesting in America's Youth: Lessons from the 2009 Recovery Act Summer Employment Initiative*, Mathematica Policy Research, February 26, 2010, http://wdr.doleta.g ov/research/FullText_Documents/ Reinvesting%20in%20America%27s%20Youth%20%20Lessons%20from%20the%202009%20Recovery%20 Act%20 Summer%20Youth%20Employment%20Initiative.pdf.

[50] Workforce3One, "Highlights of Youth ARRA (Recovery Act) Summits," December 15, 2009.

[51] Department of Labor, ETA Announces "Recovering America's Youth Summits" for Chicago (November 17-18) and Dallas (December 1 - 2)," http://www.doleta.gov/usworkforce/whatsnew/eta_default.cfm?id=2255.

[52] Department of Labor, Employment and Training Administration, Division of Youth Services, "The Work Readiness Indicator: Measuring Progress of WIA Youth," Recovering America's Youth Summits, Dallas and Chicago, December 2009, http://www.regonline.com/builder/site/tab2.aspx?EventID=776247 and http://www.regonline.com/builder/site/ tab2.aspx?EventID=777534.

[53] Department of Labor, Employment and Training Administration, Training and Employment Guidance Letter (TEGL) No. 27-09 ("Workforce Investment Act (WIA) Youth Program Guidance for Program Year (PY) 2010"), May 13, 2010, http://wdr.doleta.gov/directives

[54] Department of Labor, Office of the Inspector General, *OIG Recovery Act Plan Overview*, http://www.oig.dol.gov/ recovery/LaborOIGRecoveryActFinalWorkPlan052909.pdf.

[55] The 16 states are Arizona, California, Colorado, Florida, Georgia, Illinois, Iowa, Massachusetts, Michigan, Mississippi, New Jersey, New York, North Carolina, Ohio, Pennsylvania, and Texas. For further information, see U.S. Government Accountability Office, *GAO Tracks States' Progress Implementing the Recovery Act*, http://gao.gov/ recovery/.

[56] These states are California, Florida, Georgia, Illinois, Massachusetts, Michigan, New York, Ohio, Pennsylvania, and Ohio. For the report in July 2009, GAO also conducted oversight activities for Mississippi, New Jersey, and North Carolina.

[57] Although a more recent GAO report from December 2009 addresses implementation of ARRA, it does not provide detailed information about the Youth Activities program. See U.S. Government Accountability Office, *Recovery Act: Status of States' and Localities' Use of Funds and Efforts to Ensure Accountability*, GAO-10-231 , December 10, 2009, http://www.gao.gov/new.items/d10231.pdf.

[58] Under WIA, summer employment activities must be directly linked to academic and occupational learning. As discussed above, DOL has issued guidance stating that local programs using Recovery Act dollars for summer youth employment opportunities *may* determine whether "it is appropriate" that academic learning be directly linked to these activities.

[59] U.S. Government Accountability Office, *Recovery Act: One Year Later, States' and Localities' Uses of Funds and Opportunities to Strengthen Accountability*, March 2010.

[60] U.S. Government Accountability Office, *Recovery Act: States' and Localities' Current and Planned Uses of Funds While Facing Fiscal Stresses*, July 2009.

[61] U.S. Government Accountability Office, *Recovery Act: Funds Continue to Provide Fiscal Relief to States and Localities, While Accountability and Reporting Challenges Need to Be Fully Addressed*, September 2009.

[62] Ibid.

[63] Ibid.

[64] Ibid.

[65] Ibid.

[66] Pursuant to H.Res. 976, the House modified the Commerce-Justice-Science (C-J-S) Appropriations Act, 2010 (H.R. 2847), substituting the "Jobs for Main Street Act, 2010" as Division A of the act, and the "Statutory Pay-As-You-Go Act of 2009" as Division B. Regular appropriations for FY20 10 for activities funded in the C-J-S Appropriations Act were included in the Consolidated Appropriations Act, 2010 (P.L. 111-117).

[67] When introduced in the House, the bill was titled the Tax Extenders Act of 2009. The Senate passed an amended version of the bill as the American Workers, State, and Business Relief Act of 2010.

[68] Department of Labor, Employment and Training Administration, TEGL No. 14-08.

[69] U.S. Department of Labor, Employment and Training Administration, "American Recovery and Reinvestment Act of 2009, Monthly Participant Reports, as of March 2010," http://www.doleta .gov/Recovery/MonthlyReports/201003.cfm.

[70] This description may not capture all of the summer employment activities funded under the four laws.

[71] Some of the studies could not be directly located, and therefore, excerpts from these studies are taken from authoritative sources, such as DOL and the National Academy of Sciences, that review job training and employment programs for youth.

[72] U.S. General Accounting Office (now the Government Accountability Office), *Effectiveness and Management of the Neighborhood Youth Corps Summer Program in the Washington Metropolitan Area*, B-1305 15, May 31, 1972, http://archive.gao.gov/f0302/096548.pdf.

[73] Ibid. Data for FY1973 were not readily available.

[74] Gerald G. Somers and Ernst W. Stromsdorfer, *A Cost-Effectiveness Study of the In-School and Summer Neighborhood Youth Corps*, University of Wisconsin for the Department of Labor, July 1970, http://www.eric.ed.gov/ ERICDocs/data/ericdocs2sql/content_storage_01/0000019b/80/35/19/4f.pdf.

[75] U.S. General Accounting Office (now the Government Accountability Office), *Effectiveness and Management of the Neighborhood Youth Corps In-School Program and Its Management Problems*, B-130515, February 20, 1973, http://archive.gao.gov/f0202/094138.pdf.

[76] It does not appear that other reports specific to the summer youth program were produced. U.S. General Accounting Office (now the Government Accountability Office), *Effectiveness and Management of the Neighborhood Youth Corps Summer Program in the Washington Metropolitan Area*, B-130515, May 31, 1972, http://archive.gao.gov/f0302/ 096548.pdf.

[77] The program appears to have been also referred to as the Summer Youth Employment Program.

[78] Charles L. Betsey, Robinson G. Hollister, Jr., and Mary R. Papageorgiou, eds., *Youth Employment and Training Programs: The YEDPA Years*, National Academy of Sciences, 1985, http://www.eric.ed.gov/ERICWebPortal/ custom/portlets/recordDetails/detailmini.jsp?_nfpb=true&_&ERICExtSearch_SearchValue_0=ED265245& ERICExtSearch_SearchType_0=no&accno=ED265245. (Hereafter, Betsey, Hollister, and Papageorgiou, eds., *Youth Employment and Training Programs*.) For a critique of this study, see Vernon M. Briggs, Jr., "Youth Employment and Training Programs: A Review and a Reply Review," *Industrial and Labor Relations Review*, vol. 41, no. 1 (October 1987), pp. 141-145, http://www.jstor.org/stable/pdfplus/2523870.pdf. The response to the critique by Robinson G. Hollister is also available in the same volume of the *Industrial and Labor Relations Review*.

[79] U.S. General Accounting Office (now the Government Accountability Office), *More Effective Management is Needed to Improve the Quality of the Summer Youth Employment Program*, HRD-79-45, February 20, 1979, http://archive.gao.gov/f0302/108775.pdf.

[80] GAO observed that DOL's guidance in regulations on "meaningful work experience" was not detailed enough to evaluate the effectiveness of whether the program offered such experience, and therefore, GAO developed its own criteria for this term.

[81] A.L. Nellum and Associates, *Impacts of SYEP Participation on Work-Related Behavior and Attitudes of Disadvantaged Youth, Final Report*, for the Department of Labor, 1980. Information about the study was taken from Betsey, Hollister, and Papageorgiou, eds., *Youth Employment and Training Programs*, pp. 146-15 1. It appears that the evaluation was funded through appropriations for YEDPA.

[82] Random design assigns individuals of similar backgrounds to intervention and control groups, and can help to explain whether the intervention is effective if the outcomes are different for the two groups. Although the evaluation included treatment and control groups, the ways in which youth were assigned to the groups varied across sites. Further, the treatment and control groups differed significantly in terms of their characteristics even before the treatment group participated in the program.

[83] George Farkas et al., *Final Program Impacts of the Youth Incentive Entitlement Pilots Project*, Abt Associates and Manpower Development Research Corporation (MDRC), 1983. (Hereafter, Farkas et al., *Final Program Impacts of the Youth Incentive Entitlement Pilots Project*.) Information about the study was taken from Betsey, Hollister, and Papageorgiou, eds., *Youth Employment and Training Programs,* pp. 15 1-158. Earlier versions of the report examined outcomes for all youth.

[84] The evaluation accounted for youth who lived in the pilot communities but did not participate in the program. It is unclear whether the evaluation controlled for the fact that these other communities received funding through other YEDPA youth programs.

[85] Farkas et al., *Final Program Impacts of the Youth Incentive Entitlement Pilots Project*. Information about the study was taken from Department of Labor, Office of the Chief Economist, *What's Working (and what's not): A Summary of Research on the Economic Impacts of Employment and Training Programs*, January 1995, http://www.eric.ed.gov/ ERICWebPortal/custom/portlets/recordDetails/detailmini.jsp?_nfpb=true&_&ERICExtSearch_SearchValue_0 = ED379445&ERICExtSearch_SearchType_0=no&accno=ED379445. (Hereafter, Department of Labor, *What's Working (and what's not).*)

[86] Archived report by the Congressional Research Service, *The Job Training Partnership Act: A Compendium of Programs*. Available upon request.

[87] Jean Baldwin Grossman and Cynthia L. Sipe, *Summer Training and Education Program (STEP): Reports on Long-Term Impacts*, Public/Private Ventures, Winter 1992, http://www.ppv.org/ppv/publications/ assets

[88] The research literature shows that little is known about the effectiveness of the program. See Public/Private Ventures, *Dilemmas in Youth Employment Programming: Findings from the Youth Research and Technical Assistance Project*, for the Department of Labor, Research and Evaluation Report 92-C, 1992, p. 49, http://wdr.doleta.gov/opr/ FULLTEXT/1992_06_NEW.pdf.

[89] Jon Crane and David Ellwood, *The Summer Youth Employment Program: Private Job Supplement or Substitute?*, Harvard University for the Department of Health and Human Services, March 1984. Information about the study was taken from Department of Labor, *What's Working (and what's not).*

[90] U.S. General Accounting Office (now the Government Accountability Office), *Job Training Partnership Act: Summer Youth Programs Increase Emphasis on Remedial Education*, GAO/HRD-87-101BR, June 1987, http://archive.gao.gov/d28t5/133553.pdf.

In: Vulnerable Youth and Employment Issues
Editor: Christopher E. Perry

ISBN: 978-1-61122-020-9
© 2011 Nova Science Publishers, Inc.

Chapter 4

REINVESTING IN AMERICA'S YOUTH: LESSONS FROM THE 2009 RECOVERY ACT SUMMER YOUTH EMPLOYMENT INITIATIVE

Jeanne Bellotti, Linda Rosenberg, Samina Sattar,
Andrea Mraz Esposito and Jessica Ziegler

ACKNOWLEDGMENTS

The study team would like to thank the many individuals who contributed to the development of this evaluation report. We truly appreciate all of their efforts.

Most importantly, this study would not have been possible without the patience and generosity of the administrators, staff members, employers, and youth who participated in the study's 20 site visits. They took the time to share their experiences and respond to our requests for information during a period of intense activity and demands from many stakeholders in the workforce investment community. We appreciate the help offered by program staff in coordinating the visits, and the willingness of local employers and youth to share their personal stories with us.

A number of staff at the U.S. Department of Labor, Employment and Training Administration provided valuable input and guidance throughout the duration of this study. We especially appreciate the support and advice offered by Janet Javar, the evaluation project officer, Wayne Gordon, and Heidi M. Casta from the Division of Research and Evaluation. Gregg Weltz, Evan Rosenberg, Sara Hastings, and Charles Modiano from the Division of Youth Services provided valuable input and support from the very start of the study through the review of evaluation findings. Evan and Sara also assisted the team in obtaining state performance and draw down data to provide the national context for the study.

At Mathematica, Karen Needels and Sheena McConnell served invaluable roles as Quality Assurance Reviewer and Senior Advisor, respectively. Liz Clary, Robin Dion, Virginia Knechtel, Nora Paxton, Premini Sabaratnam, and Timothy Silman conducted site visits and took meticulous notes for the analysis. Cindy George, John Kennedy, and their staff provided editorial assistance, and Linda Heath contributed secretarial support to the study.

ABSTRACT

On February 17, 2009, President Barack Obama signed the American Recovery and Reinvestment Act into law. Passed in response to the 2008 recession, the Act's purpose was to create jobs, pump money into the economy, and encourage spending. Through the Act, states received $1.2 billion in funding for the workforce investment system to provide employment and training activities targeted to disadvantaged youth. Congress and the U.S. Department of Labor (DOL) encouraged states and local workforce investment areas charged with implementing these youth activities to use the funds to create employment opportunities for these youth in the summer of 2009.

To gain insights into these summer initiatives, DOL's Employment and Training Administration contracted with Mathematica Policy Research to conduct an implementation evaluation of the summer youth employment activities funded by the Recovery Act. As part of the evaluation, Mathematica analyzed (1) monthly performance data submitted to ETA by the states, and (2) qualitative data collected through in-depth site visits to 20 local areas. This chapter describes the national context for implementation, provides an in-depth description of the experience of selected local areas, and presents lessons on implementation practices that may inform future summer youth employment efforts.

EXECUTIVE SUMMARY

The American economy lost an estimated 7.9 million jobs between the end of 2007 and the fall of 2009 (U.S. Department of Labor 2009b). Joblessness was high for many groups, but for young adults, unemployment was particularly high and could have lasting effects. In May 2009, the jobless rate for teenagers was 22.7 percent, more than double the national unemployment rate of 9.4 percent (U.S. Department of Labor 2009b). This joblessness could have lasting effects on the young adults' future careers. Funding for youth activities through the American Recovery and Reinvestment Act of 2009 (the Recovery Act) was designed as one part of the solution and aimed to reverse the steep decline in youth employment.

Through the Recovery Act, states received $1.2 billion in funding for employment and training activities targeted to the country's disadvantaged youth. Congress and the U.S. Department of Labor (DOL) encouraged states and local workforce investment areas to use the funds to create employment opportunities for these youth in the summer of 2009. Although summer employment is made available as a component of youth activities under the Workforce Investment Act (WIA), many local areas did not provide summer jobs for significant numbers of youth after the transition to WIA in 2000 (Social Policy Research Associates 2004). Local areas had from mid-February 2009, when the Recovery Act was signed into law, to the beginning of May 2009 to design their summer youth employment activities and prepare for implementation.

To gain insights into the design and implementation of these initiatives, DOL's Employment and Training Administration (ETA) contracted with Mathematica Policy

Research to conduct an evaluation of summer youth activities funded by the Recovery Act. Although summer employment is only one component of WIA youth activities and is not funded as a separate program, the opportunities offered by local areas with Recovery Act funding in the summer of 2009 are referred to as the Summer Youth Employment Initiative (SYEI) throughout this chapter. The implementation study draws upon state performance data and in-depth site visits to 20 selected local areas (hereafter referred to as the study "sites"). The report aims to describe the national context for SYEI implementation, provide an in-depth description of the experiences of selected sites, and present lessons on implementation practices that may inform future SYEIs.

The Recovery Act Allocation for WIA Youth Activities

Although Recovery Act funds could be spent on youth activities up to June 30, 2011, Congress expressed a strong interest in the funds being used to create employment opportunities for youth in the summer of 2009. Youth would be placed in summer work experiences with local public, nonprofit, and private employers and their wages would be paid with Recovery Act funds. The Act also contained two key provisions for the WIA youth activities funded under it. First, it extended eligibility from youth ages 14 to 21 years to include those from 22 to 24 years. Second, it stated that only one key indicator—achievement of work readiness goals—would be used to measure program performance. Local areas were also required by ETA to report another performance indicator—the number of youth completing summer employment experiences. Provisions for specific aspects of initiative design included:

- **Work experience should be "meaningful" and age appropriate.** Work experiences should be age appropriate and lead to youth meeting work readiness goals. ETA encouraged local areas to expose youth to "green" (environmentally friendly) educational and career pathways. Local areas were also encouraged to match worksites with participants' goals and interests.
- **Local areas had flexibility in using classroom-based learning activities.** Local areas could decide whether to link classroom-based learning, such as occupational training, with youth's work experiences. Such a linkage was recommended for younger youth in need of basic skills and career exploration.
- **Registered apprenticeships were encouraged.** ETA suggested that local areas take advantage of local apprenticeship programs to create pre-apprenticeship opportunities.
- **Performance would be measured by one work readiness indicator.** Local areas could determine how to define the indicator but were provided with a definition for achieving work readiness goals. To encourage continued services for older youth, states could request a waiver to use only this indicator for youth who were 18 to 24 years old and who, after the summer months, participated only in work experiences.
- **WIA youth program elements were not required.** Local areas could determine which of the 10 WIA elements of youth programs to offer to participants funded by the Recovery Act. For example, this permitted local areas to determine whether or

not to provide supportive services or follow up with participants for at least 12 months after receipt of services

- **Certain groups should receive priority.** The priority service groups for WIA programs—including veterans and eligible spouses of veterans—were also priority groups for youth activities funded by the Recovery Act. As for the regular WIA youth programs, at least 30 percent of Recovery Act funding for WIA youth activities had to be spent on out-of-school youth.
- **Local areas could request waivers for contractor procurement.** States were permitted to request a waiver from the WIA requirement for service providers to be selected through a competitive procurement process, but were still required to follow state or local laws that could not be relieved by federal regulations.

Overview of the Evaluation

Six major research questions guided the evaluation. By addressing each of the following questions, the study provides policymakers, administrators, and stakeholders a better understanding of how the SYEI unfolded in 2009:

1. How did the selected sites plan for and organize summer youth initiatives with funding from the Recovery Act?
2. How did selected sites identify, recruit, and enroll at-risk youth?
3. What were the characteristics of participants nationwide?
4. What services were offered during the summer months in selected sites?
5. What types of work experiences were offered to participating youth in selected sites?
6. What lessons can be drawn about the implementation of summer youth initiatives?

To answer these questions, the evaluation draws upon two key data sources: (1) state performance data submitted monthly to ETA through December 31, 2009 that covers all youth participating in services funded by the Recovery Act from May through November 2009, and (2) in-depth site visits to 20 selected sites during July and August 2009. The state performance data describe the national scope of the initiative and provide context for the implementation experiences of the 20 selected sites. The data collected during site visits include qualitative interviews with a total of 601 individuals across the 20 sites, including 373 administrators and staff, 79 employers, and 149 youth.

The 20 local areas listed in Table 1 were selected for the study from a list of 40 local areas nominated by ETA national and regional staff as offering innovative or potentially promising approaches. ETA and the evaluation team selected the final 20 local areas using three key criteria: (1) having at least three local areas from each region; (2) choosing areas that planned to spend at least 50 percent of Recovery Act funds during the summer of 2009; and (3) including rural, urban, and suburban sites.

Table I. Sites Selected for in-depth Visits

Region	Local Workforce Investment Board	City, State
1	Regional Employment Board of Hampden County	Springfield, MA
1	The Workplace, Inc.	Bridgeport, CT
1	Workforce Partnership of Greater Rhode Island	Cranston, RI
2	Lehigh Valley Workforce Investment Board, Inc.	Lehigh Valley, PA
2	Three Rivers Workforce Investment Board	Pittsburgh, PA
2	Western Virginia Workforce Development Board	Roanoke, VA
3	Eastern Kentucky Concentrated Employment Program	Hazard, KY
3	Northeast Georgia Regional Commission	Athens, GA
3	Workforce Investment Network	Memphis, TN
4	Denver Office of Economic Development	Denver, CO
4	Montana State WIB, District XI Human Resource Council	Missoula, MT
4	Workforce Connection of Central New Mexico	Albuquerque, NM
5	Minneapolis Employment and Training Program	Minneapolis, MN
5	Workforce Development, Inc.	Rochester, MN
5	Workforce Resource, Inc.	Menomonie, WI
6	Community Development Department of the City of LA	Los Angeles, CA
6	Madera County Office of Education	Madera, CA
6	Oregon Consortium and Oregon Workforce Alliance	Albany, OR
6	Workforce Development Council of Seattle-King County	Seattle, WA
6	Worksystems, Inc.	Portland, OR

Note: The city and state reflect the location of the local area's central office.

The National Context

Enrolling more than 355,000 youth nationwide, states and local areas drew down more than $717 million through November 2009, or almost 61 percent of the national allocation of $1.2 billion in Recovery Act funds for WIA youth services. Of these participants, over 345,000 enrolled during the summer months of May through September, and 314,000 were placed in summer jobs. By comparison, local areas served a total of slightly more than 250,000 youth through comprehensive services offered by the regular WIA formula-funded youth program during the entire 2008 program year, at a cost of $966 million (U.S. Department of Labor 2009a). The higher cost for the regular WIA youth program likely results from the fact that youth receive comprehensive services for significantly longer periods of time.

States heeded the guidance provided by Congress and the ETA to focus efforts on summer employment. Large numbers of youth began enrolling in the spring, with 164,000 participants—46 percent of all youth enrolled through November—enrolling in May and June. Enrollment continued heavily through July and fell sharply in August and September, as initiatives focused on providing services to those already enrolled. Local areas also drew down funds heavily during the summer (see Figure 1). National draw downs averaged $128 million per month during the summer, peaking in August at $173 million for the month.

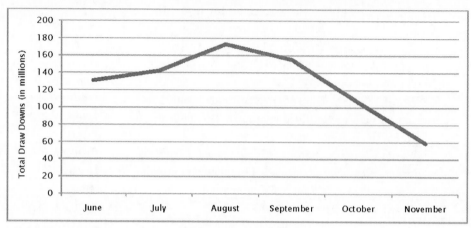

Source: Monthly draw-downs of WIA Youth Recovery Act Funds.

Notes: Draw downs reflect the actual cash drawn daily by grantees from the financial system. By comparison, expenditures are the costs reported quarterly on an accrual basis, and therefore include all services and goods received by the end of the quarter, whether or not they have been invoiced or paid. As a result, draw downs may not account for all expenditures during the reporting period. Data from March through June were only available in aggregate and are reported under the month of June.

Figure 1. National Draw Downs of WIA Youth Recovery Act Funds in 2009

The 2009 summer employment initiative enrolled a diverse array of youth (see Table 2). The majority of participants were in-school youth, a group largely composed of those ages 18 or younger. States also succeeded in enrolling a large number of out-of-school youth, a population that WIA has struggled to reach in the past but has made significant progress enrolling in recent years (U.S. Government Accountability Office 2004; U.S. Department of Labor 2009). A total of almost 9 percent of all those enrolled through November, or nearly 31,000 participants, fell within the newly added 22- to 24-year-old age range. It was challenging to enroll veterans—only 671 veterans were enrolled nationwide, or less than 0.2 percent of all enrollees through November 2009.

Employment was the main focus of local areas' efforts to expend their Recovery Act allocations. As mentioned earlier, nearly 314,000 youth, or slightly more than 88 percent of all participants enrolled through November, were placed in a summer job (see Table 2). In addition, almost 13 percent of all enrollees were placed in work experiences outside the summer months. This percentage could include participants who were also placed in summer employment, who were enrolled in services during the summer but did not work during the summer months, or who only enrolled in the WIA youth activities funded by the Recovery Act in the fall.

To streamline implementation, Congress only required states and local areas to report on one performance measure. States had to report on the percentage of participants in summer employment who attained a work readiness skill goal. Nationwide, local areas reported that just under 75 percent of youth achieved a measureable increase in their work readiness skills while participating (see Table 3). Beyond work readiness, states and local areas were also required by ETA to report on the proportion of youth who completed their summer work experience. State reports indicated a completion rate of more than 82 percent among those for whom data were available.

Table 2. Selected Characteristics of Youth Served and Services Received under the Recovery Act through November 2009

	Number of Participants	Percentage of All Participants
Total Number of Participants	355,320	100.0
Characteristics of Youth		
School Status		
In-school	224,798	63.3
Out-of-school	127,869	36.0
Not reported	2,653	0.7
Age at Enrollment		
14–18 years	228,921	64.4
19–21 years	84,539	23.8
22–24 years	30,594	8.6
Not reported	11,266	3.2
Eligible Veterans	671	0.2
Services Received		
Placed in summer employment	313,812	88.3
Placed in work experiences outside the summer months	45,407	12.8

Source: State performance reports for WIA youth initiatives supported by the Recovery Act submitted to the U.S. Department of Labor as of December 31, 2009.

Notes: Data on age could not be broken into smaller subgroups.

ETA defines the summer months as May through September.

These figures do not include the 3,763 youth served by Indian and Native American grantees as a result of reporting procedures.

Table 3. Performance Outcomes of Youth Served under the Recovery Act through November 2009

	Number Reported as Achieving Outcome	Number for Whom Data Are Available	Percentage Achieving Outcome
Increase in work readiness skills	235,043	314,132	74.8
Completion of summer work experience	242,827	294,842	82.4

Source: State performance reports for WIA youth initiatives supported by the Recovery Act submitted to the U.S. Department of Labor as of December 31, 2009.

Note: These figures do not include the 3,763 youth served by Indian and Native American grantees as a result of reporting procedures.

Data were not available for youth who were still participating in services at the time of data reporting. In addition, data were not available for some participants due to delays in state reporting.

Experiences of the 20 Study Sites

The experiences of the study's 20 selected local areas provide a rich description of the activities that underlie these national figures. The sites covered each of the ETA regions and encompassed populations of different types and sizes. Although more than half of the sites included a city, the majority had areawide populations of less than 750,000. All experienced the effects of the recession, with more than half reporting unemployment rates above 8 percent in July and August 2009. Although not representative of local areas nationwide, the sites include a diverse array of local areas and provide a picture of the SYEI in sites that ETA staff believed might offer innovative and promising approaches to disadvantaged youth.

The SYEI Goals, Context, and Organization

Selected sites reported that their primary goals for the SYEI included (1) serving as many youth as possible, (2) spending the Recovery Act funds quickly, and (3) providing meaningful summer experiences to participating youth. More than three-quarters of sites planned to spend 75 percent or more of their Recovery Act funds on the SYEI. Using those funds, they expected to enroll between 120 and 5,500 youth during the summer, with more than half of the sites planning to serve 500 or more youth.

To plan their SYEIs, the selected sites drew on their experiences providing summer work opportunities through recent programs funded by regular WIA formula funds and other resources, as well as programs under the Job Training Partnership Act (JTPA, the predecessor to WIA). Administrators in 17 sites reported that their local area had continued to provide summer work experience to youth using WIA formula funds after WIA replaced JTPA. At least nine communities also had programs that had placed more than 200 youth in summer jobs using non-WIA funds from state or local government or private sources. Most sites took the opportunity provided by the Recovery Act to expand their existing programs and make modest modifications.

Planning for the SYEI was challenging given the short timeframe and gaps in key information. More than half the sites mentioned that planning such a sizable initiative in only a few months affected their initiative designs. One-third reported that, as they started to plan for the summer, they did not know the amount of their Recovery Act allocation for WIA youth activities or were still unclear about the requirements for identifying providers.

All 20 sites, however, did successfully identify local providers and implement the SYEI. Almost half used a competitive process to identify providers. In the sites that held open procurements, some organizations that were new to WIA services received contracts. The remaining 11 sites relied on longtime providers of WIA services, either exercising waivers for the provider competition, extending existing contracts, or offering services directly through the lead agency.

Youth Recruitment and Intake Activities

An expanded SYEI required sites to quickly scale up their youth recruitment and intake activities. Sites used both media campaigns and targeted recruitment with help from local organizations to successfully reach large numbers of eligible youth. Most sites also leveraged the workforce investment system by encouraging youth already engaged with WIA to enroll in SYEI and urging adults who used One-Stop Career Centers to tell family and friends about the initiative. Sites also sought partnerships with a wide range of agencies and social service organizations that served at-risk youth, including welfare agencies, the juvenile justice system, foster care agencies, local homeless shelters, and the agencies that oversee programs such as the Supplemental Nutrition Assistance Program.

All but one site reported receiving applications from more eligible youth than they could accommodate. Sites reported that between 40 and 80 percent of applicants ultimately enrolled. Among those who did not enroll, 10 to 30 percent were clearly ineligible because their incomes exceeded the eligibility cutoff. Another 10 to 30 percent were potentially eligible but did not complete all paperwork. A majority of sites maintained waiting lists of eligible youth who could not be served, enrolling youth from the list only when an existing participant dropped out or was removed from the initiative. Two sites with excess demand did not maintain waiting lists but instead referred youth who could not be enrolled to other agencies or service providers in the area.

Although recruitment efforts were successful overall, sites had difficulty reaching some targeted populations, including veterans and their spouses, older youth, homeless and runaway youth, foster youth, and juvenile offenders. Nine sites reported a lack of success recruiting veterans and their spouses despite targeted recruitment efforts. Six sites also experienced challenges recruiting older youth because they were often no longer in school and thus were difficult to locate. Three sites said homeless and runaway youth were difficult to enroll due to lack of documentation and difficult to keep engaged in services due to their mobility. Two specifically mentioned troubles recruiting juvenile offenders and foster youth.

Nearly all sites had difficulty processing the large volume of applicants. Common challenges included the tight timeframe, the amount of paperwork involved, and difficulty collecting documentation from youth and parents. Nearly three-quarters of sites hired temporary staff to help with the intake process. Sites also used prescreening of youth and links with partners to streamline eligibility determination. At least 11 sites prescreened applications before scheduling youth for an intake appointment to weed out those likely to be ineligible. In addition, seven sites asked schools and state and local social service agencies to help verify youth's eligibility.

Youth Preparation and Support

Given the diverse array of youth enrolled in the SYEI, sites had to determine how to best prepare them for a successful work experience. Many participants had never held a job for pay and therefore did not fully understand the attitudes and skills necessary to succeed in the workplace. Even among those who had worked before, many had not explored potential career paths.

ETA required sites to conduct assessments and develop an individualized service strategy (ISS) for each SYEI participant, but gave the sites flexibility to determine what type of assessment and ISS was appropriate for each youth. Fourteen of the 20 sites used academic and career-related assessments to learn about youth's skills, interests, and needs. The six remaining sites reported not using assessments either because of the limited time available to work with youth or the lack of need since youth would not receive any services other than work placement. Across the 20 sites, a different set of 14 sites completed an ISS with every participant to get to know youth and identify their needs. In four more sites, at least one provider completed an ISS with each participant. The remaining two sites reported that the length of the summer initiative was too short to necessitate an ISS.

Although not a federal requirement for the SYEI, 16 of the 20 sites required youth to attend work readiness training. These training sessions were intended to equip youth with basic workplace skills, expose them to diverse career interests, and prepare them for the responsibilities that lay ahead. Training time in sites that used standardized curricula ranged from eight hours to two weeks. In some sites, training occurred prior to worksite placement but at others it took place throughout the summer. Some youth were assigned to work readiness tracks based on their characteristics, such as age, experience, offender status, or disabilities. Youth in almost all sites reported that this training was one of the most useful aspects of the initiative.

Nearly all sites also offered supportive services to participants once they were placed on a job. Transportation to worksites and help paying for work supplies were the most common supports. Help paying for child care was less commonly offered because sites reported that few youth required child care assistance and, if they did, other funds were available to meet this need.

Recruitment and Involvement of Employers

Employers were important partners in sites' efforts to provide youth with successful summer experiences. Though employers were receiving a summer employee whose wages were paid with Recovery Act funds, they were voluntary partners with their own interests that sites needed to address. Site staff had to recruit enough employers to place a large number of youth with wide-ranging interests and still be mindful of ETA guidance on ensuring appropriate and meaningful experiences.

Sites identified many interested employers in the public, private, and nonprofit sectors. Half of the sites focused their recruitment on a specific sector. Of particular interest, four sites heavily targeted private sector employers largely because they felt that private firms were more likely to offer participants regular positions after the summer. Almost half reported that they recruited more employers than they needed. Employer recruitment began early, often before sites began enrolling youth. Sites contacted employers they knew from previous summer programs and the regular WIA youth program, conducted media campaigns, and made direct contact with employers new to the workforce investment system.

Sites focused on carefully screening employers and orienting them to the initiative. Formal screening processes could involve a review of an employer's application (conducted at 10 sites), a visit to the worksite (conducted by at least 11 sites), or signing a worksite agreement (developed by 9 sites). Three sites chose to use all three of these techniques. More than three-quarters of sites also held formal or informal orientations with worksite supervisors to inform them of their SYEI roles and responsibilities.

Employers were eager to participate to advance their businesses but also to make a difference for youth and their communities. Respondents in nine sites reported that employers perceived the SYEI as free training of potentially permanent employees. In addition, many employers were either facing hiring freezes during the summer or could not afford to hire the extra staff they needed and thus appreciated the contributions that SYEI participants could provide. Finally, nearly all employers and staff also reported that employers felt that summer employment could improve the chances that youth would be engaged in productive work and stay out of trouble.

Youth's Summer Experiences

The heart of the summer experience did not begin until after the tremendous effort to recruit youth and employers, determine their suitability for the SYEI, and prepare them for the workplace. Although some youth were placed in academic services in the classroom, most were placed in employment. About one-third of sites emphasized work, offering few other services beyond work readiness training. The remaining two-thirds offered academics to at least some youth. Few sites offered any of the other 10 program elements required by the regular WIA youth program but optional for the SYEI funded by the Recovery Act.

Academic offerings ranged from occupational skills training to recovery of school credits. Occupational skills training was offered by 10 sites, with the training most commonly targeted to the health care, manufacturing, culinary, and construction industries as well as entrepreneurship. Less common academic programs included recovery of school credits, GED preparation programs, and remediation. Most youth were placed in jobs either after or while participating in academic offerings. However, some youth—often younger participants between 14 and 16 years of age—in five sites spent the entire summer in the classroom.

Youth worked in a wide range of industries. The most common reported by sites in the study included health care, public service, parks and recreation, and education or child care (see Figure 2). Seventeen sites placed youth in the health industry with jobs in hospitals, nursing homes, mental health centers, dental offices, and other medical facilities. Another 13 had youth working in public services with county and municipal government agencies such as the town hall, the Chamber of Commerce, the public housing department, the fire department, Veterans Affairs, or public works.

Within this wide range of industries, youth typically held entry-level jobs often involving administrative or clerical work, landscaping and outdoor maintenance, janitorial and indoor maintenance, and construction (see Table 4). Sixteen sites involved youth in administrative or clerical tasks, such as answering phones, filing, completing paperwork, and word processing. This was common within the top two industries, namely health care and public services. Another 14 sites reported that at least some youth were conducting park reclamation, green space protection, and urban forestry. Day-to-day tasks in these areas often included weeding; raising plant beds; planting flowers, bushes and trees; digging and laying recreation trails; raking; trimming bushes; and cleaning and restoring playgrounds.

Notably, youth and staff both reported that, although the daily tasks performed by participants may have been entry-level, youth were nevertheless exposed to the world of work, the work process, and careers within the industry in which they were placed. For example, a youth filing paperwork at a doctor's office learned about HIPAA regulations, observed health care workers interacting with patients, and experienced the general operations of a health care facility. Two sites also reported that some older and more experienced youth were placed in higher-level positions or supervisory roles in a range of different industries.

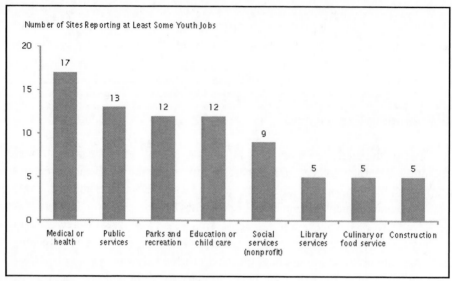

Source: Site visit interviews in 20 selected sites.

Notes: This table includes only industries mentioned by five or more sites. Industries cited by fewer than five sites include agriculture, legal services, retail, workforce development, automotive, computer services, media, hospitality, and finance. Green jobs were not categorized as a separate industry but were included in the most closely related industry listed above. These jobs are discussed in detail later in this document. N = 20 sites.

Figure 2. Common Industries for Summer Work Experiences

Table 4. Common Tasks Performed by Participating Youth at Worksites

Task	Number of Sites Reporting at Least Some Youth Performing This as Primary Task
Administrative or clerical duties	16
Park reclamation, landscaping, and outdoor maintenance	14
Janitorial or indoor maintenance	12
Construction	11
Recycling computers, paper and other materials	10
Child care, senior care, counseling at summer camps or playgrounds	10
Weatherization and energy efficiency	8
Agriculture, community gardening, and urban gardening	8
Food service	7
Service, sales, or hospitality	7
Computer repair or maintenance	6

Source: Site visit interviews in 20 selected sites.

Note: This table includes only tasks mentioned by five or more sites. Additional tasks cited by fewer than five sites include health care tasks, automotive repair and maintenance, and pet grooming or care.

N = 20 sites.

More than half the sites reported at least some success placing youth in green industries and jobs. The most common green jobs were in park reclamation, recycling, weatherization, and agriculture. A lack of guidance about what constituted a green job, however, created confusion within and across the sites, with respondents using varied definitions. For example, some referred to green jobs as those directly related to occupations in renewable energy, environmental consulting, and energy-efficient construction. Others included non-green jobs—such as administrative or maintenance tasks—within green industries or organizations. Still others talked about green exposure within non-green jobs, such as the use of recycling and environmentally friendly products in day-to-day business.

Matching Youth to Worksites

Ensuring a solid match between youth and employer was critical to both satisfying the employer's needs and maximizing the likelihood that the youth had a meaningful experience. Site staff reported four key considerations when matching youth to worksites: (1) the youth's personal interests expressed through their application, orientation, or meetings with staff; (2) direct employer feedback after a formal interview; (3) the youth's age, experience, and skills; and (4) transportation needs or other logistical issues.

Twelve sites had all or some youth formally interview with employers to simulate a real interview experience, ensure the employer was comfortable with the match, and allow the youth to become familiar with the potential work environment. Once staff members determined a potentially good employer match, most interviewing involved one-on-one personal interactions between the employer and the interested youth. Respondents in the eight sites that chose not to conduct interviews said either that the timeframe was too short or that it would have been logistically too challenging to have all youth interview.

Youth's Hours and Wages

Across the 20 sites, summer work experiences lasted an average of seven weeks at an average of 28 hours per week. Hourly wages averaged $7.75, with half the sites offering the federal minimum wage of $7.25 per hour, allowing youth to earn an average of about $1,500 if they completed summer services from start to finish. Summer experiences ranged from 3 to 20 weeks in length, with youth working 16 to 40 hours per week.

More than three-quarters of sites experienced payroll challenges due to the increased volume of workers. Logistical problems in the flow and functioning of the payroll process occurred during timesheet collection, processing of paychecks, and distribution of paychecks. Although most sites had already begun to remedy these problems by the time of the site visits, some were still considering alternative strategies to help stem the problems in future summer initiatives.

Assessing Youth Progress

Sites developed procedures to assist youth both during and after their job placements and to track their progress over time. Youth at all but one site were connected with an adult mentor—typically the worksite supervisor, a colleague, or a frontline SYEI staff member—at the start of their summer experience.

Once youth were placed in jobs, sites monitored worksites both formally and informally through in-person visits by staff. Formal visits, conducted by 11 sites, generally involved a standard protocol or monitoring checklist. Staff spoke with supervisors, spoke with youth, and observed working conditions. Informal visits, conducted by 17 sites, were more casual and typically occurred as staff picked up youth timesheets or dropped off paychecks. Staff unanimously agreed that ongoing monitoring through in-person visits was essential to ensuring high-quality experiences and heading off problems between worksite supervisors and youth before they became serious.

Every site dealt with at least some youth who performed poorly on the job. When problems could not be resolved through mentoring or guidance, youth were typically moved to a new worksite or other program activities. Despite staff efforts to mediate performance issues, all sites reported that a small portion of youth were terminated by the program, quit their jobs, or dropped out of the program.

Sites were also responsible for formally measuring growth in youth's work readiness skills for federal performance reporting requirements. Administrators and frontline staff were overwhelmingly appreciative of the limited requirements in this area for the SYEI. The flexibility given to the states and local areas, however, created inconsistency across and sometimes within sites. Most, but not all, sites measured work readiness skills before and after youth participated in activities, thereby capturing some assessment of growth or increase in skills. However, sites varied substantially in the timing of these assessments, the methods of capturing data (such as through staff observations, employer feedback, and tests of youth), and the types of skills assessed.

Overall Impressions of the 2009 Summer Experience

This evaluation documents the experiences of selected sites, paints a detailed picture of SYEI implementation, and gives a voice to the youth and employers who were at the core of this effort. Drawing from the detailed data collected, it identifies overall impressions of implementation from the perspective of local implementers, youth, and employers.

It took enormous effort to get this large initiative up and running in a short period of time. Parties at all levels of the workforce investment system—including Federal, state, and local levels—had to act quickly to ensure that the SYEI could get off the ground in time. The size of the initiative and the quick timeframe affected every aspect of planning and implementation. As a result, some sites reported having to make compromises along the way, including curbing the extent of innovation and implementing practices without exploring all possible options. Despite these limitations, administrators and staff reported pride in their accomplishments in the summer of 2009.

Although there were inevitable challenges, the SYEI was implemented successfully without any major problems. Sites were able to recruit sufficient numbers of youth to fill the program slots, to place them in employment, and to provide additional services.

Administrators and staff in the study sites reported that the SYEI had a threefold effect. First, they got money into the hands of needy families. Second, youth and their families spent the disposable income earned through SYEI jobs in their depressed local economies. Third, youth gained valuable work experience, increasing their human capital and long-term job prospects.

Youth valued the opportunity to hold a job, gain work skills, and build their résumés. They also valued the exposure to professional environments and mentoring adults. Many were enthusiastic about having money and being able to help their families in these tough economic times. In the absence of the initiative, many reported they would be competing for jobs with more experienced adult workers or doing nothing productive over their summer break. Although youth had some important feedback on key ways to improve the summer initiative, their most common complaint was that the initiative was too short and offered too few work hours.

Employers were overwhelmingly positive about the initiative. They felt that the experience of mentoring a new employee was worth the effort and almost unanimously agreed that they would participate again if given the opportunity.

Challenges and Lessons Learned

Despite the positive feedback from staff, youth, and employers, implementation of the SYEI was not without its challenges. Based on discussions with local staff, employers, and participants, as well as observation of program practices across all 20 sites, the study identifies challenges and lessons in seven key areas from implementation of the 2009 SYEI.

1. Enrollment and Eligibility Determination

Staff across all sites struggled to handle the increased volume of youth, particularly the process of determining their eligibility. For future summer initiatives, local areas should consider providing more training to less experienced staff members to prepare them for summer tasks. As did some sites in 2009, local areas should also consider relying more heavily on experienced staff to perform more complex tasks, such as eligibility determination. Local areas should also examine other possible strategies to reduce workloads and maximize staff resources such as streamlining intake procedures through prescreening applications and coordinating with schools and social service agencies to determine youth eligibility.

2. Recruitment of Veterans and Older Youth

Although overall youth recruitment efforts proved very successful, sites had difficulty reaching older youth between the ages of 22 and 24 as well as veterans and their spouses. Sites should think beyond "youth" when designing and promoting youth activities, given that many veterans and young adults have children, household responsibilities, and significant work experience. Sites reported that it was important to avoid alienating older youth by characterizing the SYEI as a youth program. Local areas should also consider developing new partnerships or reframing old partnerships with organizations that already serve these young adults. Finally, they should consider implementing strategies to differentiate services based on the unique needs of these older participants.

3. Recruitment of Private Sector Employers

Although federal guidance encouraged the involvement of private employers, some sites were hesitant about including them. Sites raised three concerns: (1) the advisability of choosing one private employer over another for a government-subsidized job, (2) the lack of sufficient information on the quality of private sector jobs, and (3) the age and background restrictions imposed by private employers. While not necessarily appropriate for all youth, the private sector can be a good source of high quality jobs for many participants, particularly older, more experienced youth. Most sites did successfully engage at least some private employers, and the private employers involved in the study appreciated the opportunity to participate and support local youth. About one-third of sites felt that private employers were more likely to hire participants permanently and were a better fit based on youth interests. In addition, sites did not report any problems or conflicts related to equity among local businesses. With sufficient planning time, local areas can address concerns about the quality of private sector jobs by sufficiently vetting potential employers and training worksite supervisors to ensure that they can provide quality tasks and professional mentoring.

4. Green Jobs

While more than half of sites reported at least some success placing youth in green industries and jobs, administrators and staff across sites and even within sites often did not use a common definition for green jobs. Respondents in three sites explicitly expressed confusion over the definition. To further expand youth opportunities in this emerging field, sites require additional guidance from ETA on what constitutes a green job. The Bureau of Labor Statistics as well as several states, foundations, and private organizations have already begun efforts to define the concept of green jobs more clearly and conduct inventories of these jobs across the country.

5. Job Matching

Some sites felt—and youth agreed—that job matching of youth to employers could have been improved by either aligning employer recruitment to the interests of youth or more closely considering data from youth intake and assessments when determining the most appropriate employer. To the extent possible, local areas should match youth to employers based on their interests and career goals to help maximize the potential for a valuable summer experience that may lead to better employment opportunities. To help achieve this goal, sites should consider using information on the types of jobs that best suited the interests of youth enrolled in the summer of 2009 to help focus initial employer recruitment efforts in future summers. In addition, if sites chose to recruit employers before enrolling youth, they should consider continuing employer recruitment as needed once youth are enrolled to accommodate the interests of as many participants as possible. Given that all matches may not be ideal, staff should also work to ensure that both employers and youth have reasonable expectations for the summer experience. In particular, staff should stress to youth that, no matter what their work assignment, they will be able to build their résumés and can learn important work skills.

6. *Measurement of Work Readiness Increases*

Sites varied dramatically in their measurement of work readiness increases among youth and sometimes used different approaches within a site. These inconsistencies make it difficult to assess the true meaning of the national performance measure. To ensure the use of a valid measure across all local areas, sites require additional guidance from ETA on standards and best practices in measuring increases in work readiness skills. This includes guidance on the timing and frequency of youth assessments, the most appropriate sources of data on youth performance, and the types of skills that should be assessed.

7. *Innovation*

Variations in the local infrastructure and economy of study sites clearly affected their implementation of the SYEI. For instance, one site reported denying services to some youth who did not live near a participating employer because the youth's community lacked a good public transportation system. However, other sites with youth in similar situations either developed their own van routes or recruited businesses within the communities where youth lived to allow them to participate. As another example, administrators in some areas said they could not place significant numbers of youth into green jobs given the lack of green industry in their local economies. Other sites in similar situations, however, developed their own green projects or tapped into the public sector for green opportunities. Addressing local circumstances may require innovation. When encountering an implementation challenge, administrators should consider new or innovative models, including looking to other sites with similar local circumstances for potential solutions.

Looking beyond Summer 2009

Although the SYEI of 2009 was a monumental effort, it was not the end of the road for participating youth. Many participants came out of the summer initiative looking for new opportunities to expand on their experiences. How they fared beyond the summer and what effect the SYEI had on their employment prospects can only be determined through long-term follow up or better efforts to track future participants. However, some sites had already begun reflecting on what worked and what could be improved for future summers.

Many youth who participated in the SYEI hoped to transition to new opportunities in the fall. The largest proportion of participants planned to return to school. Some youth could receive additional services from the workforce investment system, including the regular WIA youth and adult formula-funded programs, and from other organizations within the community. Still other youth sought to move into permanent jobs. Respondents, however, mentioned several issues that might have limited these opportunities. Although the regular WIA programs for youth and adults could serve some youth, some of these programs already had waiting lists due to excess demand. In addition, while every site expected at least some youth to enter permanent jobs, the state of the economy may have limited the number of permanent placements for youth.

Sites appeared prepared to offer summer opportunities to significant numbers of youth in 2010. During the summer of 2009, sites worked through many challenges inherent in the implementation of a new initiative and learned lessons that can be used to inform future efforts. Sites looked forward to offering summer work opportunities to youth in 2010 if funding is available. Even if dedicated funding is not available, a few sites felt the success of the SYEI in helping youth gain a better understanding of the world of work would prompt them to consider dedicating a larger portion of their regular WIA formula funds to develop summer opportunities for youth.

I. INTRODUCTION

The American economy lost an estimated 7.9 million jobs from the end of 2007 to the fall of 2009 (U.S. Department of Labor 2009b). Joblessness was high for many groups during this period, but for young adults, unemployment was particularly high and could have lasting effects. In May 2009, the jobless rate for teenagers was 22.7 percent, more than double the national rate of 9.4 percent (U.S. Department of Labor 2009b). The funding for youth activities through the American Recovery and Reinvestment Act of 2009 (the Recovery Act) was designed as one part of the solution to address this situation and reverse the steep decline in youth employment.

Through the Recovery Act, states received an additional $1.2 billion in WIA Youth funding for employment and training activities targeted to disadvantaged youth. Congress and the U.S. Department of Labor (DOL) encouraged states and local workforce investment areas charged with implementing youth activities to use the funds to create employment opportunities for these youth in the summer of 2009. Although summer employment is a component of youth activities under the Workforce Investment Act of 1998 (WIA), many local areas did not provide summer jobs for significant numbers of youth after the transition to WIA in 2000 (Social Policy Research Associates 2004). Local areas had from mid-February 2009, when the Recovery Act was signed into law, to the beginning of May 2009 to design their summer youth activities and prepare for implementation.

To gain insights into the design and implementation of these initiatives, DOL's Employment and Training Administration (ETA) contracted with Mathematica Policy Research to conduct an evaluation of the summer youth employment activities funded by the Recovery Act. Although summer employment is only one component of WIA youth activities and is not funded as a separate program, the opportunities offered by local areas with Recovery Act funding in the summer of 2009 are referred to as the Summer Youth Employment Initiative (SYEI) throughout this chapter. As part of this evaluation, Mathematica® analyzed state performance data and qualitative data collected through in-depth site visits to 20 local areas. This chapter describes the national context for SYEI implementation, provides an in-depth description of the experiences of selected sites, and presents lessons on implementation practices that may inform SYEIs.

A. Policy and Economic Context

On February 17, 2009, President Barack Obama signed the Recovery Act into law. The Act was passed in response to the economic crisis that began in December of 2007 with a housing crisis, a credit crunch, and rising unemployment across the country (U.S. Department of Labor 2009b). From December 2007 to November 2009, the number of unemployed persons in the nation rose from 7.5 million to 15.4 million, and the national unemployment rate rose from 4.5 percent to 10.0 percent (U.S. Department of Labor 2009b). With a total value of $787 billion, the Act's purpose was to create jobs, pump money into the economy, and encourage spending (U.S. Congress 2009). A key aspect of the Act was its urgency, as reflected by its enactment shortly after the start of the new Congress and administration.

In this weakened economy, youth employment rates have been at historic lows (Center for Labor Market Studies 2009). Although these rates appeared to be due to the recent economic crisis, youth employment had been decreasing steadily since 2000 (McLaughlin et al. 2009). Between 2000 and 2009, the summer employment rate for teens between the ages of 16 and 19 fell from 45 percent to 29 percent. Employment rates decreased for all gender and ethnic groups in this period, though some groups were harder hit. Although employment rates were similar for male and female youth in 2000, male employment fell by more than female employment. By 2009, the female youth employment rate was 31 percent compared with the male rate of 28 percent. African American males have historically had the lowest employment rates, and in summer 2009, African American male youth had an employment rate of 17 percent.

The dual purposes of the Recovery Act provisions targeting youth were to spur local economies and to provide employment experiences to disadvantaged youth. These employment opportunities were meant to put money directly into the hands of youth, who could both help support their families during the recession and help stimulate demand in local economies through their spending. Providing young adults with employment opportunities through the Recovery Act could also help make up for the loss of employment opportunities during the economic downturn. Without these experiences, young adults may be unable to explore future career opportunities and will be less familiar with the expectations of the world of work (Oates 2009).

B. The History of Summer Youth Programs

Starting in 1983, before the Workforce Investment Act of 1998 (WIA), the Job Training Partnership Act (JTPA) provided federal funding for employment programs aimed at disadvantaged youth. Title II-B, the Summer Youth Employment and Training Program (SYETP), was the larger of the two programs. In program year 1990, Title II-B received an allocation of $871 million and Title II-C, providing for year-round programs, received $130 million. Eligibility was restricted to low-income youth ages 14 to 21 for summer services and ages 16 to 21 for year-round services.

SYETP reflected a long-standing federal commitment to providing summer work experiences to youth (Social Policy Research Associates 1998).[1] SYETP services included basic and remedial education, on-the-job training, paid work experience, employment counseling, occupational training, preparation for work, and assistance in searching for jobs. The early 1990s witnessed a change in the program's focus from exposing youth to the world of work to linking work experiences to the youth's academic achievement. This translated into a requirement to assess the basic skills of each youth and plan a service strategy based on those assessments (Social Policy Research Associates 1998). The Title II-C year-round program provided services similar to the summer program but also provided help with transition to the working world, preventing students from dropping out of school, and mentoring.

Recognizing JTPA's lack of demonstrated success in improving youth's post-service outcomes (Social Policy Research Associates 2004; Bloom et al. 1993), WIA mandated a major refocus of youth programs. WIA required more comprehensive services focused on long-term outcomes and better aligned with youth development theory and practices. Most notably, rather than treating summer employment as a stand-alone intervention, WIA integrated it into a comprehensive program. Thus, summer work experiences became only one of 10 required elements for youth participating in programs funded under the WIA. Following the transition to WIA, a 2004 study found that youth enrollment in summer programs dropped 50 to 90 percent in most local areas (Social Policy Research Associates 2004).

Under WIA, local areas must make each of these 10 elements available to eligible youth:

1. Summer employment opportunities linked to academic and occupational learning
2. Tutoring, study skills training, and instruction leading to secondary school completion
3. Alternative secondary school offerings
4. Paid and unpaid work experiences
5. Occupational skill training
6. Leadership development opportunities
7. Supportive services
8. Adult mentoring for at least 12 months, either during or after participation
9. Comprehensive guidance and counseling
10. Follow-up activities for at least 12 months

To participate in WIA programs, youth must meet three eligibility criteria. They must be between 14 and 21 years old, qualify as low income according to WIA Section 101 (25) (U.S. Congress 1998), and meet one of six barriers to employment: being (1) a school dropout; (2) deficient in basic literacy; (3) a homeless, runaway, or foster child; (4) a parenting or pregnant teen; (5) an offender; or (6) someone who needs help completing an education program or securing and maintaining employment. In addition, WIA requires that at least 30 percent of the youth funds be spent on out-of-school youth.[2] As performance indicators, WIA enacted seven statutory measures, and DOL also added and implemented three common measures that were developed by the Office of Management and Budget (OMB)—including youth's placement in work or education, attainment of diplomas or credentials, and improvement in basic skills.

C. The Recovery Act Allocation for the WIA Youth Program

The congressional explanatory statement for the Recovery Act and ETA's Training and Employment Guidance Letter No. 14-08 (U.S. Department of Labor 2009d) laid out the key provisions for the Recovery Act's allocation of WIA youth funds. The Act indicated that the

$1.2 billion be used toward youth activities. Although the use of funds was not restricted and funds could be spent through June 30, 2011, the congressional guidance for the Act expressed a strong interest in the funds being used to fund summer employment opportunities for youth. Similar to the SYETP, youth would be placed in summer employment experiences with local public, nonprofit, and private employers and their wages would be paid with Recovery Act funds.

The Act contained two other key provisions for the WIA youth activities funded under it. First, it extended eligibility to youth up to 24 years of age. Second, the Act specified that only one indicator—achievement of work readiness goals—would be used to measure the performance of youth activities funded by the Recovery Act. Local areas were also required by ETA to report another performance indicator—the number of youth completing summer employment experiences.

ETA provided further guidance to states and local areas on the use of the Recovery Act youth funds during the summer months, defined as May 1, 2009 through September 30, 2009 (U.S. Department of Labor 2009d). These provisions included the following features:

Work experiences should be "meaningful" and age appropriate. Work experiences should be age appropriate and lead to youth meeting work readiness goals. ETA encouraged local areas to incorporate experiences in "green" (or environmentally friendly) work and skills and to introduce youth to green educational and career pathways. Local areas were also encouraged to match worksites with participants' goals and interests as much as possible.

Local areas had flexibility in using classroom-based learning activities. Local areas could decide whether or not to link classroom-based learning, such as occupational training, with youth's work experiences. Such a linkage was recommended for younger youth in need of instruction in basic skills and career exploration. Local areas could decide if the linkage was beneficial based on the circumstances of each youth, but were asked to consider academic linkages for youth without a high school diploma.

Registered apprenticeships were encouraged. Given the growing trend in registered apprenticeships, local areas were encouraged to take advantage of local apprenticeship programs to create pre-apprenticeship opportunities. These programs link out-of-school youth to technical skills training that can be translated to experience at a worksite, thus preparing the youth for formal apprenticeship programs upon completion of the summer work experience.

Performance would be measured by one work readiness indicator. Local areas could determine how to define indicators of work readiness and measure changes in the indicator but were provided with a definition for work readiness skill goals. States could request a waiver to use this indicator also for youth aged 18 to 24 years who participated in only work experiences during October 2009 through March 2010. If youth in that group received additional services during the post-summer period, they would be included in the regular WIA performance measures.

WIA youth program elements were not required. Local areas could determine which of the 10 WIA youth program elements to offer to participants funded by the Recovery Act.

For example, this provision permitted local areas to determine whether or not to provide supportive services or follow up with participants for 12 months after receipt of services. ETA also provided some flexibility regarding other design elements. While WIA requires a comprehensive assessment and individualized service strategy (ISS) for each youth participant, the Recovery Act allowed local areas to determine what type of assessment and ISS to complete for each youth that participated in the summer months only.

Certain groups should receive priority. The priority groups for WIA programs—including veterans and eligible spouses of veterans—were also priority groups for youth activities funded by the Recovery Act. ETA also noted that the extension of eligibility to 24 year olds could make more veterans eligible for summer employment. As with regular WIA youth programs, at least 30 percent of Recovery Act funding for WIA youth activities had to be spent on out-of-school youth. ETA also encouraged local areas to focus their services on groups of the neediest youth.

Local areas could request waivers for contractor procurement. States were permitted to request a waiver from the WIA requirement for service providers to be selected through a competitive procurement process, but were still required to follow state or local laws that could not be relieved by federal regulations (U.S. Congress 1999). If granted, the waiver would permit local areas to extend existing contracts for WIA services or to conduct a competition among a limited number of providers for the summer youth initiative.

D. Overview of the Evaluation

In conjunction with ETA, Mathematica designed the evaluation of the Recovery Act SYEI to provide rich information about its implementation and potential for improving the work readiness of disadvantaged youth. ETA expressed interest in learning about local areas' efforts to quickly implement a large initiative and the resulting experiences for youth, employers, and communities. However, compiling data on these experiences for all local areas was not possible within the study's scope. Thus, the study team worked with ETA national and regional staff to identify 20 areas for in-depth study (herafter referred to as the study "sites"). These sites were selected based on early indications that they could offer potentially promising approaches to delivering summer employment experiences to youth.

Although this approach limits the study's ability to draw conclusions about SYEI implementation across the country, it does provide important insights into the issues and challenges involved in providing summer work experiences to a large number of youth. In addition, the study provides information based on state-reported performance and draw down data to give some national context for the experiences of the 20 selected sites.

Furthermore, this study focused on sites' experiences preparing for and providing the work opportunities to youth during the summer of 2009. It was not designed to capture the overall quality of youth's experiences or to assess youth's outcomes as a result of their participation. Still, the information captured about the selected sites' experiences provides valuable lessons for policymakers and administrators considering implementing summer youth initiatives in the future.

1. Research Questions

Six major research questions guided the evaluation. By addressing these questions, the study gives policymakers, administrators, and stakeholders a better understanding of how the SYEI unfolded in the summer of 2009:

1. How did the selected sites plan for and organize their summer youth initiatives?
2. How did selected sites identify, recruit, and enroll at-risk youth?
3. What were the characteristics of participants nationwide?
4. What services were offered during the summer months in selected sites?
5. What types of work experiences were offered to participating youth in selected sites?
6. What lessons can be drawn about the implementation of summer youth programs?

Appendix A lists the comprehensive set of sub-questions for each major research question.

2. Selection of Study Sites

To learn about SYEI implementation, 20 local areas were selected for data collection and analysis. Based on their knowledge of local areas that offered innovative or potentially promising approaches, ETA national and regional staff nominated a total of 40 local areas for inclusion in the study. The evaluation team and ETA narrowed the list to 27 local areas using three key criteria: (1) including at least three sites from each region; (2) choosing only those sites that planned to spend at least 50 percent of Recovery Act funds during the summer of 2009; and (3) including rural, urban, and suburban sites.

In July 2009, the evaluation team conducted telephone calls with administrators in these 27 local areas to collect more information about their initiatives and discuss the feasibility of an in-person site visit. Based on these discussions and consideration of the selection criteria, Mathematica and ETA determined the final set of 20 study sites (see Table I.1).

3. Data Sources

To provide a complete picture of SYEIs in the summer of 2009, the evaluation draws upon two key data sources: state performance data and in-depth site visits. The state performance data provides the national scope of the initiative and additional context for the experiences of the 20 selected sites. During site visits, the study team collected detailed information on how the sites implemented their initiatives. Data collection for each source focused on the summer months.

State performance and draw down data. States delivered monthly performance reports to ETA for all youth participating in Recovery Act services at all local areas across the nation. The study obtained performance data submitted to ETA as of December 31, 2009 that covers implementation from May through November 2009. The data include statistics on the number of youth enrolled, their demographic characteristics, the services they received, and key performance outcomes. ETA also provided the study with data on monthly draw downs from state funding allocations for the same period of May through November 2009.

Table I.1. Sites Selected for Visits

Region	Local Workforce Investment Agent	City, State
1	Regional Employment Board of Hampden County	Springfield, MA
1	The Workplace, Inc.	Bridgeport, CT
1	Workforce Partnership of Greater Rhode Island	Cranston, RI
2	Lehigh Valley Workforce Investment Board, Inc.	Lehigh Valley, PA
2	Three Rivers Workforce Investment Board	Pittsburgh, PA
2	Western Virginia Workforce Development Board	Roanoke, VA
3	Eastern Kentucky Concentrated Employment Program	Hazard, KY
3	Northeast Georgia Regional Commission	Athens, GA
3	Workforce Investment Network	Memphis, TN
4	Denver Office of Economic Development	Denver, CO
4	Montana State WIB, District XI Human Resource Council	Missoula, MT
4	Workforce Connection of Central New Mexico	Albuquerque, NM
5	Minneapolis Employment and Training Program	Minneapolis, MN
5	Workforce Development, Inc.	Rochester, MN
5	Workforce Resource, Inc.	Menomonie, WI
6	Community Development Department of the City of LA	Los Angeles, CA
6	Madera County Office of Education	Madera, CA
6	Oregon Consortium and Oregon Workforce Alliance	Albany, OR
6	Workforce Development Council of Seattle-King County	Seattle, WA
6	Worksystems, Inc.	Portland, OR

Note: The city and state reflect the location of the local area's central office.

In-depth site visits. The study team completed visits to the 20 selected sites during July and August 2009, while youth were being served. Each visit, conducted by one member of the study team, lasted an average of 2.5 days. Site visitors spoke to a total of 601 individuals across the 20 sites, including 373 administrators and staff, 79 employers, and 149 youth. Appendix B provides the demographic characteristics of the youth who participated in focus groups. The interviews and focus groups conducted during these site visits were the main source of information for this study.

4. Analytical Approach and Limitations

The two data sources required different analytical approaches. For the state performance and draw down data, the analysis was intended to provide a larger picture of SYEI implementation across the country. The analysis was purely descriptive. State-specific statistics were aggregated to produce national frequencies. The team also analyzed enrollment patterns over time. Given that states provided only aggregate data, analyzing subgroups was not feasible.

For the in-depth site visits, the analysis focused on the study's key research questions as the evaluation team searched for themes, patterns, and relationships that emerged both within individual sites and across sites. The analysis considered models of program organization, outreach, and recruitment; similarities and differences in service offerings; approaches to work readiness; and the range of summer work experiences. The study also looked across sites at the common lessons learned, challenges faced, and suggestions for structuring an improved SYEI.

The analysis of qualitative data went beyond the national data and explored, in great detail, the experiences of a subset of local areas. Throughout the analysis, the site served as the unit of analysis, even when multiple providers or employers at a site reported different approaches or opinions. We account for these differences by reporting when a particular practice occurred site-wide and when it varied from provider to provider within a site. Given that the evaluation team was not always able to meet with representatives from all local providers, the analysis does not include the full range of site experiences. In addition, employers and participants were purposefully selected by the principal contact in each site and are not representative of all those involved in the initiative. Despite these limitations, the study gathered the perspectives of a large number of diverse respondents.

Throughout the report, local practices and youth perspectives are highlighted in text boxes. The practices described in these boxes are not intended to represent promising or high quality strategies. Instead, they provide concrete examples of the general trends across sites or unique practices adopted by one or more local initiatives. Sites are referenced by the city and state where the central office is located although practices are generally implemented in the wider service area. Similarly, the quotes provided by youth from focus groups are not intended to be representative of all youth, but rather to enable the reader to hear the voices and perspectives of some youth participating in the initiatives.

E. Organization of the Rest of the Report

The purpose of this chapter is to provide a rich description of the implementation of SYEIs funded by the Recovery Act in the summer of 2009. The report continues in Chapter II with a snapshot of the initiative nationwide, using state performance and draw down data. The remainder of the report focuses on the implementation experiences of the 20 selected sites. Chapter III describes the selected sites and their strategies for organizing and planning the summer initiative Chapter IV describes the sites' effort to reach out to prospective youth participants and their processes for enrolling participants. Chapter V examines the strategies used to prepare eligible youth for the worksite placements. Chapter VI discusses the recruitment of employers to provide summer jobs. Chapters VII and VIII explore the range of summer experiences and how local areas monitored youth progress. Finally, Chapter IX provides lessons about the successes and challenges that local areas experienced in implementing the summer youth initiative.

II. THE NATIONAL CONTEXT

Nationwide, local areas served more than 355,000 youth through November 2009 using Recovery Act funding. To document the use of these funds in a timely fashion, ETA required that each state and outlying area[3] submit monthly performance reports on their youth initiatives. Although the overall number of data elements was kept to a minimum to reduce the burden imposed on state and local areas, the data provide an overview of how the summer youth initiative unfolded nationally. The evaluation gathered youth performance data submitted to ETA by the states on youth activities from May through November 2009.

Although the rest of the report discusses qualitative findings from 20 sites, this chapter uses national data to look at the SYEI across all local areas. It examines the use of Recovery Act funds, how many and what types of youth were served, what services they were provided, and what outcomes the youth experienced. Section A begins by examining the monthly trends in national funding draw downs and enrollment in youth employment initiatives. Section B examines who was served in these initiatives during the summer of 2009[4] and the extent to which key target populations, such as veterans, were reached. Section C looks at the types of services youth received that summer, including summer employment, education services, and other supports. Section D concludes with outcomes experienced by the youth served by these initiatives.

KEY FINDINGS: THE NATIONAL CONTEXT

- **States and local areas enrolled more than 355,000 youth nationwide from May to November 2009 using Recovery Act funding.** Enrollment was heaviest in May, June, and July, reflecting the fact that states and local areas heeded federal guidance to focus efforts on summer employment opportunities. By comparison, the regular WIA youth program served slightly more than 250,000 youth during the entire 2008 program year.

- **National draw downs totaled more than $717 million through November 2009, accounting for almost 61 percent of the nearly $1.2 billion in Recovery Act funds.** The proportion of funds drawn down by each state within this timeframe varied from 33 to almost 93 percent.

- **Out-of-school youth accounted for 36 percent of participants nationwide.** The economy as well as the decision to expand eligibility by allowing enrollment of young adults up to age 24 may have contributed to this success.

- **More than 88 percent of participants were placed in summer jobs.** Of those in summer jobs, states reported that over 82 percent completed their summer job experience. States also reported that 75 percent of all youth achieved a measureable increase in their work readiness skills.

A. National Patterns of Enrollment and Draw Downs

Enrolling more than 355,000 youth nationwide, states and local areas drew down more than $717 million through November 2009, or 61 percent of the $1.2 billion in Recovery Act funds targeted for WIA youth services. The proportion of funds drawn down by states varied dramatically from a high of 93 percent in Idaho to a low of 33 percent in Hawaii (see Appendix C). By comparison, local areas served a total of slightly more than 250,000 youth through the regular WIA program during the entire 2008 program year with a budget of $966 million (U.S. Department of Labor 2009a).[5]

As shown in Figure II.1, states heeded the guidance provided by Congress and ETA to focus efforts on summer employment initiatives rather than comprehensive services. Large numbers of youth began enrolling in the spring, with 164,000 youth enrolling in May and June.[6] This initial enrollment accounted for 46 percent of all youth enrolled through November. Enrollment continued heavily through July with another 133,000 youth entering the initiatives. New enrollments fell sharply in August and September as initiatives focused on providing services to those already enrolled; in many cases, initiatives only enrolled new participants in these months by taking youth from waiting lists when participating youth dropped out. As discussed in Chapter IV, administrators from selected local workforce investment areas reported beginning recruitment of youth as early as March and April, often before local funding allocations were made by states, although official enrollment often did not begin until May and June.

National draw downs averaged $128 million per month during the summer period and peaked in August at $173 million per month (see Figure II.2). The peak in draw downs trailed enrollment slightly. This likely reflects the fact that local areas incurred significant costs in youth wages only after youth were officially enrolled, took part in early preparation activities, and were placed at worksites.

B. Characteristics of Youth Participants

The 2009 summer employment initiative enrolled a diverse array of youth, in terms of gender, race, education level, and age (see Table II.1). Females and males participated at similar rates. African Americans made up 45 percent of all participants through November 2009. Whites were the second largest racial group, comprising 38 percent. Other ethnic groups made up less than 5 percent of participants. The racial background of more than 12 percent of participating youth is unknown. States also reported that nearly 25 percent of participants were of Latino or Hispanic origin. The majority of participants were in-school youth, a group largely comprised of those ages 18 or younger (see Table II.1).

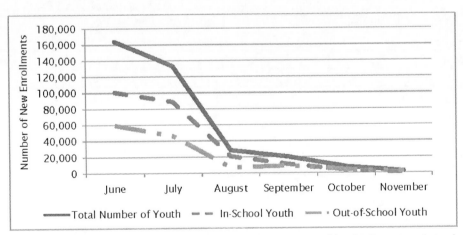

Source: State performance reports for WIA youth initiatives supported by the Recovery Act submitted to the U.S. Department of Labor as of December 31, 2009.

Note: States submitted their first performance reports in June with aggregate data for youth enrolled in May and June.

Figure II.1 WIA Youth Enrollment in 2009 Under the Recovery Act

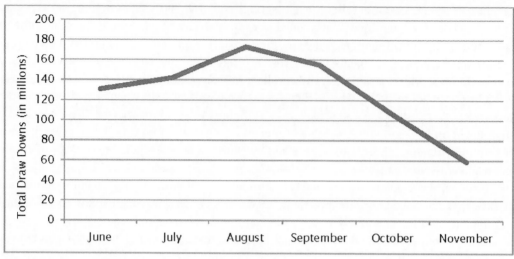

Source: Monthly draw downs of WIA Youth Recovery Act Funds.

Notes: Draw downs reflect the actual cash drawn daily by grantees from the financial system. By comparison, expenditures are the costs reported quarterly on an accrual basis, and therefore include all services and goods received by the end of the quarter, whether or not they have been invoiced or paid. As a result, draw downs may not account for all expenditures during the reporting period. Data from March through June were only available in aggregate and are reported under the month of June.

Figure II.2 National Draw Downs of WIA Youth Recovery Act Funds in 2009

Table II.1. Characteristics of Youth Served under the Recovery Act through November 2009

	Number of Participants	Percentage of All Participants
Total Number of Participants	355,320	100.0
Gender		
Male	175,239	49.3
Female	179,496	50.5
Not reported	585	0.2
Race		
Black or African American	158,914	44.7
White	136,563	38.4
American Indian or Alaska Native	7,145	2.0
Asian	6,329	1.8
Hawaiian Native or Other Pacific Islander	2,149	0.6
Not reported	44,220	12.4
Latino or Hispanic Origin	86,859	24.4
School Status		
In-school	224,798	63.3
Out-of-school	127,869	36.0

Table II.1. (Continued)

	Number of Participants	Percentage of All Participants
Not reported	2,653	0.7
Age at Enrollment		
14–18 years	228,921	64.4
19–21 years	84,539	23.8
22–24 years	30,594	8.6
Not reported	11,266	3.2
Education Level at Enrollment		
8th grade or under	45,302	12.7
9th to 12th grade	204,378	57.5
High school graduate or equivalent	81,372	22.9
1–3 years of college or full-time technical or vocational school	20,506	5.8
4 years college or more	1,366	0.4
Not reported	2,396	0.7
Individuals with Disabilities	45,125	12.7
Eligible Veterans	671	0.2

Source: State performance reports for WIA youth initiatives supported by the Recovery Act submitted to the U.S. Department of Labor as of December 31, 2009.

Notes: Data on age could not be broken into smaller subgroups.

These figures do not include the 3,763 youth served by Indian and Native American grantees as a result of reporting procedures.

Analysis of data on those served during the summer months of May to September 2009 result in differences of less than one percentage point in all categories when compared with November statistics presented in the table.

States also succeeded in enrolling a large number of out-of-school and older youth. Out-of-school youth included dropouts as well as youth who had received a high school diploma or its equivalent but were not enrolled in postsecondary education and needed assistance securing or holding employment. ETA placed particular emphasis on this population by requiring that states expend a minimum of 30 percent of their funds, both Recovery Act funds and WIA-formula funds, on this group. The WIA program has struggled to reach this critical high-risk population in the past (U.S. Government Accountability Office 2004). However, the program has made significant progress enrolling out-of-school youth in recent years, with this group accounting for 42 percent of youth served during program year 2008 (U.S. Department of Labor 2009).

Using Recovery Act funds, out-of-school youth accounted for 36 percent of those enrolled through November. Although this proportion remained relatively steady through the early summer months, it began to rise to nearly 50 percent in September (not shown). This suggests that out-of-school youth received additional priority as in-school youth returned to the classroom. Success with out-of-school youth recruitment may have resulted from the increase in unemployment among youth due to the recession. The Recovery Act also expanded eligibility to allow young adults between the ages of 22 and 24 to enroll. In fact, nine percent of all those enrolled through November—nearly 31,000 participants—fell within this age range. Site visits to selected areas suggest that most of these older participants were not attending educational programs at enrollment.

As expected given the high proportion of in-school youth, 70 percent of enrolled youth had less than a high school diploma (Table II.1). Another 23 percent had received their high school degree or equivalent. Local areas were also able enroll a portion of more highly educated participants: the remaining seven percent of participants had at least some postsecondary education at enrollment.

Youth with disabilities accounted for about 13 percent of participants. As defined for performance reporting, a disability is "a physical or mental impairment that substantially limits one or more of the person's major life activities." These activities can include a wide range of functions such as "caring for one's self, performing manual tasks, walking, seeing, hearing, speaking, breathing, learning, working, and receiving education or vocational training" (U.S. Congress 2000).

Veterans and their spouses were given priority of service as a result of the high incidence of unemployment immediately upon discharge from the military. Evaluation site visits revealed that this was one of the most challenging populations to reach. State data reflects this pattern, with only 671 veterans, or less than 0.2 percent of all participants, enrolled nationwide. ETA did not require states to report on the number of participants who were spouses of veterans, so such data are not available.

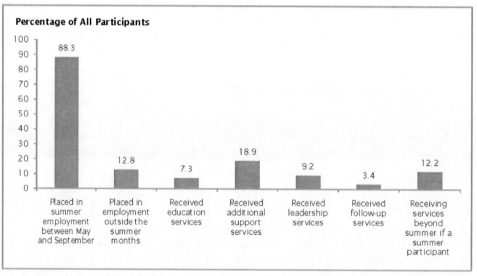

Source: State performance reports for WIA youth initiatives supported by the Recovery Act submitted to the U.S.

Department of Labor as of December 31, 2009.

Notes: ETA defines the summer months as May through September.

Data on those "placed in employment outside the summer months" can include participants who were also placed in summer employment.

N = 355,320;.data on those "receiving services beyond the summer if a summer participant" pertain only to 345,394 youth who participated during May through September.

These figures do not include the 3,763 youth served by Indian and Native American grantees as a result of reporting procedures.

Figure II.3. Youth Services Received under the Recovery Act through November 2009

C. Patterns of Service Receipt among Participating Youth

Youth employment clearly served as the focus of local efforts to expend Recovery Act allocations. Nearly 314,000 youth—88 percent of participants—were placed in a summer job (see Figure II.3). In addition, 13 percent of all participants were placed in work experiences outside the summer months. This percentage could include participants who also were placed in summer employment, those who participated in WIA youth activities funded under the Recovery Act but did not work during the summer, and those who did not enroll until the fall. Although the data does not allow for subgroup analyses, patterns of enrollment suggest a surge in fall work experience placements among out-of-school youth as in-school youth returned to school. Appendix D provides employment rates and other key statistics by state.

Smaller proportions of youth were exposed to a range of other services. As mentioned in Chapter I, of the 10 youth service elements associated with the regular WIA youth program, ETA only required work experience for these summer initiatives. However, many local areas chose to provide at least some other services—including education services, support services, leadership development, and follow-up services—to a proportion of youth.

Educational services were provided to a small proportion of youth. Slightly more than 7 percent of youth received education services, including but not limited to "tutoring, study skills training, and instruction leading to secondary school completion" (U.S. Department of Labor 2009e). As discussed in Chapter VII, evaluation site visits suggest that the some of the most common educational activities included occupational skills training, GED preparation, recovery of school credits, and remediation.

Additional service offerings included support services and leadership development activities. Almost 19 percent of youth received some sort of support service. ETA guidance allows for a broad interpretation of support services but provides examples such as adult mentoring and comprehensive guidance and counseling. As discussed in Chapter V, local areas involved in the study appeared to use this category mostly to capture transportation assistance, clothing and tools, and child care. Slightly more than 9 percent of youth also participated in leadership development activities. These types of services aim to "encourage responsibility, employability, and other positive social behaviors." (U.S. Department of Labor 2009e) Leadership development activities also include service learning projects, peer-centered activities, and teamwork activities.

Local areas continued to track very few summer participants into the fall. Chapter VIII suggests that few local areas chose to exercise the option to follow summer participants for 12 months after enrollment to assess their progress over time. Nationally, local areas report formally following only 3.4 percent of youth served under the Recovery Act as of November 2009.

A larger fraction of summer participants, however, continued to receive at least some services beyond September. Specifically, 12.2 percent of participants enrolled during the summer months received services in the fall through either Recovery Act initiatives or regular WIA programs. This could include WIA youth services for those aged 14 to 17, WIA adult services for those aged 22 to 24, or either youth or adult services for youth falling in the middle range of 18 to 21.[7] As a way of encouraging states to continue providing services to older youth, states were allowed to apply for waivers on performance reporting requirements through March 2010 for summer participants between the ages of 18 and 24 who participated in work experience from October 2009 through March 2010.

D. Short-term Outcome Measures

To streamline implementation, Congress only required states and local areas to report on one performance measure for youth served with Recovery Act funds. States had to report on the percentage of participants in summer employment who attained a "work readiness skill goal." Nationwide, local areas reported that almost 75 percent of youth achieved a measureable increase in their work readiness skills through summer employment (see Table II.2).

To provide context for this statistic, ETA guidance specifies the following:

"A measurable increase in work readiness skills includ[es] world-of-work awareness, labor market knowledge, occupational information, values clarification and personal understanding, career planning and decision making, and job search techniques (resumes, interviews, applications, and follow-up letters). The[se skills] also encompass survival/daily living skills such as using the phone, telling time, shopping, renting an apartment, opening a bank account, and using public transportation. They also include positive work habits, attitudes, and behaviors such as punctuality, regular attendance, presenting a neat appearance, getting along and working well with others, exhibiting good conduct, following instructions and completing tasks, accepting constructive criticism from supervisors and coworkers, showing initiative and reliability, and assuming the responsibilities involved in maintaining a job. This category also entails developing motivation and adaptability, obtaining effective coping and problem-solving skills, and acquiring an improved self image." (U.S. Department of Labor 2006)

ETA gave local areas discretion over how and when to measure this outcome. A report on the use of Recovery Act funding by the Government Accountability Office (U.S. Government Accountability Office 2009) suggests that this flexibility may limit the usefulness of the data as it impairs the comparability and rigor of the data. Chapter VIII discusses the issue further and provides details on how the 20 selected local areas chose to measure increases in work readiness.

Table II.2. Performance Outcomes of Youth Served under the Recovery Act through November 2009

	Number Reported as Achieving Outcome	Number for Whom Data Were Available	Percentage Achieving Outcome
Increase in work readiness skills	235,043	314,132	74.8
Completion of summer work experience	242,827	294,842	82.4

Source: State performance reports for WIA youth initiatives supported by the Recovery Act submitted to the U.S. Department of Labor as of December 31, 2009.

Notes: These figures do not include the 3,763 youth served by Indian and Native American grantees as a result of reporting procedures.

Data were not available for youth who were still participating in services at the time of data reporting. In addition, data were not available for some participants due to delays in state reporting.

Beyond the Congressional requirement, ETA also required states to report the proportion of youth who completed their summer work experience. Although data were not available for all 314,000 youth who participated in summer employment, state reports indicate that more than 82 percent of those for whom data were available completed their summer job. Site visits suggest that the remainder of summer work participants either dropped out or were terminated for worksite performance issues.

III. THE SYEI CONTEXT AND ORGANIZATION

The previous chapter presented the national picture for the SYEI; this chapter begins the focus on the 20 selected sites through information collected during in-depth site visits. Similar to local workforce investment areas across the country, the selected study sites brought their particular characteristics and past experiences to bear in developing their Recovery Act SYEIs. Reflecting the study's selection criteria, the sites represented all regions of the country as well as different service delivery models. For example, local areas' Workforce Investment Boards (LWIBs) could choose to deliver SYEI services directly to youth or contract out the services to youth providers. In part, these decisions reflected areas' existing organizational structures for the WIA youth program.

Before turning to key aspects of the sites' SYEIs, this chapter provides the background for the selected study areas. Section A presents a few select characteristics, such as the population size and economic situations, of the selected sites. Section B discusses the planning phase, including when the initiatives were designed and by whom, the influence of sites' previous experiences on program design, and the challenges the sites faced. Finally, Section C presents four models of how the SYEI was organized across the sites and how sites worked with providers and staffed the initiative.

KEY FINDINGS: CONTEXT AND ORGANIZATION OF STUDY SITES

- **Planning for the SYEI was challenging given the short-time frame.** Sites dealt with this challenge by leveraging existing relationships and ensuring open communication with new implementation partners.
- **The LWIB or its administrative agent led the planning efforts.** Youth Councils provided the most input into local sites' plans; youth providers and employers were rarely involved.
- **SYEI providers included a mix of new and experienced WIA youth providers.** Three sites chose to administer the program solely through the LWIB or its administrative agent. The remaining 17 sites contracted SYEI services to local providers, including 9 that contracted with at least some providers that were new to WIA.

A. Characteristics of Selected Local Areas

Reflecting the evaluation's site selection criteria, the study's local sites were diverse on several dimensions. In addition to representing each ETA region, the sites encompassed populations of different types and sizes. As Table III.1 indicates, more than half of the sites encompassed a city, although most of these also provided services to youth in neighboring counties. Respondents in sites with a city and surrounding counties often reported that the counties had very different characteristics from their major central city. For example, the Central New Mexico workforce investment area includes the city of Albuquerque but also three rural counties. These differences could have implications for the worksites that are available and accessible to youth. A majority of sites had area-wide populations of less than 750,000.

All of the sites reported experiencing the effects of the current recession. Most sites described large businesses failing and the resultant toll on the community. However, respondents in about a third of the sites reported that the consequences for their areas were not as severe as elsewhere either because a diverse economy helped them weather the current downturn or because the local economy was already suffering when the recession started. While respondents in almost half of sites reported local unemployment rates of 8 to 10 percent, about a third reported unemployment rates of over 10 percent. By comparison, the national unemployment rate reached 9.4 and 9.7 percent in July and August 2009, respectively.[8]

Echoing recent research on the effects of the recession on youth employment (Center for Labor Market Studies 2009), respondents in over half the sites volunteered that youth employment opportunities had become more limited due to the recession. In particular, the jobs that would traditionally be offered to youth were being offered to underemployed or unemployed adults. Employers were not willing to hire inexperienced youth when experienced adult workers were also looking for work.

Table III.1. Selected Characteristics of Study Sites

Characteristic	Number of Sites
Type of Area	
City	3
City and surrounding county(counties)	8
Suburban towns / communities	3
Rural counties / communities	6
Population of Area (estimate)	
Less than 500,000	8
500,000-749,999	3
750,000-999,999	5
1,000,000 or more	4

Source: The primary source of data for "area type" is local respondents. "Population size" data are from the U.S. Census Bureau 2009.

Note: N = 20 sites.

B. Planning for Recovery Act SYEIs

Following enactment of the Recovery Act in February 2009, sites began an intensive planning period. They had only a few months to gear up to provide work experiences to many more youth than had been served in recent summers. The short planning time and federal guidance affected sites' goals for the summer initiative, their plans to scale up existing programs or to create new ones, and the level of involvement of stakeholders.

1. Goals for the Summer of 2009

The goals of the 20 selected sites for their Recovery Act–funded SYEI tended to mirror the goals set in the congressional explanatory statement and ETA's guidance for the use of the funds. First, the pressure on sites to spend their allocations in the summer of 2009 was linked to the number of youth they targeted to serve. Several sites reported that they did not know their allocation until late spring. However, prior to learning their allocations, sites projected how many youth they could serve, given the basic parameters of their summer youth initiatives, such as length of summer work experience and average wages. The 20 selected sites planned to enroll a total of 22,600 youth, with the smallest targeted enrollment of 120 and the largest of 5,550. Nine areas planned to serve fewer than 500 participants, while six planned to serve more than 1,000 (see Table III.2). According to estimates obtained during site visits, the sites were well on their way to reaching their goals by July and August 2009. All 11 sites with actual enrollment statistics at the time of the site visits had surpassed their enrollment targets.

Second, as discussed in Chapter II, states and local areas nationwide responded to the federal guidance by spending a majority of their allocation by November 2009. Study sites' commitment to spending a majority of their Recovery Act youth allocation in the summer of 2009 is shown in Table III.2. Indeed, they were initially selected, in part based on their plans to spend at least 50 percent of their allocation during that summer. In addition to complying with federal guidance, administrators were intent on helping their local youth, families, and economy by injecting Recovery Act funds into their communities. For these reasons, 12 sites indicated that they planned to spend 90 percent or more of their youth allocation in the summer of 2009.

Administrators' other goals for their SYEIs also drew on the federal guidance they received. One goal mentioned by administrators in 11 sites was to provide the youth with a meaningful summer work experience in which they could either explore career interests or become able to put actual work experience on their résumés or both (see Table III.3). An administrator in one of these 11 sites stated that one of the site's major goals was to provide youth with a "life-changing opportunity." Similarly, in citing goals for their SYEIs, site administrators acknowledged the Recovery Act's one required indicator, achieving work readiness. WIA administrators in 7 sites identified improving participants' work readiness skills through training or work experience as an important goal or emphasis. Other goals mentioned by administrators in a smaller number of sites included involving the private sector in work experience opportunities, transitioning older youth into permanent work or other meaningful activities after the summer, and providing employers with positive experiences with the area's youth.

Table III.2. Study Sites' Plans for their Recovery Act Youth Allocations

Characteristic	Number of Sites
Number of Youth Planned to Serve	
Fewer than 250	3
250-499	6
500-999	5
1,000-2,499	3
2,500 or more	3
Proportion of Allocation Planned to be Spent on SYEI	
Less than 75	4
75-89	4
90-99	4
100	8

Source: Site visit interviews in 20 selected sites.
Note: N = 20 sites.

Table III.3. SYEI Goals Cited by Site Administrators

Goal	Number of Sites
Serve as many youth as possible	12
Spend Recovery Act money quickly	12
Provide a meaningful summer work experience	11
Improve participants' work readiness	7
Transition older youth to additional opportunities	7
Involve private employers	3
Provide employers with positive experiences	2

Source: Site visit interviews in 20 selected sites.
Notes: N= 20 sites.
    In each site, several administrators responded to an open-ended question about their goals for the
    SYEI, and each administrator often cited multiple goals. The analysis categorized these responses
    into the seven different goals identified in the table and, if any administrator in a site mentioned the
    goal, the site was counted as having that goal.

2. Previous Summer Experiences

To plan their SYEIs, the sites drew on their experiences providing summer work opportunities through recent programs funded by regular WIA formula funds and other resources, as well as programs under the Job Training Partnership Act (JTPA). As discussed in Chapter 1, until the summer of 2000, when WIA was implemented across the country, JTPA had funded a stand-alone summer youth employment and training program. Under WIA, summer work experiences became one of the 10 components that local areas were required to make available as part of youth programs. Administrators in 17 study sites reported that their local area continued to provide summer work experiences to youth using WIA formula funds after the transition from JTPA. These experiences were not generally offered as part of a separate program, but were opportunities extended to youth served through the regular WIA program. By and large, these programs were small. Although data were not available from all sites, 11 of the 17 sites with data reported an average of 184 youth served in summer work experiences through WIA-formula funds.

Summer work opportunities were also available to youth in the study areas from other sources. At least 9 communities had programs that placed more than 200 youth in summer jobs using funds from state or local government or private sources. In about half of these communities, the same agency that led implementation of the Recovery Act SYEI was involved in these programs. In the remaining communities, a different entity, such as a separate city agency, had responsibility for the summer initiative. For example, Los Angeles and Seattle both offered sizable programs to help youth find jobs (see Box III.1). Respondents in other communities mentioned other smaller programs, most often offered by local providers.

BOX III.1. SUMMER YOUTH PROGRAMS WITH NON-WIA FUNDING SOURCES

Los Angeles, CA. The Summer Youth Employment Program, which is one component of a city initiative called HIRE LA to help youth find jobs, had historically received city and county funding. The program was run by the city's WIA administrative agency and placed 10,000 youth in subsidized and unsubsidized employment in the summer of 2008. The mayor began the initiative in 2005 to combat high rates of youth unemployment in the city.

Seattle, WA. For at least 12 years prior to passage of the Recovery Act, the city of Seattle, a 2009 SYEI contractor, funded a summer youth program that provided approximately 300 jobs each year. The program was targeted to in-school youth, and focused more on academics than on employment, including dropout prevention and preparing youth for entering college to gain job-related skills.

Most sites with existing programs took the opportunity provided by the Recovery Act to expand those programs. For example, the 11 sites that reported serving an average of 184 WIA-funded youth in prior summers planned to provide summer work experiences to an average of 1,033 participants in the summer of 2009 with their Recovery Act youth allocations alone. About half of these 11 sites also continued to fund the summer work experiences for youth enrolled in the regular WIA program using WIA formula funds. This included one site that continued to provide jobs to about 250 youth enrolled in the regular WIA youth program services and planned to offer work experiences to 850 additional youth through the Recovery Act. In other sites, administrators reported that the Recovery Act paid for all summer work experiences, as WIA-formula funds were reserved for providing other services to youth enrolled in regular comprehensive services. For example, administrators in one site reported that they shifted the WIA-formula funds to hire staff to implement the SYEI.

In addition to increasing the number of youth served by existing summer youth programs, sites took the opportunity provided by Recovery Act funding to modify existing programs. For many sites, program changes were modest. For example, one site added a pre-apprenticeship program that it could not afford previously (discussed in more detail in Chapter VII), and another offered office-based experiences in addition to the conservation-related experiences that had been part of the program in previous summers. Another site reported offering the same basic opportunities as in previous summers but stated that Recovery Act funding allowed it to increase the number of weeks that youth could participate and to add academic courses to the curriculum. Four sites changed their employer focus: one site focused more on opportunities for youth in high-demand industries and three sites focused more on private, for-profit employers than they had before.

Two sites took unique approaches to developing their SYEIs in light of their own past experiences. One site used the Recovery Act funds to invigorate its summer program and encouraged providers responding to a request for proposals to be innovative. As a result, youth in this site had the opportunity to participate in diverse activities such as indoor and outdoor maintenance work, high-tech digital arts, and entrepreneurship. Administrators in the second site decided to leverage the existing city-funded summer program instead of scaling up the WIA- formula funded summer program (see Box III.2). As a result, the joint program funded through the city and the Recovery Act was able to fund approximately 3,300 youth, extend the weeks of a youth's experience from 6 to 10, and extend eligibility to counties beyond the city limit.

BOX III.2. THE MEMPHIS SUMMER YOUTH PROGRAM

Prior to the Recovery Act summer youth program, the LWIB fiscal agency and the city of Memphis had separate summer youth programs. The LWIB provided a four- to six-week summer work experience to about 250 regular WIA youth participants. The city summer youth program, begun in 1993, annually served 500 to 600 youth who were selected by lottery. In the city program, following an orientation, older youth received a work placement while younger youth were placed in a school-based program.

The LWIB and city joined together to administer the 2009 SYEI using a combination of city and Recovery Act funds. The city took responsibility for the younger youth in the school-based experiences and the LWIB for the older youth in work experiences. However, the LWIB funded both older and younger youth meeting the WIA eligibility requirements, while the city funded youth who were not eligible for WIA. As a result of this joint effort, about 2,700 youth were supported through Recovery Act funds and 600 through the city funds.

---

3. Planning for the SYEI

The SYEI planning process started for a majority of sites as they witnessed passage of the Recovery Act in February 2009. More than half the sites reported that they began planning in February or March, shortly after the bill was signed into law. Several other sites started planning even earlier, either in response to the expectation of a federally funded program or because they intended to revamp an existing program. One site reported starting planning as late as April.

Generally, the LWIB or its designated administrative agency (hereafter referred to as the "lead agency") led the planning process with help from other stakeholders.[9] Administrators in all sites but one said the Youth Council had some role in the Recovery Act–funded SYEI. In more than half these sites, the Youth Council's role was largely advisory. For example, administrators in one site described the role of the Youth Council as providing some feedback and advice as the WIA administrative agency moved forward with its plans. In other sites, the Youth Council had a larger role. Administrators in these sites reported that their Youth Council was involved in the process of procuring contractors for the SYEI by reviewing proposals and recommending which providers should be awarded contracts. For example, the lead agency in one site worked directly with the Youth Council to procure youth providers for the SYEI. A subcommittee of the council reviewed and commented on a request for proposals developed by the lead agency. The subcommittee also reviewed and ranked all proposals before presenting the top proposals to the full council for approval.

The SYEI timeline did not appear to provide much opportunity for states to provide additional guidance to local areas. Although sites mentioned taking part in conference calls and webinars with state officials, only five reported that their state required or strongly recommended any specific program components. One reason for the lack of state input, as mentioned by one administrator, was that the lead agency had to move quickly in order to implement the initiative and could not wait to receive formal guidance from the state.

Youth providers tended to have a minor role in planning the SYEI, if they played any role at all. Youth providers had an early role or say in the design of the SYEI in only five sites, according to administrators and provider staff. Three of these sites were those with one main provider, and the LWIB appeared to rely on that provider for its expertise. In the other two sites, the providers' role was smaller, giving the lead agency feedback on its plans through provider focus groups.

Employers were also not an integral part of the planning process. In eight sites, respondents mentioned that employers were involved only in their capacity as LWIB or Youth Council members. Administrators in two other sites reported that they did a quick survey of employers to learn about job availability before the summer began. Respondents in other sites did not report any employer involvement during the planning phase.

4. Planning Challenges

Administrators identified two key planning challenges. The first involved the pressures of planning a sizable initiative in only a few months. More than half the sites mentioned that the tight time line affected the initiative's design phase and its implementation. However, all sites did successfully implement the SYEI. Administrators in one site said that they were still able to implement the initiative because they enjoyed a positive relationship with the existing provider of youth programs. Respondents in another reported that the short time frame prevented them from developing as strong a classroom training component as they would have liked, and those in a third did not involve the Youth Council as fully as they would have done had more time been available.

A second challenge affecting initiative design was gaps in information. About one-third of sites reported that they lacked information needed to effectively design their initiatives. Of these sites, four mentioned that they did not know how much money they would receive until after planning had begun, with one receiving substantially less than expected and another receiving twice the expected amount. Another three sites reported being unclear during the planning phase about the requirements for identifying providers through a competitive procurement process and how the funds were to be used.

C. The Organization of the Recovery Act SYEI

Although most sites had some experience providing summer work experiences to youth, they still needed to determine how to organize the much larger summer 2009 initiative. Their decisions largely followed their existing structure for providing services to regular WIA youth. However, even though ETA's guidance permitted states and local areas to apply for waivers to dispense with normal competitive bidding processes, many local areas chose to hold open competitions, often engaging organizations that were new to the workforce investment system. All sites also hired new temporary staff to scale-up implementation of their initiative.

1. Organizational Models

Local sites had flexibility in organizing their SYEIs. Administrators of the lead agency could decide to directly provide all or most services to youth or to contract with one or more providers to deliver the services. Based on these decisions, the 20 study sites fell into one of four organizational models in which the lead agency: (1) provided direct services with no contractors, (2) provided some direct services and used contractors to deliver specific services, (3) contracted with a single provider to deliver services, and (4) contracted with multiple providers (see Figure III.1).

Each of the four models is described in the following list:

1. **No contractors.** The lead agency in three areas did not contract with providers, opting instead to deliver the services directly. For all three sites, this is the same model used for their regular WIA youth program.
2. **Specialized contractors.** The lead agency in two sites delivered most services directly but contracted with providers for specific functions. In one site, three providers ran two-week health and manufacturing academies to a subset of participants before those youth were placed at their worksites. The lead agency, however, was responsible for placing the participants at the worksites and monitoring their work there. In the second site, five outside providers offered a one week 15-hour work readiness training to participants while the lead agency directly provided all other services.
3. **One contractor.** Four areas elected to contract with one provider to administer the SYEI. In all of these sites, this contractor was also the main contractor for the provision of regular WIA youth services. One of these contractors used subcontractors to administer a subset of services.
4. **Multiple contractors.** More than half the sites (11 out of 20) contracted with multiple providers to deliver most SYEI-related services. The number of providers ranged from 2 to 23, with an average of 11. Box III.3 describes two sites with multiple contractors.

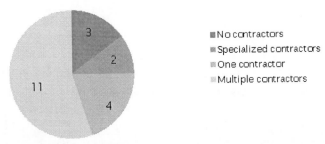

Source: Site visit interviews in 20 selected sites.
Note: N= 20 sites.

Figure III.1. Study Sites' Organizational Models

Table III.4. Number of Contractors

	Number of Sites
Number of Contractors	
0	3
1 - 5	8
6 - 10	3
11 - 23	6

Source: Site visit interviews in 20 selected sites.
Note: N= 20 sites.

The 17 sites that contracted out some services used an average of eight contractors. Nine sites had six or more contractors (Table III.4). There did not appear to be a direct relationship between the planned number of SYEI participants and the number of contractors. Of the three largest sites, one had 15 contractors, another had 9 contractors, and the third provided services directly.

BOX III.3. SITES WITH MULTIPLE PROVIDERS

Minneapolis, MN. Minneapolis Employment and Training Program (METP) is the fiscal and administrative entity for the Minneapolis LWIB, known as the Minneapolis Workforce Council. Through an open procurement process, METP contracted with 11 nonprofit organizations to provide SYEI services. All providers were on METP's preexisting master contract list and had executed METP contracts in the past. Some had served as regular WIA youth providers; others had contracted with METP to provide other youth or adult services. All providers had implemented similar programs in the past and knew what to expect during the summer. In addition, they all had existing networks of youth and employers. The providers had sole responsibility for recruiting youth and worksites. Each of these 11 providers focused on recruiting youth and employers from a certain neighborhood or section of the city in order to maintain METP's commitment to community-based service delivery. Two of the providers were contracted to provide services to Somali and Hmong youth.

> *Portland, OR.* Worksystems, Inc. (WSI), is the operating agency for the Portland LWIB. Under an ETA procurement waiver for the Recovery Act SYEI, WSI contracted with the 12 providers that had been operating their regular WIA youth program. Many of these local providers were alternative high schools or organizations with GED programs, and all but one offered comprehensive education components as part of their SYEI. Though WSI gave overall guidance about the program, local providers had relative autonomy in terms of program design. Providers were largely responsible for youth and worksite recruitment, although WSI did conduct some site-wide recruitment activities.

2. Identification of Summer Providers

Acknowledging the pressures on local areas to implement a summer initiative in a few short months, ETA encouraged states and local areas to explore emergency procurement processes or to apply for a waiver allowing local areas to extend existing contracts or to hold a competition with a limited number of providers (U.S. Department of Labor 2009d). Alternatively, local areas could move ahead with a competitive selection process or directly provide services, as did the three sites that followed the first model described previously.

Almost half of the study sites completed a competitive request for proposal (RFP) process to identify providers for the SYEI (see Table III.5). Of these nine sites, three held a competition for SYEI providers even though their states applied for a procurement waiver. An administrator in one of these sites explained that they moved forward with the RFP out of concern that they would not hear in time to conduct the process if the waiver was denied. In the end, this site awarded the contract to its regular WIA youth contractor, which was the only provider that submitted an application. From discussions during site visits, it appears that the other two sites went ahead with a procurement process because they were not certain of the federal requirements for procuring providers for the SYEI.

Sites that conducted a procurement competition often completed the process shortly before the summer months, leaving little time for selected providers to start their initiatives. Seven of the nine released their RFPs between March 13 and April 15, and one released its RFP in May. Most awards were made in May. However, in at least one site, a contractor reported not receiving the signed contract until July 14. The ninth site released its RFP in October 2008 in anticipation of its regular summer youth program. Because of delays in approval of its annual WIA plan, however, contracts at this site were not awarded until the beginning of July 2009.

Table III.5. Sites' Processes for Identifying Summer Providers

Process	Number of Sites
Competitive procurement process	9
Waiver	5
Extended contracts with existing provider(s)	3
None (provides services directly)	3

Source: Site visit interviews in 20 selected sites.
Note: N= 20 sites.

About half the sites that used a competitive procurement effort reported that the RFPs generated a lot of interest among local organizations. For example, in Rhode Island, 200 organizations attended a bidders' conference jointly run by the state's two LWIBs. According to administrators, the Greater Rhode Island LWIB received 18 high-quality RFPs and funded them all. Two sites were able to fund less than half of the submitted proposals. In Lehigh Valley, 130 organizations attended the bidders' conference, and 15 of 70 applications were funded. Administrators reported that the response was "unprecedented." Minneapolis funded 11 of 36 applications. The other half of sites with procurement processes had fewer than 10 applicants and funded all or most of them.

Sites that exercised a waiver in place of issuing RFPs stated that they had recently held a competition or knew that there were no providers other than those with which they had active contracts. For example, one site had just completed the competition for its five-year procurement cycle in 2008. An administrator of the LWIB administrative agency in another site reported that, through the two-year procurement cycle, the agency had developed a strong set of youth providers that were knowledgeable about the WIA program. To allow other organizations the opportunity to compete for an SYEI contract, the administration said the RFP process would have had to begin in January to allow sufficient time for new providers to prepare a credible bid.

Administrators in three remaining sites neither exercised a waiver nor used a competitive procurement process. Administrators in these sites reported that they had recently held a competitive procurement process or that their service areas did not have viable providers other than those with which they already contracted.[10] All three of these sites were in largely rural areas.

3. Characteristics of Summer Providers

The 17 study sites with at least one contractor engaged a total of 130 providers. Eight of these sites continued to contract exclusively with their regular providers of WIA youth programs. Not surprisingly, these sites included seven that exercised a waiver or claimed they did not need one. Also among these eight sites was the site described above that conducted an RFP process for a subset of services but contracted with its main WIA youth provider for the bulk of SYEI services. Contracted providers in these eight sites accounted for 31 percent of the total of 130 providers.

The remaining nine sites contracted with a combination of existing WIA providers and some new to the WIA system.[11] For example, the Pittsburgh site funded 12 organizations that had provided WIA services before and 5 that were new to WIA. In Denver, two of the three providers had previous contracts for regular WIA youth programming; the third was a new contractor. Eight of the 15 providers in Los Angeles were also regular WIA youth providers, but all 15 had experience contracting with the city.

Providers across the sites included nonprofit organizations, schools and school districts, and government agencies. Five sites had contracts only with nonprofit organizations, such as community action agencies, and one only contracted with government agencies. The other 11 sites contracted with a combination of providers. For example, the 14 providers used by one site included a government agency, a hospital, a community college, three technical schools, five community-based organizations, a union, and two public school systems.

4. Relationships between Lead Agencies and Providers

Regardless of the site's organization model, the LWIB or its administrative agency supervised the SYEI. From discussions with site administrators, it appeared that the LWIB in seven sites was active in the ongoing administration of the SYEIs. In five of these sites, the LWIB was the administrative agency for the WIA program and directly provided services or supervised the SYEI providers; in the other two, the LWIB set policies for the administrative agency to carry out. In the remaining 13 sites, the administrative agency appeared to be the driving force of the SYEI, although recommendations and advice were provided by the LWIB and Youth Council.

Typically, the relationship between the lead agency and the providers was smooth. As described above, many of the sites had existing relationships with all or some of their contractors prior to creation of the SYEI. In addition, most areas employed a youth services coordinator (or a staff member in an equivalent position) who was in regular contact with providers to discuss the ongoing operations of the SYEI and address any issues that arose. Respondents in four sites reported that a key to their success was strong collaboration between the lead agency and providers and between the providers themselves. In one of these areas, the youth services coordinator called each provider weekly for updates and met monthly with providers to discuss their progress. The coordinator reported that these regular interactions were invaluable.

In three sites, however, at least one provider felt that more collaboration would have improved the initiative. Providers in two of these sites reported that they had never met before the site visit's provider focus group and had missed opportunities to benefit from each other's experiences. As a result, problems were not uncovered and handled promptly or consistently for all providers. In the third site, one provider felt that better communications would improve the quality and consistency of service provision in the future.

5. Summer Staffing Arrangements

The increased scope of the 2009 SYEI, compared with past summer programs, required organizations in every study site to hire temporary staff. This included as few as a single hire in one area to as many as 63 in another. In the former site, the administrative agency hired the summer youth program coordinator to oversee day-to-day operations and manage the lead agency's relationship with the providers. The site's local providers did not hire temporary staff but borrowed staff members from other programs. In the latter site, the administrative agency hired one temporary staff person to oversee the SYEI and the local providers hired 62 temporary staff, including clerical staff and worksite supervisors and monitors.

Two types of individuals were commonly hired as temporary SYEI staff. At least four sites hired teachers or school district staff to work during their summer recess. One of these sites hired staff that were laid off from the Head Start program for the summer. Another common source of temporary staff was college students or recent graduates. Seven sites mentioned recruiting these individuals, in part as an extension of their mission to provide work experiences to young entrants into the workforce. Only one site reported targeting dislocated workers for the temporary SYEI positions.

Sites hired temporary staff to fill a variety of roles, including oversight and clerical positions. Nine sites hired temporary staff to be involved in the worksite experiences by working as monitors, job coaches, or crew leaders. A different set of nine sites also recruited temporary staff to assist in the upfront tasks of the SYEI, including assisting with youth recruitment, intake, assessment, and orientation. Additional information about staff roles in upfront and work experience tasks can be found in Chapters IV and VII, respectively.

IV. YOUTH RECRUITMENT AND INTAKE ACTIVITIES

An expanded SYEI required sites to quickly scale up their youth recruitment and intake activities. With only a few months of preparation, sites had to recruit the youth and determine the eligibility of each youth under WIA rules and regulations. They also had to reach out to key populations they had targeted for services as well as those identified in the ETA guidance. To ensure that these populations were served, they had to establish procedures for providing priority to members of these groups.

This chapter discusses how the study sites approached these tasks, the challenges they faced, and the characteristics of participants they recruited. Section A describes the flow of youth into the SYEI, from first finding out about the initiative to the point of being enrolled. Section B describes how sites recruited youth for the SYEI, and Section C describes how they determined youth's eligibility. Section D discusses some of the barriers youth in the study sites faced and their reasons for participating in the SYEI. Post-enrollment activities are discussed in Chapters V and VII.

KEY FINDINGS: YOUTH RECRUITMENT AND INTAKE ACTIVITIES

- **Except for some targeted populations, sites successfully recruited youth.** Staff used media campaigns and targeted recruitment with help from local organizations to successfully reach large numbers of eligible youth. However, some target populations, such as veterans and older youth, were difficult to recruit.
- **Nearly all sites found it difficult to process large volumes of applicants.** Strategies to deal with the number of applicants and the paperwork included hiring temporary staff, prescreening youth, and linking with partners to streamline eligibility determination.
- **SYEI participants expressed a need for financial support and work experiences.** Youth expressed appreciation for the SYEI, given their employment barriers and the tight labor market.

A. The Flow of Youth into the SYEI

The entry of youth into the SYEI followed a similar pattern across the sites. Although no two sites implemented the exact same intake process, the processes shared many common elements. The types and number of local staff members that the prospective participant could meet along the way, however, varied with the site's organizational structure. For example, a prospective participant for a SYEI run by the LWIB or its administrative agency might only be able to apply for the initiative through one central access point. By contrast, an applicant for a SYEI contracted out to many local providers might apply through the lead agency or directly through a local provider.

Figure IV.1 depicts the flow of youth into the SYEI. The process began when a youth became aware of the SYEI and expressed interest in participating. In many cases, the youth's name and contact information were shared with a participating agency by a referring party such as a school counselor or case worker. At this point, an intake staff member at the lead agency or a local provider might prescreen the youth to determine his or her eligibility for the initiative based on initial information, such as income and barriers to employment. If the youth passed this prescreening, then his or her application and required documents were reviewed more closely as a formal application.

Formal applications were processed either by a provider or non-provider agency. As discussed in Chapter III, the LWIB or its administrative agency served as the main provider in 5 of the 20 sites. The remaining 15 sites contracted with local organizations to serve as providers. These provider agencies often conducted intake directly. Those youth determined eligible were either enrolled or placed on a waiting list.

In cases in which the lead agency contracted out administration of the initiative to local providers, the lead agency (a non-provider) might also receive and process applications. These agencies would either refer eligible youth to a provider for enrollment or place that youth on a waiting list.

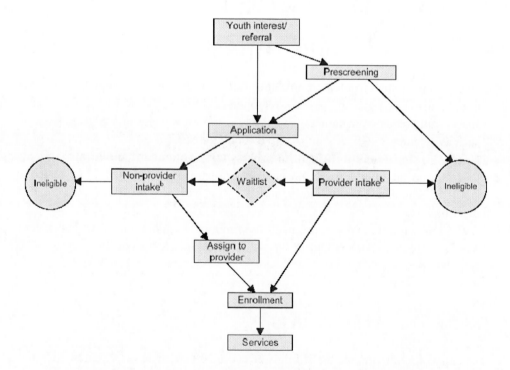

[a] This figure reflects the majority of scenarios in our 20 sites but does not capture all variations.

[b] A non-provider can be the WIB, WIB agent, or any entity not providing post-intake services to youth. A provider can be the WIB, WIB agent, or contracted provider that will be providing services to the youth after intake into the SYEP.

Figure IV.1. Possible Routes of Entry into the SYEI[a]

B. Recruitment of Eligible Youth

All study sites focused largely on youth recruitment during the early months of the initiative. Indeed, almost three-quarters of sites began recruitment by April. As discussed in Chapter III, regardless of whether sites already had administered a summer program, they had to recruit many more youth to fill the increased number of slots made available by the funding through the Recovery Act. Hence, they needed to start early. Local staff used multiple strategies to reach out to eligible youth, including particular target groups. Although these efforts were largely successful, sites found the time line and recruitment of particular populations to be challenging.

1. Targeted Youth Populations

Youth eligibility for SYEI generally followed the eligibility requirements for regular WIA youth programs. Eligible youth had to have low household incomes and demonstrate at least one of six barriers to employment. The six barriers included being (1) a school dropout, (2) deficient in basic literacy, (3) a homeless, runaway, or foster child; (4) a parenting or pregnant teen; (5) an offender; and (6) one who needs help completing an education program or securing and maintain employment. Sites had flexibility to define the sixth barrier to meet the needs of youth in their communities. In addition, 30 percent of regular WIA and Recovery Act youth funds was to be spent on out-of-school youth and both gave priority to eligible veterans and their spouses. However, the Recovery Act expanded eligibility from past WIA definitions of youth (ages 14-21) to allow the SYEI to serve young adults ages 22 to 24.

Within these eligibility parameters, local areas had flexibility to identify priority youth populations. In over half the sites, LWIBs, Youth Councils, or fiscal agents were involved in selecting key target populations. States were only cited as providing guidance by a quarter of sites. In addition, local providers often had some flexibility in determining which youth to target. In a few cases, the selection of specific providers helped the site target key populations. For example, providers in at least two sites were selected because of their history serving particular high-need populations, such as foster children or out-of-school youth.

Specific target populations were defined by youth's demographics, age, and socioeconomic characteristics. Sites did not limit their enrollment to the populations they targeted, but they did make special efforts to increase the participation of those populations. Table IV.1 lists populations that sites or providers mentioned as targeted groups.

About a quarter of sites also limited their recruitment and enrollment to certain age groups. Three sites excluded the youngest youth—those between 14 and 15 years old. Two of these sites had already moved away from serving the youngest youth in their regular WIA program. Another site chose not to serve youth older than 21 years of age. A fourth site excluded both 14–15 year olds and those older than 21 years of age. One administrator at this site reported that the site did not want to serve older youth who would normally receive services through the WIA adult program.

Defining the sixth eligibility barrier was another strategy for identifying the types of youth that would be targeted for the SYEI. A majority of sites defined this barrier to include more than one category of youth, ranging from very specific descriptions to more broad categories. Common interpretations of the sixth barrier included youth with a disability, those behind grade level in school, or those with a lack of work history or skills (see Table IV.2).

Table IV.1. Target Populations Identified by Sites

Abused children
Children of incarcerated parents
Children of veterans
Gang-affiliated youth
Indians/Native Americans
Latinos
Migrant and refugee
Persons with an individualized education program (IEP) or a disability
Sex workers
Specific age groups (e.g., 14-18 years, 16-21 years)
Substance abusers
Temporary Assistance for Needy Families (TANF) recipients
Veterans and their spouses
Youth running out of unemployment insurance (UI)
Youth with limited English proficiency (LEP)

Source: Site visit interviews in 20 selected sites.

Note: Populations are listed alphabetically and not in order of prevalence.

Table IV.2. Sites' Interpretations of the Sixth Barrier to Employment or Education

Barrier	Number of Sites
Youth with a disability or IEP through the public school system	11
Behind one or more grade levels	7
Lack of work history/work maturity	7
Limited English proficiency	6
Failed high school graduation exam	4
Receiving public assistance	3
History of substance abuse	3

Source: Site visit interviews in 20 selected sites.

Note: N = 20 sites.

2. Youth Recruitment Efforts

Outreach methods were diverse and relied on multiple organizations to reach targeted youth. Provider and agency staff recruited youth through formal advertising as well as by partnering with organizations such as the workforce investment system, other governmental agencies, and community-based organizations. Initial outreach activities were apparently successful in generating a critical volume of interest given that 15 of the 20 sites reported that word-of-mouth became a significant source of referrals over time. Box IV.1 provides examples of specific recruitment strategies.

Responsibility for youth outreach depended on whether the initiative was contracted out to providers or administered through the lead agency. Of the 15 sites in our sample that contracted out operation of the program to providers, 6 sites mentioned that both the providers and the lead agency shared responsibility for reaching out to youth. In another seven of these sites, providers were solely responsible for recruiting youth, sometimes with help from city officials in developing media campaigns. The remaining two sites contracted with local organizations that had a sufficient volume of existing youth clients to fill Recovery Act slots. The lead agency was solely responsible for recruiting youth only in the five sites that had no major providers directly serving youth.

Three distinct approaches to outreach emerged across the sites. First, a total of 14 sites mounted publicity campaigns. These sites used the media to reach out to the public. Specific strategies included placing advertisements on local television and radio stations and in local newspapers; using social networking sites; staffing booths at music events or local malls; and distributing fliers or conducting mailings. Six of these sites also mentioned news coverage or press conferences that were designed to generate general community awareness.

Box IV.1. Innovative Strategies to Recruit Youth

Use of mass media
Hazard, KY. The site designed a media blitz to cover the large geographic area they served. They produced six television commercials using youth volunteers and aired them during primetime programs, *The Tonight Show*, and televised coverage of the NCAA basketball tournament. The site also ran 60-second spots on local radio stations, and posted information on the internet sites MySpace and YouTube.

Lehigh Valley, PA. The LWIB designed a marketing strategy that would appeal to youth and create a fresh image for the program. They placed advertisements at bus stops and on buses and sponsored booths at local malls and popular music events. An electronic application was placed on the agency's website for the first time, making it easier for net-savvy youth to apply.

Partnerships with community organizations
Pittsburgh, PA. Administrative staff worked with local city officials to arrange for the city's welfare office to send letters to their clients notifying them about the SYEI. Letters were sent to all households on the welfare rosters that included youth of the eligible ages.

Second, many sites leveraged the workforce investment system to recruit youth. As described in Chapter III, the lead agency for the WIA youth program was the main provider of SYEI services in five sites and the main contractors were also regular WIA youth providers in another eight sites. In other sites, a mix of new and experienced youth providers was involved. These organizational structures clearly gave many local SYEI recruitment staff access to youth already participating in the regular WIA program and to the families of potentially eligible youth. Adults who used a One-Stop Career Center were encouraged to tell their family and friends about the SYEI.

Finally, partners and organizations in the surrounding community were a significant source of potential participants in all sites. Local staff reported that promoting the initiative in schools was often the most effective method. Some public school districts, alternative schools, and colleges served directly as SYEI providers and were able to recruit from their own in-house programs. In areas where schools did not act as providers, lead agencies and WIA youth providers typically had strong relationships with K-12 and postsecondary schools.

Local staff used their contacts with teachers, guidance and career counselors, principals, and other school officials to advertise the initiative. Staff also attended job fairs, set up information tables, or made presentations at schools and colleges to recruit youth to the initiative. For example, outreach staff at one provider set up information stations in schools before the second semester ended and handed out intake paperwork for students to complete while SYEI staff members were present.

Sites also sought partnerships with a wide range of social service organizations that served at-risk youth. Sites that targeted juvenile offenders worked to establish partnerships and referrals through the juvenile justice system. For example, they contacted truant and probation officers and sought out judges and case workers in juvenile and family courts. Sites that targeted homeless, runaway, and foster care youth contacted case workers at foster care agencies and local shelters. Sites also contacted local government agencies such as those providing rehabilitative services and benefits under Temporary Assistance for Needy Families (TANF), Supplemental Nutrition Assistance Program (SNAP), and Supplemental Security Income (SSI). Local staff from various sites reported distributing fliers to these agencies and requesting referrals from staff and counselors. Staff also contacted nongovernmental organizations that provide social services to youth to obtain referrals and to spread the word about the initiative to eligible youth.

3. Hard to Reach Populations

Sites found certain key target populations—including veterans; older youth; homeless, runaway, and foster youth; and youth offenders—to be the most difficult to identify and recruit. Given the high unemployment rate among veterans returning to the civilian workforce, ETA designated veterans and their eligible spouses as a priority group for the SYEI (U.S. Department of Labor 2009c). The expansion in the maximum participant age to 24 years also increased the proportion of veterans who could be potentially eligible. Only one site, however, reported success enrolling a few veterans through its connection with the local office of the Department of Veterans Affairs (VA). Another nine sites reported a lack of success despite targeted recruitment. Staff in one of these sites reported reaching out to the local VA office but found that most veterans were not ready for or interested in employment services soon after discharge from the military.

Older youth were also challenging to reach. Six sites reported that older youth were often no longer in school and, thus, difficult to locate. Another reason may be that staff administering the initiative did not typically serve youth aged 22 to 24 years and therefore had fewer local recruitment contacts for this group. One site reported that, although older youth expressed interest in the initiative, many did not follow through with the application process. Several sites that reported some success with older youth found that it was important to avoid characterizing the SYEI as a "youth" initiative. Many older participants had children, household responsibilities, and significant work experience. The message that was given to these groups was critical in affecting their perception of the initiative and their willingness to participate. To specifically target this population, one site developed a special poster and displayed copies in tattoo parlors, bars, grocery stores, laundry mats, temporary housing, clothing stores, garages, pool halls, and anywhere they thought older youth would congregate.

Another reported that "walking the neighborhoods" and marketing through television and radio spots were more likely to attract older youth.

Smaller numbers of sites also mentioned difficulties recruiting homeless, runaway, and foster youth; and youth offenders. Three sites said that homeless and runaway youth were difficult to enroll due to lack of proper documentation to verify eligibility for services and keep engaged due to their mobility. Two sites mentioned difficulty recruiting youth offenders and foster youth.

C. Youth Intake and Enrollment Process

The early part of the summer was an active time for all sites as they rushed to implement new or modified eligibility determination systems, establish eligibility of recruited youth, and reach their target enrollment numbers. These activities often occurred at the same time that sites were training new employees. Sites needed to find ways to efficiently handle the intense demand for services and the complex eligibility process. Key strategies that emerged from site visits included prioritizing certain youth, maximizing staff resources, and streamlining determination of applicants' eligibility.

1. Enrollment Numbers and Priorities

All but one site in our sample reported receiving applications from more eligible youth than they could accommodate. Sites reported that between 40 and 80 percent of applicants ultimately enrolled in the initiative. Among those who did not enroll, 10 to 30 percent were clearly ineligible because their incomes exceeded the eligibility cutoff. Another 10 to 30 percent were potentially eligible but did not complete all paperwork. At the time of the site visits, 10 sites stated that they had enrolled more youth than originally planned, and 4 additional sites were still enrolling youth.[12] The total number of enrolled youth varied tremendously across the 20 selected sites, from a low of 80 to a high of more than 5,500.

A majority of sites also had waiting lists of eligible youth. Sites generally enrolled a youth from the waiting list only when an existing participant dropped out or was removed from the initiative. Two sites with excess demand did not maintain waiting lists. Instead, these sites referred youth they could not enroll to other agencies or service providers in the area.

In choosing youth for enrollment, almost half the sites gave priority to certain populations during the intake process. Nine sites prioritized populations such as homeless and foster youth, youth offenders, youth with disabilities, or out-of-school youth. These groups generally reflected the sites' recruitment priorities. Nine other sites reported that they did not give priority to any groups and described their intake process as first-come, first-served. One additional site with multiple providers allowed those providers to set their own policies regarding priorities. The last site had a unique process. Eligible youth who applied before a certain date were sorted by zip code. Within each zip code, youth were assigned by lottery to the provider in that zip code or to a waitlist. After the initial lottery, youth were enrolled from the waiting list if a slot became available.

Even though most sites reached their target enrollment numbers, providers in four sites reported that the income eligibility guidelines prevented them from meeting their enrollment targets. One site was able to fill only 75 percent of its available slots by July due to the high number of applicants ineligible on the basis of income. Another three sites met overall enrollment targets but individual providers reported having difficulty enrolling enough youth because of the income eligibility guidelines. In one of these sites, the slots that could not be filled by one provider were reallocated to providers that had youth waiting to be served.

2. Staffing Strategies for Youth Intake

In anticipation of much larger caseloads than they had experienced in prior summers, site administrators adopted one of three staffing approaches to handle intake and eligibility determination. First, nine sites hired temporary staff members to help existing staff conduct upfront activities such as meeting with youth and parents, documenting eligibility, and completing paperwork and data entry. At one site, two existing staff members worked part-time on SYEI, while four temporary hires conducted intake activities full-time. At a second site, most eligibility staff members were temporary hires.

Second, five sites hired temporary staff to conduct nonintake activities, freeing up existing experienced staff to focus on determining eligibility. For example, at one site, existing WIA specialists determined eligibility while the temporary hires handled logistics and dealt more directly with youth and employers during the summer. In explaining this staffing decision, administrators often cited the resources that would have been required to train new hires on WIA's complex eligibility rules.

Finally, six sites relied on existing WIA or other experienced staff to conduct SYEI intake. One site contracted with neighborhood centers that already served eligible SYEI youth to process paperwork and determine eligibility. Once determined eligible, the youth were assigned to a provider. Initiatives in the other sites relied exclusively on staff at existing WIA youth programs or One-Stop Career Centers to conduct intake and eligibility, calling on these workers either part- or full-time during the summer.

In addition to these three basic models, three sites added a second level of eligibility determination for quality-control purposes. In these sites, frontline staff processed paperwork and conducted initial eligibility determinations. However, the final determination of a youth's eligibility was done by a specialist at the lead agency who was experienced in WIA eligibility decisions. This approach served as a safety precaution given the high volume of applications being processed quickly and sometimes by inexperienced workers.

3. The Eligibility Determination Process

The eligibility determination process involved considerable paperwork and many types of documentation from youth participants and their families. As a result, sites and providers developed ways to facilitate the intake process. Most importantly, the initiatives sought to limit the amount of resources that had to be spent tracking down youth's paperwork. They often did so by relying on other government agencies and school staff instead of youth and their parents. Sites also used prescreening to winnow the number of applicants scheduled for intake appointments. Finally, sites offered evening and weekend hours to accommodate the school and work schedules of youth and their parents.

Seven sites reported using partnerships with other social service agencies to help streamline eligibility determination for youth (see Box IV.2 for discussion of two examples). At least one provider or the lead agency in six of these sites mentioned that SYEI staff sent lists of applicants to state and local agencies or schools to solicit help verifying eligibility. For example, one provider sent a list of SYEI applicants to the local Supplemental Nutrition Assistance Program office to determine that the families were receiving assistance, automatically verifying the youth's income eligibility. Three of the six sites also mentioned working with schools to gather documentation, such as an IEP, which provided evidence of a disability. In the seventh site, the state welfare office provided SYEI staff with a list of individuals aged 14 to 24 whose families were receiving public assistance and might be eligible for the initiative. Staff could check an applicant against this list to verify that they were receiving assistance.

Box IV.2. Streamlining Eligibility

Bridgeport, CT. The LWIB worked with the local Department of Children and Families (DCF) to verify eligibility for SYEI applicants. LWIB staff provided DCF with a list of applicants who had indicated they were receiving services from DCF, and DCF provided a verification letter for each youth that indicated if he or she was receiving cash payments. DCF case managers regularly accompanied youth to their first SYEI intake appointments.

Cranston, RI. Youth center staff reached out to local schools to recruit youth and assist with documenting eligibility for applicants. Schools regularly had parents sign releases allowing the school to share information from a student's file, and the school could copy these documents for the youth center to prove a student's eligibility.

Prescreening also helped streamline the process of determining eligibility. At least 11 sites mentioned prescreening youth by making phone calls, using a preapplication, or reviewing an application before scheduling the youth for an intake appointment. The pre-application gathered basic information without documentation, such as the youth's date of birth, household income, educational background, work history, and job interests. Screening out youth likely to be ineligible reduced the number of youth that frontline staff would have to meet with and assess for eligibility. It also prevented the possibility of some youth and their families taking the time to assemble the necessary paperwork only to be found ineligible.

Beyond partnerships with other public agencies, six study sites added evenings or weekend hours to manage the increased workload and to provide more convenient times for youth or their parents to meet with staff. Extended hours allowed parents of minors to complete paperwork during non-work hours and youth to complete paperwork after school.

4. Intake and Enrollment Challenges

Administrators and frontline staff reported that it was often challenging to process paperwork for large numbers of youth given the short period and amount of paperwork required. Local staff described difficulties establishing eligibility for applicants and accessing key documentation from parents. Thirteen sites mentioned having at least one challenge related to income determination.

In seven sites, staff reported that the time frame was too short for the eligibility process, which was time-consuming and often plagued by many delays. Even if local staff were familiar with the WIA eligibility process, staff members were often using new forms created especially for SYEI and dealing with a slightly different set of requirements than those for the regular WIA program. Staff in these sites felt the eligibility and enrollment process involved too much documentation for an initiative that provided participants with only a few weeks or months of services. In at least four sites, youth under the age of 18 also had to obtain a work permit before being assigned to a worksite.

Staff in 11 sites reported difficulty collecting documentation from youth and parents. Five of these 11 sites reported problems gathering financial information from parents or involving parents in the eligibility determination process at all. Income eligibility determination required public assistance documents, Social Security numbers, pay stubs, or other forms of documentation. These documents sometimes had to be produced for every adult member of the youth's household. This requirement often made the process time consuming for both staff and the families of applicants. Similarly, five sites reported challenges getting youth or parents to produce documents to show evidence of one of the qualifying barriers. This was particularly difficult when the documentation had to come from a local government agency, such as a welfare or foster care agency, as those agencies needed time to supply the needed documents. Sites in our sample estimated that between 10 and 30 percent of potentially eligible applicants dropped off without completing their paperwork.

5. Youth with No Documented Barriers

If a youth met the income requirements for the initiative, local staff members in some sites were likely to try to identify a qualifying barrier. Frontline staff in one site shared that youth were often unwilling to talk about their background or history, especially about situations that would normally be considered a disadvantage for a job, such as being homeless or a youth offender, but are eligibility criteria for the SYEI. As a result, staff would have to find other ways to identify barriers for those youth.

At least six sites had some applicants take academic aptitude tests in math or English or both that could document a basic literacy deficiency. These tests were often the only assessment done for youth. In most cases, this testing was reserved for income-eligible youth with no documented barriers. However, one site tested all youth prior to eligibility determination in case the scores could be used for eligibility. The tests commonly used were the CASAS, TABE, and WRAT tests (Comprehensive Adult Student Assessment Systems 2010; CTB McGraw-Hill 2010; Psychological Assessment Resources, Inc. 2010). More information on assessments can be found in Chapter V.

D. Youth Characteristics

Based on discussions with staff in 20 sites and participating youth in 19 sites, many of the youth served by the study sites were disadvantaged and faced multiple obstacles to employment. On top of their personal challenges, these youth faced a market in which jobs were scarce and youth were competing for jobs against older, more experienced workers.

Youth appeared to greatly appreciate the opportunities offered by the SYEI and welcomed the help finding summer employment or other opportunities.

1. Employment Barriers

The most common barriers for youth cited by site administrators and frontline staff included lack of education and basic literacy skills, criminal involvement, teen pregnancy, and lack of transportation. These barriers were cited by staff in at least half the sites studied. Other barriers mentioned often but by less than half the sites included gang involvement, substance abuse, lack of work skills or work maturity, lack of work experience, being in foster care, and homelessness. Smaller numbers of sites also mentioned that youth with disabilities, youth in single parent homes, youth with limited English proficiency, and refugees and immigrants faced unique challenges. Most sites mentioned 5 or 6 different barriers, but two sites cited up to 10.

Information gathered from focus groups with youth reinforced several of these barriers.[13] Thirty-eight percent of youth in these groups reported never holding a job for pay before participating in SYEI. This was the case for 15 percent of the out-of-school youth and 45 percent of the in-school youth. Nine percent of the youth reported experiencing mental, physical, or emotional health problems that limited the kind or amount of work or training they could perform. Youth also said that their personal histories, such as a juvenile record, elicited negative responses from employers, creating a major challenge to being offered a job.

2. Youth's Reasons for Participating

Although focus group participants reported many reasons for enrolling in the SYEI, two primary reasons emerged. First, the wages earned from a summer job meant immediate cash in their pockets, often for the first time. The majority of youth in one-third of sites and at least several youth in all but one of the remaining sites mentioned that earning money was a primary motivation for participating. Second, many youth felt that exposure to a professional environment and mentoring adults could help them develop a résumé and lead them to a career.

Wages were especially important given the toll that the bad economy was taking on their households. Many youth reported having parents out of work or in risk of losing work and that summer employment was difficult to find. Youth in five sites specifically mentioned needing to earn money to help support family. In-school youth also reported needing to help their families pay for books, school supplies, and transportation when they returned to school in the fall.

YOUTH PERSPECTIVES: REASONS FOR PARTICIPATING IN THE SYEI

"I am in it for money, and also I heard they help you, they support you in all your dreams and goals, to reach your goals."

"Just having a job, trying to be responsible, to have my own money."

"It was a good way to make money over the summer, and it was just for the summer, so if we're still going to school, it kind of ends and gives a little break to get ready for school."

> *"Mainly the experience. . . . Because, I mean, the money is all right, but it's not gonna last that long . . . but if we get the experience and we can put that on a résumé and get a better job for more money, then that's fine, too."*
>
> *"I joined the program to see what's out there, like different jobs, and seeing what I was capable of doing, and like my best ability."*
>
> *"[To] find yourself. Like say if you didn't know what you wanted to do and you come to the program and you're like wow, I really like culinary arts or something, it gives you kind of a heads up of what you're good at and what maybe you should do in the future."*

YOUTH PERSPECTIVES: PAST EXPERIENCES LOOKING FOR WORK

> *"I'd still be looking for a job, trying to figure out a way how to get a job and get around the felonies that I've got, and trying to go crazy to find a job and not knowing what to do to get one. . . ."*
>
> *"There are older people, too, that lost their jobs and are now working at a lot of places where we used to work at. So, that's a big problem too."*
>
> *"There's very little jobs for people who don't have high school diplomas. . . . I'm 17 and I've got to graduate still. So there's no jobs for me. And places I've applied, they want experience, but I can't have experience until they hire me, and they won't hire me because I don't. It's a vicious cycle."*
>
> *"A lot of the reason why I couldn't get a job was I had a good job working with mentally disabled, taking care of them, but made a mistake, got a DUI, lost my job. Then because of that, it was hard for me to find jobs within my career path I wanted. . . ."*

Focus group participants also indicated that they applied for the initiative to build their résumés, explore careers, obtain references, network, and help them get a better job later in life. At least one youth in most sites reported that they were interested in gaining experience. As mentioned above, the SYEI work experience was a first job for many participants and, as a result, the start of their résumés. Youth in at least three sites reported their interest in obtaining permanent placement.

Beyond money and work experience, the youth mentioned other reasons for participating. One common reason was that it was a way to keep busy and stay out of trouble. Youth also mentioned the desire to develop soft skills, such as having a sense of responsibility, developing a strong work ethic, and learning to manage their time and money. In addition, youth mentioned that the initiative would help support their life goals and their desire to grow mentally and professionally.

3. Summer Alternatives to the SYEI

Although the study cannot know for sure what SYEI participants would have been doing without the initiative, it was able to collect focus group participants' impressions about their alternatives. Many youth did not think they would have been working had they not participated in the initiative. They mentioned looking for work prior to enrolling in the SYEI but were largely unsuccessful. Without SYEI, those same youth may have given up looking or continued to look for a job throughout the summer months without ever finding one. At least one youth from most of the sites reported that they would not be doing anything productive during the summer in the absence of SYEI. Youth commonly said they would be sleeping, watching TV, or hanging out. In more than half the sites, youth commented that they would still be looking for work but were not optimistic that they would have found a job. This latter appears to be a widespread sentiment. As one youth commented, "That's all everybody talks about: looking for a job." Youth in six sites indicated that they would probably have been taking classes if they were not participating in the initiative.

Focus group participants who thought they might have found work on their own believed these work experiences would have been less rewarding than the SYEI experience. Youth in eight sites speculated that they would have found jobs as retail cashiers, fast-food cashiers or food handlers, landscapers, lifeguards, babysitters, or manual laborers. Three youth reported that they would be working at previously held jobs, although their hours in these jobs would have been reduced and the work would not have been related to their career interests.

V. Youth Preparation and Support

Given the diverse array of youth enrolled in the SYEI, sites had to determine how to best prepare participants for successful participation in summer work experiences. Many participants had never held a job for pay and therefore did not fully understand the attitudes and skills necessary to succeed in the workplace. Even among those who had worked before, many had never explored potential career paths. As a result of these gaps of experience, sites found it important to prepare youth before sending them to worksites and then support them while they were on the job.

This chapter describes the sites' activities aimed at preparing and supporting youth in summer activities. Section A begins with the first activities that youth completed after they were recruited, as staff provided information and assessed their skills, interests, and needs. Section B turns to the training given to the youth to prepare them for work. Section C discusses the support services that initiatives provided the youth once they were placed in jobs.

KEY FINDINGS: YOUTH PREPARATION AND SUPPORT

- **In most sites, staff conducted assessments and developed an ISS for each youth.** Fourteen sites used academic and career-related tools to identify each youth's skills, interests, and needs. Across the 20 sites, a different set of 14 sites completed an ISS for each participant.

- **Although readiness training was not a federal requirement, most sites required youth to attend work readiness training sessions.** Youth focus group participants reported this training to be one of the most useful aspects of the program.

- **More than three-quarters of sites offered participants transportation services and access to work supplies.** Although providers tried to match youth to jobs in accessible locations, providers in 17 sites found that youth often needed help getting to work. Sixteen sites also helped youth purchase needed works supplies, such as clothes and tools.

A. Initial Preparation Activities for Youth

Although the SYEI was a new experience for most lead agencies and providers, it was also a new experience for many participants. Many had not previously been enrolled in WIA programs and had little or no work experience. As a result, staff found that they needed to prepare many participants for the initiative and what would be expected of them at worksites. At the same time, staff often felt that they had to learn more about each individual participant to help make the summer rewarding for all, including youth, employers, and staff.

1. Youth Orientation Activities

Sites commonly held an orientation for new participants at the beginning of the initiative. The main goals of the orientation were to introduce the participants to staff, inform them of the initiative's requirements and expectations, and review a participant handbook. Half the sites met these goals through a stand-alone orientation, while six other sites integrated the goals into other activities, such as work readiness training (discussed later in this chapter). Although the practice was not standardized within the four remaining sites, at least one provider in each of these sites also reported offering a stand-alone orientation session.

In the sites with stand-alone sessions, orientation was structured as either a group or one-on-one activity. Sessions were typically held just before or after participants' eligibility was determined. The length of orientations varied widely, ranging from 15 minutes to 4 days.

Six sites chose not to set aside a specific time for orientation. Four of these sites indicated that their work readiness training served the purpose of an orientation. Two of the six sites made an effort to orient youth to the initiative during the intake session.

2. Academic and Career Assessments

Although ETA instructed sites to provide some form of assessment for all youth, some sites did not conduct any assessments. ETA's guidance stated that "although some level of assessment...is required, a full objective assessment...as specified in the WIA regulations is not required for youth served only during the summer months" (U.S. Department of Labor 2009d). Administrators in 14 sites reported that staff formally assessed youth at some point during SYEI enrollment. Six sites reported that they did not provide assessments to all of their participants, citing either the limited amount of time available to work with youth or the lack of need for formal assessments since youth would not be receiving any services other than work placement.

Of the 14 that conducted assessments, 12 sites assessed youth with tools that measured their need for services as well as their preparedness for and interest in work. These needs assessments included career and academic interest inventories, needs assessments, skills assessments, and goal planning tools. Site staff often used the results of these tests to place youth in appropriate work experiences or job readiness classes and to identify support services that might be needed by the youth or the youth's family.

Six of the 14 sites, including 2 of those sites that administered work- or service-related assessments, carried out academic assessments. Academic assessments could include tests such the Test for Adult Basic Education, the Wide Range Achievement Test, and tests developed by Comprehensive Adult Student Assessment Systems. As discussed in Chapter IV, some sites used testing results to qualify youth for the initiative under the eligibility criterion of basic skills deficiency. Others used assessments to determine the participant's need for education services offered through the SYEI.

3. Individual Service Strategies

As with assessments, not all sites reported completing an individual service strategy (ISS) for every participant, despite federal requirements. ETA specified that an ISS must include results from youth assessments and age-appropriate goals. However, local areas had the flexibility to design their own ISS for the SYEI. Respondents from 14 sites reported that all participants completed an ISS, and in 4 other sites at least one provider completed the ISS with its participants. The ISS often recorded youth's career and educational goals, academic and career interests, skill levels, and transportation or other support needs. Staff in these sites reported that preparing the ISS was useful both for getting to know the youth and for determining an appropriate work placement. Sites completed the ISS at various times—during intake, after eligibility was determined, during orientation, or during work readiness training.

In the two sites where no providers completed an ISS for participating youth, administrators reported that the timeframe of the SYEI was too short to necessitate an ISS. They felt that the enrollment process was already too time intensive to add another lengthy procedure. These two sites both enrolled large numbers of participants compared to most other sites; however, staff in sites that completed an ISS for participants reported spending only 5 to 30 minutes on each ISS.

B. Work Readiness Training

Because the SYEI focused on placing participants in meaningful summer work, ETA suggested that sites consider strategies to help participants prepare for these experiences. Federal guidance acknowledged that many participants may need assistance "refining [their] attitudes, values, and work habits which will contribute to their success in the workplace" (U.S. Department of Labor 2009d). In addition, the Recovery Act specified that the work readiness indicator would be the only measure used to assess performance. For these reasons, sites worked to improve youth's work readiness skills during the summer months through formal workreadiness training provided in classroom settings.

Table V.1 Work Readiness Training

Training	Number of Sites
Required	16
Type of Curriculum (across providers within site)	
Standard	8
Varied	8
Not required	4

Source: Site visit interviews in 20 selected sites.
Note: N = 20 sites.

1. Site Requirements for Youth Attendance at Training

In 16 of the 20 sites, all participants attended work readiness training. The lead agency of the four remaining sites did not require providers to offer work readiness training, although at least one provider in each site did so. Administrators in two of the sites that did not require training reported that, in light of the short timeframe, they chose to focus exclusively on providing high quality work experiences. A respondent from one of these sites stated that a key to the successful implementation of their initiative within the abbreviated timeframe was their focus on work experience. One provider in a third site chose not to offer any formal training because SYEI participants, many of whom were also participants of an in-house program, had already been adequately prepared for work through other services. Staff from two additional providers that did not offer work readiness training commented that preparing the youth too much for their work experiences "may take away from the experience itself." They also felt that youth would develop work readiness skills on the job.

2. The Use of Standardized Work Readiness Curricula

In half of the 16 sites that required training, providers used a common curriculum for all youth within the site (see Table V.1). In each of the eight sites with a standard curriculum, participants were exposed to the same content and hours of training, although sometimes at different stages in the initiative. Three sites used an off-the-shelf curriculum that the lead agency purchased, while the remaining sites used locally developed training materials. Training time in these eight sites ranged from eight hours to two weeks. In five of the eight sites with required training, all youth received the training at the beginning of the summer. One site offered training weekly throughout the summer. Youth in two other sites received training at different times. For example, in one site, staff at different locations had discretion to offer the two-day training before the youth started work, later in the summer, or over the course of the summer.

The curriculum varied across providers within the remaining eight sites. In these cases, the lead agency gave flexibility to providers regarding training design and administration. In three of these eight sites, the lead agency did, however, dictate the amount of work readiness training required. Providers in the remaining five sites had the flexibility to also determine the timing, duration, and intensity of the training. As a result, the training varied widely within some sites. For example, at one site, training ranged from informal one-on-one meetings with youth at one provider to a 16-hour training session at another. Work readiness training offered by providers at another site ranged from 6 to 48 hours. Five of these eight sites tended to hold the training at the beginning of the summer; and one conducted training throughout the summer. Timing in the remaining two sites varied by provider.

3. Work Readiness Tracks Based on Youth Characteristics

Participants came to the SYEI with different experiences. Some had previous work experience, but others did not. In addition, participants fell within an 11-year range, from young teenagers to adults. This resulted in mixed levels of maturity and life experience. At least one provider in nine sites accommodated this diversity by tailoring work readiness offerings based on participants' age, previous work experience, criminal history, or disability status.[14]

Across all 20 study sites, at least one provider in seven sites grouped youth for work readiness by age. In three of these seven sites, the training largely served as all or most of the younger youth's summer experience. In addition to classroom training, these youth participated in community service activities as their work experience (see Box V.1). The older youth in these sites participated in less formal training and spent most of their time at worksites. In two of the seven sites, all or some of the providers exposed all youth to the same curriculum, but focused the training differently depending upon the age of the youth. For example, in one site, the lead agency did not feel it was appropriate for 24-year-olds to attend the same training session as 14-year-olds, so they held two different training sessions using a modified curriculum. Since many of the older youth had some prior work experience, their training was more fast-paced than in the younger group and incorporated role-playing activities. Finally, in three of the seven sites, all or some providers reported grouping youth by age, although it was unclear how the youth's experiences in the training differed.

BOX V.1. WORK READINESS TRAINING SERVED AS THE WORK EXPERIENCE FOR YOUNGER YOUTH

Albany, OR. Many 14- and 15-year-olds participated in camps designed to develop work readiness skills and provide career exploration activities. One provider offered a three-week program during which youth could chose three career clusters to explore. Youth also participated in field trips and community service projects such as landscaping at a community college and removing graffiti. The youth were paid a stipend of $150 per week. One provider noted that they chose this program model because they anticipated that it would be difficult to place younger youth with employers.

Memphis, TN. All youth aged 14 to 15 attended a career exploration program run by the city and participated in weekly community service projects such as volunteering at the food bank and working at a nursing home. The training, based on an off-the-shelf curriculum, ran 10 weeks, and youth were paid $7.25 per hour for participating.

Menomonie, WI. Many youth aged 14 to 16 participated in career academies operated by technical colleges and the Red Cross. The academies provided career exploration activities, job search training, and work readiness instruction focused on developing youth's self-confidence, teamwork, and interpersonal skills. Youth also volunteered at the humane society, a food pantry program, and Habitat for Humanity. The program ran 8 to 10 weeks, and youth were paid $7.25 per hour.

Although age was the most common characteristic by which youth were grouped for training, some youth in four sites were assigned based on other characteristics. In one site, different providers offered separate training sessions based on previous work history, offender status, and disabilities. For example, a modified work readiness training for youth with disabilities was taught by a certified teacher funded by the school district. One provider in the second site grouped youth with criminal histories to tailor the work readiness training to that population and to avoid mixing the youth offenders with other youth. In the two other sites, older youth with previous work experience could be exempted from training altogether.

4. Common Work Readiness Training Topics

Work readiness training covered a wide range of topics from basic interviewing tips to teen fitness. At least one provider in the majority of the 20 study sites addressed soft skills, job preparation, career exploration, and financial literacy during work readiness training (see Table V.2). Other less common topics included work orientation, basic skills, and green jobs. Box V.2 provides descriptions of training structure and content in two sites.

To capture the attention of youth, providers tried some unique approaches to delivering their main training messages. For example, one provider showed a 20-minute work readiness video made by youth participants from a previous summer program. The video discussed interviewing, dress, attitude, program expectations, timesheets, grievance policies, and payroll. In another site, a provider gave each youth a flash drive containing the résumé and cover letter that the youth developed during training as well as additional materials.

BOX V.2. EXAMPLES OF WORK READINESS TRAINING

Albuquerque, NM. The Basic Skills Employability Training (BEST) curriculum for work readiness has been used and updated by the SYEI provider for the past 15 years. Each 10-hour class had 12–15 youth participants and was held during the first five weeks of the summer, mostly before work experiences began. Every youth was required to attend this training, but training time was unpaid. The classes included a mix of reading, interactive exercises, and hands-on experiences. Staff administered pre- and posttests to participants. The BEST curriculum includes the following modules: employer expectations, substance abuse and mental health education, career strategies, identification of occupations of interest, preparing a résumé, the job search, the interview process, basic computer skills, and sexual harassment.

Rochester, MN. Youth participants were required to attend the Blueprint for Success work readiness training program, held for two weeks at the beginning of the summer and administered by staff at a One-Stop Career Center. Youth were paid $200 for completing the training but were penalized for lateness or absences. Training took place in groups of 15 to 25 participants, separated by age groups or background. The curriculum for Blueprint for Success was designed to meet ETA's definition of work readiness, and includes a pre- and postassessment. The curriculum covered the following topics: self-discovery; managing your time effectively; realities of the job market; workplace skills for today's employee; effective communication; contacting employers; preparing for the job interview; getting hired: workplace issues, paperwork, and finances; and keeping your job.

---

5. Incentives to Encourage Attendance

Given the importance that sites placed on preparing youth for the workplace, sites devised strategies to encourage attendance at work readiness training. Site staff felt this was particularly important given that many in-school youth did not want to be in the classroom during their summer break. Although respondents in most sites reported little drop-off during work readiness training, staff in two sites reported that some youth attempted to skip these sessions.

Table V.2 Common Topics Addressed in Work Readiness Training

Topic	Areas Covered	Number of Sites[a]
Soft Skills	Communication, teamwork, decision making, problem solving, conflict resolution, business etiquette, work habits, responsibility, integrity, leadership, customer service, self-esteem, time management	18
Job Preparation	Résumés, job search, references, applications, cover letters, interviewing, entrepreneurship, how to dress, networking, goals, attendance, punctuality	16
Career Exploration	Interest inventories and career assessments, options after high school, further education, field trips, guest speakers	13
Financial Literacy	Budgeting, use of credit, opening a bank account	11
Work Orientation	Sexual harassment, employment law, payroll, expectations, schedules, taxes, cashing paychecks	6
Basic Skills	Computer literacy, math and reading skills	4
Green Jobs	Green industries, green aspects of jobs, environmentalism	4
Miscellaneous	Substance abuse/mental health education, community awareness, nonviolent social change, teen food and fitness, communication with police, advocacy	4

Source: Site visit interviews in 20 selected sites.
Note: N = 20 sites.
[a]At least one provider in the site reported addressing the topic in the work readiness training.

Table V.3. Incentives Offered for Work Readiness Training

Type of Incentive	Number of Sites Offering Incentive[a]
Any Incentive[b]	16
Monetary Incentive	14
Type of Monetary Incentive[b]	
Wages	6
Stipends	6
Gift Cards	3
Nonmonetary Incentive	8
Type of Nonmonetary Incentive[b]	
Certificate of completion	7
Timed training to encourage participation	3

Source: Site visit interviews in 20 selected sites.
Note: N = 20 sites.
[a] At least one provider in the site offered the incentive.
[b] In some sites, providers used more than one form of incentive.

Providers in 16 sites used incentives, such as hourly wages, stipends, gift cards, and certificates of completion to encourage youth to participate (see Table V.3). Providers in 14 of these sites offered an hourly wage or a stipend. In six of these sites, at least one provider paid youth a standard wage ranging from the minimum wage of $7.25 to $10 per hour for their participation. In six other sites, one or more providers gave youth a stipend—ranging from $25 to $200 and averaging $110—for participation in training. One provider offered a stipend of $450 to those youth for whom the training encompassed the majority of their summer experience. Two sites offered an hourly stipend of $7.25 per hour for training rather than paying regular wages so the earnings would not be taxed.

In three sites, at least one provider gave youth gift cards for attending work readiness training. In one of these sites, the gift cards were used to encourage the youth to complete the homework assignments. In another site, one provider surprised the youth with gift cards following the training, so the cards served as a reward rather than an incentive. The $10 to $25 gift cards were often for local retail chains and restaurants and in one case for movie theaters.

Eight sites also used other nonmonetary forms of encouragement. From at least one provider in seven of the eight sites, youth received a certificate specifically created for the initiative. One provider noted that the certificate was designed to serve as a signal to potential employers that the youth was a good employment investment as a result of having work readiness training. As another form of encouragement, at least one provider in three sites scheduled training sessions so that youth would be obligated to attend. For example, several providers in one site held work readiness trainings on Mondays and Fridays. Since the youth picked up their timesheets on Monday and dropped them off on Fridays, this schedule motivated them to attend the training sessions to ensure timely payment of their wages. In another site, at least one provider distributed paychecks during work readiness workshops. According to youth from a third site, if they missed a work readiness workshop, they were not allowed to work the following week, although the provider manager reported that they gave the youth some leniency with regard to this rule.

YOUTH PERSPECTIVES: EXPERIENCES IN WORK READINESS TRAINING

Résumé Building

"I never knew what a résumé was until I actually did one, and I used to hear about it so much, and I'm a senior now and I'm like, "What is a résumé?" . . . There were some jobs I tried to apply for online and it says, "Please post your résumé." I'm like, "Résumé? What résumé?" . . . I actually learned it and I actually have one now."

Financial Literacy Training

"[In this economy]. . . you have to think about how you're going to manage your money and where it's going to go, and if you really need to spend it on something that you don't really need and stuff, so that helps."

"[I really liked] the two budgets. The first one was a large amount. The second was a lower amount, and the first one was for somebody who graduated college, and the other one was for somebody who didn't go to college. So that was real good because it really gave us a perspective."

Guest Speakers "We had city officials. We had managers, owners of private businesses and entrepreneurs. Different people with different career paths who came in *and told us about their stories, the choices they made and just basically told us the basic foundations for creating your own business or even just doing, you know, making correct choices, if you will."*

"[My] supervisor tries to get people to come in and talk to us about . . . their majors and their jobs and what they're doing, what they're going to school for, and that gives us a little clue of what we might want to do. And we can ask questions to them too and we'll get answers. And it kind of like opens your eyes to other opportunities that way."

Other Activities

"We had the opportunity to rate yourself, like if you were a social person, artistic and things like that. So then you could look at the occupation and things like that and see what you worked best with, so that you could basically understand that it's important to get a job that you are interested in and not something that you're not, so that you have a good time as well."

"They taught us stuff like what type of communication person that you are. Like they had it separated up into several color groups, and depending on what color you were, what communication you were. And that's helpful to find out how your supervisor communicates, so that we know how to communicate better with that person. So that was interesting."

6. Youth Impressions of Work Readiness Training

Participants in the youth focus groups had mostly positive reactions to work readiness training. In almost all sites, youth reported that the training was one of the most useful parts of the summer initiative. Participants in about one third of the sites discussed the value of the specific soft skills they developed, citing enhanced communication, time management, and teamwork skills.[15] In five of the 11 sites that offered financial literacy as part of the training, the youth expressed appreciation for that part of the instruction. Participants of five focus groups also commented that they appreciated the opportunity to draft their résumé and cover letter and found interview tips and mock interviews helpful.

Even though they found the work readiness experience useful, participants from half the sites that discussed the training felt that improvements could be made. In particular, some participants reported that the training was boring, reflected simple common sense, or presented material they already knew through school or their participation in WIA programs. To address these issues, they suggested tailoring the training based on youth's previous work experiences (as some sites did) and grouping youth for the training by their work assignment.

C. Supportive Services

Although sites were not required to offer supportive services to participants, many SYEI providers had extensive experience working with disadvantaged youth and recognized the need for additional support for youth to overcome their employment barriers. In the 20 study sites, staff most often reported helping youth to resolve transportation issues, to acquire appropriate work clothing and tools, and to gain access to child care. Providers from all but one site reported supplying youth with needed support services either in-house or through referrals to community partners. Administrators in the remaining site that did not connect youth with other services felt the summer focus on work left no time for other services or referrals.

1. Transportation and Work Supplies

Sites reported giving participants help getting to and from their worksites, purchasing needed work supplies, and gaining access to child care (see Table V.4). Transportation services were most common, with 17 sites reporting that they help youth get to and from their summer worksites. In most cases, these services were offered after an initial assessment of the participant's needs. Staff often reported trying to find worksites that were within walking distance of youth's homes, yet transportation was still either a common or major barrier for many youth. Youth in rural areas often did not have a driver's license, access to a car, money for gas, or available public transportation. Youth in cities often did not have disposable income to purchase bus passes or tokens, and public transportation was simply not accessible to some. A provider at one site even noted that the site considered the location of a youth's residence and his or her access to transportation as a factor for enrollment, denying enrollment to some youth who could not access available worksites.

Transportation assistance took several forms. Providers in eight sites issued bus passes and tokens. Since public transportation was not readily available in other areas, providers from at least seven sites provided youth with gas money or shuttled them to and from their worksites in vans. As discussed in Chapter III, some sites included both urban and rural areas. For that reason, providers in at least five sites offered both types of assistance, providing shuttle rides or gas money to some youth while giving bus passes to others. The remaining two sites that provided youth with transportation help did not specify the form this assistance took.

Other common supports included assistance purchasing work supplies and obtaining child care. Providers from 16 sites helped youth purchase needed supplies for work such as clothing, tools, boots, and safety goggles. These providers either directly purchased the materials for youth or referred them to partners, such as Dress for Success and Gentlemen's Closet. Providers from 10 sites stated that, when necessary, they helped youth obtain child care. However, most noted that, given the age of the participants, this was not often necessary. For example, staff in one site indicated that they could use other funds to help youth pay for child care but few needed it.

Table V.4. Supportive Services Offered

Service	Number of Sites
Offered Services Directly or by Referral	19
Offered Transportation Support	17
Bus passes/tokens	8
In-house vans/gas money	7
Type of support unspecified	2
Offered Money for Work Supplies	16
Offered Help Obtaining Child Care	10

Source: Site visit interviews in 20 selected sites.
Note: N = 20 sites.

2. Local Emphasis on Supportive Services

Sites differed in their focus on supportive service. Several sites appeared to highlight them. For example, three sites included line items in providers' budgets for these services. In one of these sites, the providers' budgets included three line items for supportive services: one for a $100 work-support payment that each participant received upon completion of the work readiness training, one for transportation-related costs, and one for supplies. Providers at the other two sites could use the funds to help youth obtain any service need to be able to work successfully.

Providers from six other sites indicated that, if they had had more time, they would have placed a greater emphasis on connecting youth with supportive services. The youth services coordinator at one site thought that the workload was so high they did not have time to take a proactive approach to identifying and meeting supportive service needs.

VI. The Recruitment and Involvement of Employers

Employers were important partners in sites' efforts to provide youth with successful summer experiences. Though employers were receiving a summer employee whose wages were paid with Recovery Act funds, they were voluntary partners with interests that could diverge from those of the sites. Thus, sites' recruitment efforts needed to address employers' reasons for participating. At the same time, site staff had to recruit enough employers, with sufficient jobs, to satisfy the large number of youth with wide-ranging interests while also being mindful of ETA guidance on ensuring appropriate and meaningful experiences.

This chapter discusses how sites succeeded in recruiting employers. Section A describes employer recruitment strategies, including when sites began this process, what employers and economic sectors they targeted, and some of the challenges they faced in this aspect of their initiatives. Section B reviews sites' processes for screening and orienting employers after recruiting them. Finally, Section C describes sites' understanding of employers' motivations for participating.

KEY FINDINGS: EMPLOYER RECRUITMENT AND INVOLVEMENT

- **Sites successfully recruited interested employers.** Sites contacted and recruited employers they knew and those new to the workforce investment system through direct contacts and broad media campaigns. More than half the sites focused their recruitment on particular sectors of the economy, and almost half reported that they recruited more worksites than they needed.
- **To ensure appropriate work experiences for youth, sites screened and oriented employers.** Formal screening processes involved such steps as reviewing an employer's application, visiting the worksite, and signing a worksite agreement. Most sites also provided worksite supervisors with an orientation to their SYEI roles and responsibilities.
- **Employers were eager to participate to benefit their businesses and their communities.** Employers reported appreciating the free summer help during lean times and the opportunity to mentor the youth.

A. Employer Recruitment

Although many sites had existing relationships with local employers, all sites had to conduct some recruitment activities to generate the number of worksites needed for the expected volume of participants. In addition to determining when to conduct this recruitment, sites made decisions about how to reach out to the business community and whether to target specific sectors of the economy. Most sites reported that they recruited sufficient numbers of employers to accommodate participating youth.

1. Timing of Employer Recruitment

Staff of the participating organizations—often the lead agency along with their providers—began recruiting employers even before they approached youth about participating. In 15 sites, staff began their efforts early to have enough employer worksites to meet the expected demand for work placements. In 1 of these 15 sites, the lead agency required prospective providers to include a list of confirmed employer worksites in their bids to become a SYEI provider. In 5 of the 20 study sites, one or more providers reported waiting to recruit employers until after they had begun recruiting youth.

At least eight of the study sites continued to recruit employers once they had started recruiting youth. Site administrators reported using this strategy because they had insufficient time to recruit enough employers before the initiative started or because they wanted the interests of enrolled youth to drive at least some of the employer options. For example, in one site, several participants indicated an interest in the law, which was not represented in the set of employers initially recruited. To meet this interest, staff successfully recruited local law firms.

2. Employer Recruitment Strategies

To recruit employers, sites relied on two main strategies: (1) reaching out to employers who had existing relationships with the workforce investment system, and (2) promoting the SYEI more broadly to the employer community. Sixteen sites reported capitalizing on their existing relationships with employers (see Table VI.1). They contacted employers that had previously worked with the LWIB or its providers, either as a youth employer or in some other capacity. To advertise the initiative to a wider range of potential employers, sites also reported asking members of the LWIB to reach out to their own employer networks and using employer listservs maintained by their own business services units.

Table VI.1. Employer Recruitment Strategies

Strategy[a]	Number of Sites
Outreach to Existing Employer Contacts	16
Outreach to Broader Employer Community	14
Direct phone or in-person contacts	14
Broad media/other campaigns	6
Chamber of Commerce resource	6

Source: Site visit interviews in 20 selected sites.
Note: N = 20 sites.
[a]Sites used multiple outreach strategies.

The lead agencies and providers also served as a potential source of worksites. In five sites, at least one provider served as the primary worksite for SYEI participants. These arrangements for youth job placements at the providers were agreed upon with the lead agency before the provider was awarded the SYEI contract. For example, a provider in one site was a nonprofit community action agency with its own organic farm that supplied meals and produce to families in need. The provider was able to employ all of its youth participants at the farm and farm stand and did not need to recruit any worksites. In another site, a local public university that was a long-time provider of summer youth placements assigned a majority of its participants to work within its own departments. To place the remaining youth, the provider recruited worksites from the surrounding community. In addition, many other providers from across the sites hired small numbers of youth to work in their own organizations doing clerical work or documenting the summer through marketing materials, while referring most youth to outside employers.

Most sites also reached out to the broader employer community. Fourteen sites reported directly contacting employers that they did not know to gauge their interest in participating in the initiative. One common approach was "cold calling" employers by phone, but, according to staff in one site, this was the least effective recruitment strategy. Another common strategy was to personally visit local businesses. At least one site felt that this was their most effective recruitment method. Six sites sought to recruit employers through marketing campaigns. They reported a range of promotional activities, including issuing press releases, placing newspaper and television advertisements, sending mass mailings and emails, maintaining a website, and distributing fliers. In addition, six sites reported that the local Chamber of Commerce was a helpful resource, and one site used a directory of social service organizations that serve youth to find potential employers. Box VI.1 provides an example of multiple employer recruitment strategies used in a single site.

BOX VI.1. COMBINING MULTIPLE STRATEGIES TO RECRUIT EMPLOYERS

Bridgeport, CT. The recruitment of employers at the Bridgeport, CT, site was a joint effort between LWIB leadership, the youth coordinator at the LWIB, and the LWIB's marketing division. Information was sent to 5,000 employers that had had previous contact with the LWIB. Fliers were also distributed through the local Chamber of Commerce, and a PowerPoint presentation, along with a handout responding to frequently asked questions, was developed to be used in presentations to potential employers. The marketing materials presented the program as career exploration opportunities for youth and an opportunity for employers to train and vet possible employees. Staff highlighted that employers would bear no costs for the program.

Beyond broader outreach campaigns, city officials and union leaders provided support. According to administrators, unions rarely opposed offering youth summer employment experiences. Five sites reported that SYEI administrators had regular contact with union leaders and either kept them informed of initiative activities or received input from them on summer programming. Three sites reported successfully negotiating agreements with union representatives or members that allowed the site to place youth at particular worksites. In addition, 7 of the 20 sites reported that they received positive support from city mayors or other local politicians, and that such support was often instrumental in encouraging employers to participate in the initiative and the community to back it. One site made efforts to keep local officials informed about the progress of the initiative.

3. Efforts to Engage Particular Economic Sectors

Although all sites successfully recruited employers from the public, nonprofit, and private sectors, more than half of sites or their providers focused recruitment on one sector or another. Staff in eight sites reported a focus on creating meaningful experiences for the youth regardless of the employer's sector (see Table VI.2). (Note that some of these sites might have included targeting efforts that were not revealed during site visits because those individuals or providers who carried them out were not among those interviewed.) Thus, neither the lead agency nor the providers targeted any particular sector. Across the three economic sectors, youth could participate in jobs at employers ranging from city government to community action agencies to local construction companies. (Chapter VII discusses participants' work experiences in more detail.)

By contrast, particular providers or the lead agency focused recruitment efforts on the private sector in at least six sites. Within these, the emphasis was sitewide in four sites and provider-specific in two others. One common reason given for this emphasis was that, in the current economy, staff considered private sector firms more likely to offer participants regular positions after the summer. Another reason given was that private sector worksites might also be more relevant to the long-term career interests of participating youth. For example, based on their conversations with youth, staff in two sites reported that most youth were not interested in working for nonprofits. The sites that targeted the private sector did not appear to have any particular characteristics that distinguished them from other sites, and, in fact, all sites had at least some private sector employers participate. All recruitment efforts in at least five sites and efforts of specific providers in least one other site targeted the public and nonprofit sectors. The reported reasons for focusing on these sectors ranged from general unease about choosing one private employer over another for a government-subsidized job, lack of sufficient information on the quality of private sector jobs, and restrictions placed by private sector employers on the age and background of the youth they were willing to hire. Sites also felt that public and nonprofit organizations were more familiar with occupational safety and child labor laws, had a better understanding of disadvantaged youth, and tended to be in more accessible locations. Staff in one site also felt that public and nonprofit employers had organizational missions that aligned more closely with the SYEI, making them easier to work with and more likely to offer youth placements.

4. Challenges to Employer Recruitment

Sites generally reported success recruiting a sufficient number of employers for the SYEI, although they faced challenges along the way. At least 7 of the 20 study sites reported recruiting more potential employers than actually needed. Only four sites reported not being able to match all youth to a worksite. As discussed in Chapter VII, three of these sites reported that some youth interviewed poorly with prospective employers and were unable to secure jobs despite the availability of positions, and the fourth site reported an insufficient number of employers given the volume of youth they ultimately enrolled.

Table VI.2. Targeting Employer Recruitment on Particular Sectors

Targeting	Number of Sites
No Targeting	8
Targeting Private Sector	6
Sitewide	4
By particular providers	2
Targeting Public and Non-profit Sectors	6
Sitewide	5
By particular providers	1

Source: Site visit interviews in 20 selected sites.
Note: The data presented is based on interviews with staff of lead agencies and specific providers. Since all providers across the 20 sites were not interviewed, it is possible that particular providers in additional sites targeted sectors that were not accounted for in this table.
N = 20 sites.

Despite their success, at least some staff in 16 sites reported challenges due to employer expectations, the timing of the recruitment, and the economy. In nine sites, at least some staff reported that employers had unrealistic or incompatible requirements for the youth they would be willing to hire. In particular, sites found it challenging to identify employers willing to hire youth under the age of 18. As a result, one site placed younger youth in camps where they were provided with work readiness training. (These camps are discussed in Chapter V.) Staff in four sites also discussed the difficulty of finding appropriate employers for certain types of youth. Three reported that it was hard to find employers to work with youth who had criminal records or could not pass a drug test. Another site found it difficult to recruit employers that would hire youth with a disability, such as autism.

Staff across the study sites also indicated that the initiative's short timeline affected their ability to recruit placements that were appropriate for youth. Because most employer recruitment occurred before youth enrolled, the staff did not know their eventual participants' abilities or interests. Three sites specifically mentioned this as a challenge, and interviews in other sites indicated that youth were sometimes placed at worksites that did not match their interests because of a lack of suitable choices.

Six sites mentioned that recent layoffs by employers in their areas hampered their ability to recruit employers. Because of the weak economy in many local areas, companies were either reducing hours for employees or laying off workers completely. Either of these situations made an employer ineligible for participation as an SYEI worksite, as discussed in the ETA guidance and the Workforce Investment Act (U.S. Department of Labor 2009d; U.S. Congress 1999). A seventh site also mentioned not being able to place youth at an employer that had recently laid off workers, but stated that single instance did not affect their recruiting strategy or the number of available worksites. Another site also reported some community concerns that SYEI youth were taking jobs away from workers, so staff asked employers to certify that this was not the case before accepting them into the initiative.

B. Screening and Orienting Recruited Employers

Most participating employers, whether or not they had prior involvement with the workforce investment system, were new to the SYEI. As a result, site staff had to screen employers and their proposed work placements to ensure that they would be appropriate opportunities for participants. In addition, employers required guidance on what their responsibilities would be as part of the initiative. Holding an orientation session was the most common method for informing employers about these responsibilities.

1. Employer Screening Strategies

Most sites formally screened employers before accepting them into their initiative. However, sites appeared to be less stringent about screening employers who had hired youth in the past through other youth employment programs. In these instances, staff felt they had sufficient knowledge about the worksite and supervisors.

The employer screening process included from one to three different steps, including an application describing the potential work experience and work environment, an in-person visit to the employer, and the signing of a worksite agreement.

- **Application.** At least 10 of the 20 sites had an application or registration form for employers to use to express their interest in the SYEI. These applications typically asked for a description of the worksite environment, the jobs to be given to youth, and the employer's requirements for those positions. At least three sites maintained the form on their website for electronic submission; staff in one of these site reported that online applications likely increased the number of employers that applied to the initiative. Other sites mailed applications to interested employers.
- **In-person visits.** In-person visits were part of the screening process for at least 11 sites. At least one provider or the key administrator mentioned vetting employers through these visits. This allowed staff to develop a personal relationship with the worksite supervisor and get a first-hand look at the work environment. Staff did not visit all employers; as mentioned earlier, staff often felt they were sufficiently familiar with employers that had hired youth in previous summers.
- **Worksite agreements.** Nine sites reported asking employers that passed the screening process to sign worksite agreements. The worksite agreement normally did not guarantee that any participants would be placed with the employer but described the employer and worksite supervisor's responsibilities should they receive any participants. The worksite agreement was either signed during an in-person visit or mailed to the employer for signature.

Through each of these steps, site staff used a range of criteria to assess the appropriateness of a worksite (see Box VI.2). Staff reported looking for meaningful experiences where youth could learn skills, have an effective mentor and attentive supervisor, and work in a safe and protected environment. Staff also considered whether there were recent layoffs at the site, the accessibility of the location, and the reasonableness of the employers' preferences for and expectations of the youth. Six sites had more specific criteria that employers needed to meet, such as a supervisor-to-youth ratio of one to five, compliance with labor laws, and assurances that assigned youth would not have family members employed at the same site.

Box VI.2. Screening Employers for the SYEI

Madera, CA. The provider at this site reported receiving about 225 responses to a mass mailing sent to approximately 3,200 local employers. All employer applications to the program were screened by staff to ensure that worksites were suitable for youth. Screening criteria included the worksite's location, required work hours, availability of adequate supervision, job description, layoff history, accessibility for individuals with disabilities, and previous experience as a youth employer. Staff called employers that passed the screening to discuss their participation and the nature of the job to ensure that the work would be meaningful to participants and help them develop marketable skills.

Although site staff generally appeared satisfied with their sites' screening process, some staff at two sites raised some concerns. These staff members reported that, in the SYEI's initial phase, they were more focused on recruiting sufficient numbers of employers than on the quality of worksites. Given more time, they said they could have been more selective and weeded out employers that were less likely to provide youth with meaningful experiences.

2. Employer Orientation and On-going Support

Relationships between local staff and employers were critical to the success of youth's summer experiences. Most sites felt it was important to discuss with employers their SYEI responsibilities when youth were placed at their worksites. After youth began working, local staff typically maintained regular communication with worksite supervisors throughout the summer.

Employer orientation was commonly used to ensure that employers understood their roles and responsibilities. These orientations typically consisted of reviewing a supervisor handbook, timesheets, labor laws, wages, workers' compensation laws, supervision policies, and workplace safety, among other topics. More than three-quarters of the study sites held group or one-on-one orientations for employers who were assigned a participant. Ten sites oriented employers primarily through one-on-one sessions or during worksite visits, and five held larger group orientations. These five sites also held one-on-one orientations with those employers that were unable to attend the group sessions or were recruited after those sessions had been held. Only one site reported that the group orientation was mandatory for employers.

Four sites did not hold employer orientations. Of these sites, three provided printed orientation packets or a supervisor handbook. In a fourth site, at least one provider reported that they knew their employers through previous experiences so an orientation was not necessary.

Beyond orientation, employers in all 20 sites reported positive ongoing relationships with staff. Staff in most sites maintained regular contact with employers through regular monitoring visits to the worksites (see Chapter VIII for more details on such monitoring). Through these visits and phone availability, staff learned about problems, such as issues with participants' attendance or behavior, and could try to resolve them. One site also reported providing ongoing training and guidance to worksite supervisors given variation in their experiences working with youth. Another site made special efforts to maintain contact with employers at which disabled youth were placed (see Box VI.3).

Box VI.3. Providing Additional Support to Employers Working with Disabled Youth

In *Bridgeport, CT*, staff worked closely with employers at which disabled youth were placed to provide clear instructions on how best to work and support youth with disabilities. For example, staff asked an employer who hired a youth with a memory disability due to an accident to write down instructions rather than provide verbal instructions. As needed, these youth were also assigned a job coach to help support both the employer and the youth at the worksite. In one case, a job coach spent one hour each work day helping the employer acclimate and mentor two blind youth at their worksite location.

Despite an overall positive experience, discussions with selected employers indicated that communication processes could have been improved at some sites. For example, one employer thought that having input into the job-matching process would have improved the placements and helped supervisors become more familiar with their youth.

C. Employer Motivation

Sites' efforts to engage employers in the SYEI benefited from an understanding of why employers would be willing to participate. Across the sites, employers were interested in the opportunity to help their communities and to support their own businesses. Employers felt that the experience was worth the effort of mentoring a new employee and almost unanimously agreed that they would participate again given the opportunity.

1. Employers' Reasons for Participating

Based on focus groups conducted with small groups of employers in each site and interviews with site staff, employers appeared to have been motivated largely by a desire to give back to the community and also by the wish to receive extra help in a tight economy. Of course, employers had varied reasons for participating, but employers from all sectors across all sites believed it would benefit the youth, their businesses, and the community as a whole.

The three most frequently mentioned reasons given for participation, according to staff and employers, were to help youth succeed, take advantage of subsidized summer help, and vet future employees without any commitment or cost. Staff reports echoed these same sentiments. First, respondents in 19 sites reported that employers wanted to mentor the youth and give them an opportunity to build their résumés and work skills. They felt that the disadvantaged youth served by SYEI might not otherwise have these opportunities to be engaged in productive work and stay out of trouble.

Second, although companies that recently experienced layoffs were generally not a part of the SYEI, many public, nonprofit, and private firms that were involved either faced hiring freezes during the summer or could not afford to hire the extra staff they needed. Administrators or employers in 17 sites reported that employers often needed the help that SYEI participants could provide. That extra help was a "life-saver," according to one employer. This sentiment prevailed even though employers recognized that hosting the youth meant closely supervising them and working with them to develop professionally. Staff in these sites also reported that having additional help at no cost was a strong motivator, though not the primary motivator for all. Employers also appreciated that the SYEI providers typically bore the responsibility for worker's compensation and general liability claims.

Finally, hiring a SYEI participant was ideal for the employers that planned on adding to their workforce and could afford to do so. Respondents in nine sites reported free training of potentially permanent employees was a motivation for employer participation. During the summer, the employer could evaluate and train the potential employee with no obligation to hire the worker and without incurring the costs usually associated with on-the-job training. Though detailed numbers were not available from most of the 20 sites studied, anecdotal reports suggest that some employers took advantage of this opportunity and hired their SYEI participants on a permanent basis after the summer. (See Chapter VIII for more information on permanent placements.)

To reinforce this last benefit to employers, 16 sites reported discussing the potential for permanent placements with employers during the recruitment process. For example, frontline staff at four of these sites encouraged employers to think of the youth initiative as free employee training. At the remaining four sites, permanent placements were either not an initiative goal or were not a salient issue given that the site primarily served younger youth still in school.

2. The Work Opportunity Tax Credit

In hopes of translating youth's summer experience into a permanent job placement, staff in four sites reported that they discussed the Work Opportunity Tax Credit (WOTC) with employers.

The WOTC is a federal tax credit that private businesses can claim if they hire employees from 12 designated groups that experience barriers to employment. A WOTC can be for as much as $2,400 for each eligible employee's first year of employment.[16] Employers would not be eligible for the WOTC while wages were subsidized by Recovery Act funds, but rather could claim the credit if they hired youth permanently. Two of the 12 eligible groups were covered under the SYEI funded by the Recovery Act: unemployed veterans and disconnected youth. ETA encouraged sites to recruit youth from these groups and to discuss the WOTC with employers as a benefit to hiring youth in these targeted groups as permanent employees.

Among the sites that promoted the WOTC, three mentioned discussing the credit with all employers. In the fourth, only one of providers mentioned discussing the WOTC. The provider that did discuss the WOTC, however, was unaware of the recent changes in the policy that applied to the SYEI. Despite holding these discussions, administrators in one of these sites thought that employers were unlikely to take advantage of the WOTC given the amount of paperwork involved. By contrast, an administrator in another site believed that the hiring of participants on a permanent basis would be significant—possibly 90 percent of for-profit worksites.

Staff in most other sites reported that they did not discuss the WOTC with employers either because they did not feel the WOTC was relevant to the SYEI employers or they lacked enough knowledge about the WOTC to present it to employers. Many staff said that the WOTC was not relevant for their public or nonprofit agencies or that the participating youth were not technically employed by their summer worksites. Staff in two sites acknowledged that the WOTC might become relevant if youth were hired after the summer but still did not feel it was necessary to discuss the credit with employers. In addition, staff said they did not discuss the WOTC with employers because they felt uninformed and unclear about the conditions or requirements. The SYEI coordinator in one of these sites felt that the WOTC was too difficult to understand and that there was a general negative perception that it involved too much paperwork.

VII. YOUTH'S SUMMER EXPERIENCES

The true heart of the summer experience did not begin until after the tremendous local effort to recruit youth and employers, determine their suitability for the SYEI, and prepare them for the workplace. Although some youth were placed in academic services in the classroom, most were placed in employment. These jobs were usually at entry level, but they had the potential to accomplish two important goals. One was to influence youth's views about the world of work, the work process, career development, and the need for further education. The other was to stimulate the economy by getting cash into youth's pockets.

KEY FINDINGS: THE RANGE OF SUMMER EXPERIENCES

- **About one-third of sites emphasized work, offering few other services.** The remaining two-thirds offered academics to at least some youth. Few sites offered any of the other 10 program elements required by the regular WIA youth program but optional for Recovery Act programs.
- **Half of sites offered occupational skills training.** The most common industry covered by training was health care, followed by manufacturing, culinary, construction, and entrepreneurship. Other academic offerings included GED preparation, remediation, and recovery of school credits.
- **Health care, public services, parks and recreation, and education and child care were the most commonly reported industries for summer jobs.** Youth most often performed administrative or clerical tasks, landscaping and outdoor maintenance, janitorial and indoor maintenance, and construction work. Although youth's daily tasks may have been at entry level, participants were nevertheless exposed to careers within the industry where they were placed in a summer job.
- **Youth could work an average of 200 potential hours over seven weeks at $7.75 per hour.** This resulted in average potential earnings of $1,500 per youth over the course of the summer.
- **More than three-quarters of sites experienced at least some payroll problems.** The most common problems involved timesheet collection, paycheck processing, and paycheck distribution.

This chapter explores the common patterns and unique variations in how sites developed and structured youth's summer experiences. Section A begins by discussing local strategies for serving youth through worksites, the classroom, or a combination of both. Section B describes the types of activities and tasks that youth were doing on a daily basis through the SYEI. Section C analyzes the strategies and factors that influenced how youth were matched to academic programs and employers. Finally, Section D discusses the hours that youth worked and the wages they received through Recovery Act funds.

A. Local Strategies for Serving Youth

The focus of summer initiatives administered through the workforce investment system has shifted over time. As discussed in Chapter I, the JTPA Summer Employment and Training Program focused initially on employment. However, the early 1990s saw a shift to ensure linkage between youth's work experience and their academic achievements. With the passage of WIA, summer employment became only one of 10 required program elements. In contrast, the Congressional explanatory statement for the Recovery Act stated that "the conferees are particularly interested in these funds being used to create summer employment opportunities for youth." At the same time, ETA allowed "the flexibility to determine whether it is appropriate that academic learning be directly linked to summer employment for each youth" (U.S. Department of Labor 2009d).

1. The Focus on Employment

In identifying their service delivery strategies beyond work readiness training, sites took one of two approaches. About one-third focused largely on work experience, offering few other services beyond work readiness training. The remaining two-thirds offered work experience as well as academic experience to at least a subset of youth. Very few sites offered any of the remaining 10 service elements that are required through regular WIA youth programs but made optional for the SYEI funded by the Recovery Act (see Chapter I for a list of the 10 elements).

About one-third of sites chose to emphasize on-the-job experience through work site placements (see Table VII.1). Six of these seven sites offered jobs to all youth; one focused on work for older youth and required academic activities for all younger youth. Site administrators in these sites gave two common reasons for their choice of service model. First, they believed that the model complied with the true intent of the Recovery Act to stimulate the economy and put money directly in the hands of youth. Second, they felt the implementation time frame was too tight either to logistically coordinate an academic component with local partners or to ensure a reasonable impact on youth who participate for less than two months.

2. Provision of Academics and Other Services

Thirteen sites offered some form of academics to at least a subset of youth. Six of these offered area-wide programs to all interested youth before they were placed in a job. Although available to all, sites typically reported that less than 10 percent of youth in these sites expressed interest and enrolled in academics. For those youth who did enroll in academics, either the summer began with occupational skills training before placement in a related employment opportunity or the skills training occurred simultaneously with a relevant job.

Some sites also allowed youth to participate in remediation, recovery of school credits, or GED preparation while working in their summer jobs. Those youth who were not interested in academics were matched immediately to employment.

The academic offerings in the seven remaining sites varied by youth providers within sites and were not necessarily available to all youth enrolled across the site. In some cases, an emphasis on innovation resulted in service offerings that were dramatically different from one provider to the next. For example, a single site had one provider that offered entrepreneurship training, another that offered occupational skills training in computer technology, another that offered remediation, and yet another that offered high-tech digital arts education. Another site offered leadership skills training in one service location, CPR and first aid training in another, and fire suppression certification in another. The content, duration, and intensity of academic programs are discussed in detail below.

Beyond academics and work experience, the 20 sites offered few of the remaining 10 elements of the regular WIA program. Supportive services, discussed in Chapter V, served as the only other major service offering. Two sites offered summer components that involved leadership development opportunities. One site reported offering a behavioral adjustment program. Another offered dropout prevention, violence prevention, and fatherhood services. The evaluation revealed no sites offering mentoring beyond the worksite or counseling such as for drug and alcohol abuse.

Parent involvement was also limited, with 16 sites reporting that it was not encouraged beyond providing intake paperwork. Six of these sites, however, stated that some parents either contacted the site about youth paychecks or to check on their child's progress. Three of these sites also involved parents if youth had behavior issues or became involved in worksite conflicts. Of the remaining four sites, two invited parents to attend orientation and/or work readiness training. One of these plus another two sites also invited parents to a summer graduation, recognition, or culmination ceremony at the end of the initiative.

B. The Content of Summer Experiences

To the extent possible, most sites tried to tailor these experiences to the needs and interests of each individual youth.

Table VII.1. Local Strategies for Serving Youth through the SYEI

Strategy	Number of Sites
Employment with Few Other Services	7
Employment plus Academics	13
Extent of Academic Offerings[a]	
Offered site-wide to interested youth	6
Offered only to a subset of youth	7

Source: Site visit interviews in 20 selected sites.
Note: N = 20 sites.
[a]Pertains only to those sites that offered employment plus academics.

Given this customization, it is important to understand not only the types of activities to which youth were exposed but also the day-to-day tasks they accomplished and their perceptions of the overall experience.

1. Types and Content of Academic Offerings

In those sites that offered classroom activities beyond work readiness training, academics ranged in both content and intensity. Some youth spent very few hours in academics before moving to a worksite; others spent the entire summer in the classroom and did not participate in summer employment. The content varied from occupational skills training to GED preparation and recovery of school credits.

Table VII.2 Industries for Occupational Skills Training

Industry	Number of Sites Offering Training
Health	4
Manufacturing	2
Culinary	2
Construction	2
Entrepreneurship	2
Renewable energy	1
Keyboarding, computer system building	1
Retail	1
Green career paths	1

Source: Site visit interviews in 20 selected sites.
Note: Total number of sites offering training = 10.

BOX VII.1. OCCUPATIONAL SKILLS TRAINING IN THE HEALTH CARE INDUSTRY

One provider in the *Denver, CO*, site developed a "pre-professional occupations" program, which staff called "the health care academy." Nearly 50 students participated in the program, which was "designed to provide youth exposure to health occupations and the opportunity to become certified in various industry-recognized certifications that will attempt to facilitate future success within the health care sector." Youth spent time at two hospitals in the region over six weeks and completed the following components: (1) industry-recognized training and certification (including training in the Health Insurance Portability and Accountability Act (HIPAA), cardiopulmonary resuscitation—health provider, first aid, and blood-borne pathogens), (2) SafeServ certification, (3) wheelchair transport, (4) oxygen safety, (5) hospital/medical terminology, (6) scope of practice, (7) careers within health care, and (8) "other related work skills." The program also included job-shadowing opportunities, exposure within health settings (including emergency rooms, supportive programs, front desk ambassadors, environmental services, cardiology, pulmonary physiology, minimally invasive diagnostic center, nursing, rehabilitation, imaging and food services), and networking and career mentorship.

At least some youth in five sites spent the entire summer in academic activities. As discussed in Chapter V, three sites reported that younger youth (aged 14, 15, and sometimes 16) spent the summer in work readiness training. A fourth site offered arts education to 12 youth as their summer work experience. This involved training in high-tech digital arts, including digital imaging, software programs, journalism, and desktop publishing. They worked on developing portfolios and documented a local music festival. Finally, a fourth site worked with a professor at a local four-year college to develop a college-level leadership development course for 21 youth. The program was based largely on team work activities and included work site field trips and community service projects.

BOX VII.2. ONE SITE OFFERED STRONG INCENTIVES FOR PARTICIPATION IN SUMMER EDUCATION

The site in *Albuquerque, NM*, placed a strong emphasis on the importance of education. It accomplished this in two ways. First, all youth who were assessed below a 12th-grade level on the Test of Adult Basic Education were encouraged to participate in a Key Train remediation course throughout the summer experience. Second, the site encouraged participation in other academic programs through a monetary incentive. Youth were given an additional $1 per hour in summer wages if they enrolled in a GED preparation course, postsecondary education, or an academic program that would result in a credential from an acceptable institution. In addition, youth received a $100 bonus upon completing one of these programs and receiving the related certification. As of the evaluation site visit in August 2009, the site reported that 85 percent of youth enrolled in the educational incentive program.

Ten sites offered occupational skills training to a portion of participating youth. The most common industry covered by training was health care, followed by manufacturing, culinary, construction, and entrepreneurship (see Table VII.2). Box VII.1 provides an example of training in the healthcare industry. Training programs lasted between one and six weeks and were typically administered by community colleges or local nonprofit organizations that served as summer providers or subcontractors. Three of the sites administered their occupational skills training programs as a component of pre-apprenticeship activities, discussed later in this chapter. Although figures were not available from all sites, most sites reported that between 5 and 10 percent of youth attended occupational skills training. To encourage participation in academics, one site used strong financial incentives (see Box VII.2).

Other academic offerings were less common. Two sites offered recovery of school credits, two offered GED preparation, and one offered remediation. At least one provider in three sites offered participating youth the opportunity to complete a 10-hour training certification from the Occupational Safety and Health Administration (OSHA). One site offered other certifications as part of the summer experience, including training in CPR, first aid, and babysitting.

YOUTH PERSPECTIVES: CERTIFICATIONS FROM THE OCCUPATIONAL SAFETY AND HEALTH ADMINISTRATION

"... OSHA helped a lot of people realize ... they were like, 'I didn't know that could happen.' So now I got my goggles on, my facemask and my gloves on, 'cause I'm not playing no games with chemicals and stuff."

"We got that certificate for doing OSHA. Like it makes you feel good, like you actually accomplished something, like you're not doing this for no reason."

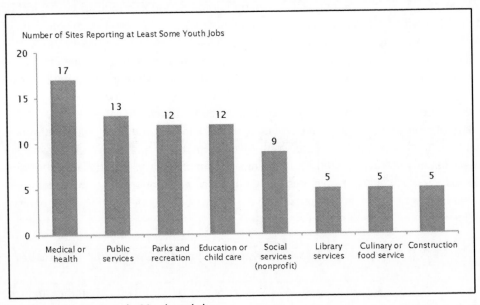

Source: Site visit interviews in 20 selected sites.

Notes: This table includes only industries mentioned by five or more sites. Industries cited by fewer than five include agriculture, legal services, retail, workforce development, automotive, computer services, media, hospitality, and finance. Green jobs were not categorized as a separate industry but were included in the most closely related industry above. These jobs are discussed in detail later in this chapter.

N = 20 sites.

Figure VII.1 Common Industries for Summer Work Experiences

2. Industries and Tasks of Youth's Summer Jobs

Youth were placed in a wide range of industries and occupations during their summer work experiences. As mentioned in Chapter VI, sites targeted the public, private, and nonprofit sectors when recruiting employers. The most common industries reported by site visit respondents—including LWIB and provider administrators, case managers, worksite recruiters, worksite supervisors, and employers—involved health care, public services, parks and recreation, and education/child care (see Figure VII.1). Seventeen sites placed youth in the health industry, with jobs in hospitals, nursing homes, mental health centers, dental offices, and other medical facilities. Another 13 had youth working in public services with county and municipal government agencies such as town hall, the chamber of commerce, the public housing department, the fire department, Veterans Affairs, or public works. Twelve developed programs in parks and recreation, which are discussed below in the section on green jobs. A comparable number of sites placed youth in educational institutions such as the superintendent or board of education offices, high schools, alternative schools, middle and elementary schools, and child care centers.

Within this wide range of industries, the most common duties that youth performed included administrative or clerical tasks, landscaping and outdoor maintenance, janitorial and indoor maintenance, and construction (see Table VII.3). Sixteen sites involved youth in administrative or clerical tasks, such as answering phones, filing, completing paperwork, and word processing. This appeared to be common within the top two industries: medical/health and public services. Another 14 sites reported that at least some youth were conducting park reclamation, green space protection, and urban forestry. Day-to-day tasks in this area often included weeding; raising plant beds; planting flowers, bushes, and trees; digging and laying recreation trails; raking; trimming bushes; and cleaning and restoring playgrounds. Two sites also reported that some older youth or youth with more work experience were placed in higher-level positions or supervisory roles in a range of different industries.

Information gathered from the youth who participated in focus groups mirrors these patterns quite closely. Among these youth, over 87 percent reported working as part of the summer initiative (see Table VII.4).[17] The most common industries included health care and social assistance, education services, and public administration. The most common job descriptions were office and administrative support; education, training, and library; and building and grounds cleaning and maintenance.

Table VII.3. Common Tasks Performed by Participating Youth at Worksites

Task	Number of Sites Reporting at Least Some Youth Performing This as Primary Task
Administrative or clerical duties	16
Park reclamation, landscaping, outdoor maintenance	14
Janitorial or indoor maintenance	12
Construction	11
Recycling computers, paper and other materials	10
Child care, senior care, counseling at summer camps or playgrounds	10
Weatherization and energy efficiency	8
Agriculture, community gardening, urban gardening	8
Food service	7
Service, sales, or hospitality	7
Computer repair or maintenance	6

Source: Site visit interviews in 20 selected sites.

Note: This table includes only tasks mentioned by five or more sites. Additional tasks cited by fewer than five sites include health care tasks, automotive repair and maintenance, and pet grooming or care.

N = 20 sites.

Table VII.4. Summer Work Experiences of Focus Group Participants

	All Participants (Percentages)
Working as part of the Recovery Act SYEI	**87.9**
Industry[a]	
Healthcare, social assistance	30.7
Education services	28.2
Public administration	9.7
Arts, entertainment, recreation	6.5
Retail trade	4.0
Administration and support, waste management, remediation services	2.4
Accommodations and food service	2.4
Other	4.8
Not specified	11.3
Occupation[a]	
Office and Administrative Support	27.4
Education, Training, and Library	24.2
Building and Grounds Cleaning and Maintenance	19.4
Personal Care and Service	5.7
Health Care Practitioners and Technical and Health Care Support	4.0
Food Preparation and Serving Related	3.2
Sales and Related	3.2
Community and Social Service	2.4
Arts Design, Entertainment, Sports, and Media	0.8
Installation, Maintenance, and Repair	0.8
Transportation and Material Moving	0.8
Not Specified	8.1
Sample Size	**124**

Source: Information forms completed by youth who participated in site visit focus groups.

Notes: Those who did not report working may have been enrolled in an academic program or may not have been assigned to an employer by the time of the site visit.

Data on industry were coded according to the North American Industry Classification System and occupations were coded based on the Standard Occupational Classification System.

[a] Data pertain only to those youth who reported working as a part of the Recovery Act SYEI at the time of the site visit.

Notably, both youth and staff reported that although youth's daily tasks may have been at entry level, participants were nevertheless exposed to careers within the industry where they were placed in a summer job. For example, a youth filing paperwork at a doctor's office learned about HIPAA regulations, observed health care workers interacting with patients, and experienced the general operations of a health care facility. A youth answering telephones at a nonprofit agency learned about the needs of the agency's clients, the array of services available to meet those needs, and strategies that case managers used to match clients to the most appropriate services. These experiences were reported as valuable in exploring career options and considering future jobs.

Table VII.5. Characteristics of Pre-Apprenticeship Programs

Site	Local Partner	Number Enrolled	Trades Covered During Training	Type of Work Experience
Seattle	South Seattle Community College and Manufacturing Industrial Council	100	Cement masonry, carpentry, drywall, energy auditing, weatherization, power utility work, heating and cooling, energy-efficient window-glazing	Private sector employers
Lehigh Valley	United Community Services	12	Building and construction trades	Visitors and field trips to worksites
Roanoke	Labor Local #980	10	Electrical, brick laying, sheet metal, carpentry and concrete	Habitat for Humanity

3. Pre-apprenticeship Programs

Across the 20 sites, only three sites developed pre-apprenticeship programs to support youth development in the trades (see Table VII.5). The Seattle program built upon an existing relationship; Lehigh Valley and Roanoke developed new programs from the ground up. In describing the motivation for developing a new pre-apprenticeship program, one site administrator explained that the region expects widespread retirement among baby boomers to create more demand for skilled workers in the building and construction industry.

Each pre-apprenticeship program lasted seven to eight weeks and covered a range of building and construction trades (see Table VII.5). All three targeted older youth: one enrolled only 17- and 18-year-olds, and two enrolled only those 18 or older. The two new programs enrolled small numbers; the existing program in Seattle enrolled 100 summer youth.

All three programs balanced classroom activities with practical hands-on experience. The Roanoke program consisted of four weeks in training followed by three weeks of on-site job training at a Habitat for Humanity construction site. The Seattle program involved three weeks of classroom training followed by worksite placements at private sector employers. Finally, the Lehigh Valley program involved two days per week in the classroom, one day per week with visitors who work in the field, and one day per week of hands-on activities during field trips.

Participants who completed two of these programs received an industry-recognized certification. In particular, one program included the 10-hour OSHA training that resulted in certification. The other site's program involved certifications in CPR and flagging for construction sites.

4. Green Jobs

Given the focus of the Obama administration on training workers for green jobs, the guidance provided by ETA placed a strong emphasis on "incorporating green work experiences" in SYEIs. This included both conservation and sustainable practices. Suggested areas included "retrofitting of public buildings, the construction of energy-efficient affordable public housing, solar panel installation, reclaiming of public park areas, or recycling of computers" (U.S. Department of Labor 2009d). Local areas were also encouraged to partner with community colleges to identify training opportunities or coursework that could be infused with green components.

Despite this guidance, study respondents across sites and even within sites often did not use a common definition for *green jobs*. What one person considered green, another did not. Administrators and staff in three sites explicitly expressed confusion over the definition. Many other sites categorized a range of different activities as green. For example, some sites considered green jobs to be those directly related to occupations in renewable energy, environmental consulting, and energy-efficient construction. Others discussed non-green jobs, such as administrative or maintenance functions, within green industries or organizations. Still others talked about green exposure within non-green jobs, such as the use of recycling and environmentally friendly products through day-to-day business practices. This mimics the findings presented by the GAO suggesting that local areas were unclear about what constitutes a green job (U.S. Government Accountability Office 2009). As a first step in defining the concept of green jobs, the Bureau of Labor Statistics developed new O*Net occupational classifications, released in summer 2009, to define green jobs.[18]

Keeping in mind local variation in the definition of green jobs, nine sites reported little success in placing summer youth in the green sector. Four of these reported that because the local area contained very little green industry, they were unable to tap into an existing market. Three felt that the time frame for implementation was too tight to develop jobs in new industries, including the green industry. One site also said that 80 percent of job placements were made in the nonprofit and public sectors; most local green jobs were found in the private sector. The remaining two sites had planned to identify green jobs but could not report why it was not happening. Despite their reported lack of success, all these sites were able to engage at least a small number of youth in green jobs.

By contrast, 11 sites reported success in developing green jobs for the summer. Some were not able to identify as many as they had planned but were still pleased with the proportion of youth who were exposed to a green work experience. Specific reports were not available from all sites, but five reported placing between 10 and 48 percent of youth in green jobs. The site reporting 48 percent involved youth in a large conservation effort.

Green jobs across all 20 sites were identified within the private, nonprofit, and public sectors. For example, youth were placed at for-profit organizations such as environmental consulting firms, a manufacturing facility that makes products to aid in oil cleanup, retailers selling organic and recycled products, and a company selling energy-efficient two-wheeled vehicles. Nonprofit worksites that involved green concepts included urban gardens, an agency focused on the fair production and distribution of food, and community development organizations doing graffiti removal and neighborhood beautification. Other sites partnered with government agencies—such as Parks and Recreation, the Forestry Department, and the Bureau of Land Management—to develop green jobs. Three sites developed their own conservation corps to do community cleanup without the assistance of other agencies, and one site partnered with the public housing authority to do energy audits.

Across all 20 sites, the most common green jobs included park reclamation, recycling, weatherization and energy efficiency, and community gardening (see Table VII.3). Less-common jobs were in industries such as construction, manufacturing of green building materials, and the energy sector, including solar and wind energy. As discussed above, some of these jobs involved administrative or maintenance tasks within a green industry, but youth were nevertheless exposed to the field. Park reclamation and related jobs appeared to involve the largest number of youth across sites. Box VII.3 provides some examples of green jobs reported across the sites.

BOX VII.3. EXAMPLES OF GREEN JOB PLACEMENTS

The site in *Bridgeport, CT,* partnered with the mayor's office on a green initiative. Several youth accompanied city staff as they visited local residents from door to door. The team talked to residents about energy efficiency strategies and made simple conservation efforts such as changing light bulbs.

In *Springfield, MA,* 30 youth helped to turn a dump site into an outdoor amphitheater for local concerts and events. On the worksite, they performed cleanup, made art out of recycled junk, and helped with community gardening.

The site in *Albuquerque, NM,* partnered with a local housing authority that received Recovery Act funds to support weatherization of homes. Several youth were placed at this site to answer telephone inquiries from residents and help them complete applications to receive weatherization services.

In *Pittsburgh, PA* , 140 youth who were served by the Student Conservation Association spent the summer building a playground for a new green development that serves homeless mothers and their children, building new recreation trails through low-income neighborhoods, building rock steps and tinder bridges, removing invasive plant species, and using global positioning systems to plot different tree species.

Two youth in *Lehigh Valley, PA,* performed administrative duties at an environmental consulting group aimed at "building stewardship" by helping academic, nonprofit, and professional clients develop environmentally sustainable practices and facilities.

Seven sites also tried to reinforce green concepts during classroom activities. As discussed in Chapter V, four sites discussed green concepts such as recycling and energy conservation in the work readiness training provided to all participating youth. Another site offered an occupational skills training in construction that discussed green technology, materials, and building techniques. Another site worked with the local community college to offer a two-week training course on green career paths. Finally, one site developed a program where students could receive college credits for the exploration of water quality jobs.

5. Community Service Activities

Many participating youth contributed to community service projects through their worksite placements and training activities. For example, occupational skills training in one site and a pre-apprenticeship program in another culminated in a community service project. Youth in career academies in two sites also participated routinely in these projects throughout the summer. Two other sites reported that, as part of their paid work experience, some youth volunteered at the local senior center, humane society, food pantry, community arts center, and Habitat for Humanity. Most of the parks reclamation and community cleanup activities were also considered service learning opportunities.

Only two sites, however, actively encouraged service learning beyond the worksite and classroom. In particular, one site offered a wage incentive of an extra $1 per hour to those youth who committed to completing 20 hours of community service over the course of the summer. Front-line staff developed lists of potential community service sites by contacting local nonprofit organizations. They also encouraged youth to identify their own opportunities through local churches and schools. Youth were required to have the community service supervisor sign a log tracking the hours completed. A provider in the second site encouraged volunteering through its health care program. Youth were taught the importance of volunteering, and staff helped them fill out a volunteer application at the local hospital so they could begin unpaid volunteer work outside their summer experience.

6. Youth Impressions of Summer Employment

Although the study is not designed to rigorously assess whether the tasks performed by youth provided "meaningful" work, youth in 19 of the 20 sites provided their perspectives during focus groups on the usefulness to them of their summer work experiences. Youth were largely positive, citing noticeable improvements in their soft skills, work performance, and resumes. They also expressed appreciation for the income. However, a smaller number of youth were unhappy with aspects of their summer jobs and suggested improvements to the summer initiative.

When asked what was most useful about their summer experience, at least some youth in 11 sites mentioned that it helped build their résumé and prepare them to find better jobs in the future. Youth in seven focus groups mentioned developing networking skills, contacts within the professional community, and solid references. Youth in six groups reported that their jobs were directly related to their long-term career goals. Finally, at least some youth in five sites were placed in jobs that were not related to their interests but felt that they still learned valuable lessons and skills.

Despite the largely positive response, at least one youth in seven sites expressed dissatisfaction with the work experience. Some complained that the work was boring, they did not like the work, or they did not have enough work to keep busy. Others said their jobs did not match their interests, and they were not learning useful skills. Two youth in one focus group also reported that they were paid less and worked fewer hours than they were promised during the application process. These youth suggested that to help improve the summer experience, sites should work harder to find the right employer match given youth interests and ensure that there is enough interesting work at each employer to justify a summer job.

YOUTH PERSPECTIVES: PERCEIVED BENEFITS OF WORK EXPERIENCE INCLUDE CONNECTIONS TO CAREER GOALS

"I want to be a writer, and this documentary, or the things that they have me doing, gives me the opportunity to get comfortable with using my voice and putting my ideas and my views out there. So, just a great experience on so many levels."

"My major is pre-social work, and I want to work for an adoption agency or foster care. And at the children's home [where I work], they have an adoption program and foster care, and I have had the opportunity to learn about the adoption process there."

"Hopefully I will be like an anesthesiologist. So that's why I'm majoring in chemistry. It's pre-med. [This summer] is like a shadowing experience, because I actually do go in during different surgeries, and I get to like see firsthand if I could see myself doing this."

"I work in the resource room, and I'll help customers do job search, if they need to make résumés. I really love it because I get to help people who don't have jobs who are looking for jobs and who really need help. . . . It's not what I wanted to do, [but] I kind of think I can make a career out of this, 'cause I really do enjoy it."

"There are the people that study the immune system and find the vaccinations. So I've been working with CMV—that's herpes—and cancer. Just trying to like basically connect all the dots so that they can find the vaccinations for herpes right now. I'm interested in immunology, so that was neat that I got that job, because that's like specifically what I am interested in."

"I don't ever want to be a landscaper. . . . The way it did help me was, because of this experience, now I know I would never want to do that. . . . I don't think there are negative parts about the job. I mean, the work is hard, but we learned, like, this is not what we want to do in the future."

YOUTH PERSPECTIVES: PERCEIVED BENEFITS OF WORK EXPERIENCE SUCH AS INCREASES IN PROFESSIONALISM, INTERPERSONAL SKILLS, AND LEADERSHIP

"This is like a perfect first job because like you learn like your responsibilities, you learn how to work with other people, your communication skills. . . .I'm like all excited about it. My first check came. It was exciting. . . .And I feel like after this I will find another job, since I have a reference."

"It didn't help me exactly with the career field I want to do, 'cause I want to do something in the medical field. The OSHA helped a little bit with like the medical stuff, but like I think it's more of the experience. Like you learn to adapt to different situations and how to deal with different people and how to be professional, and that helps you in any career."

"Usually I talk to people that I have something in common with. And so, like, now I work with people that I don't know, that I don't have anything in common with, that I normally wouldn't even talk to. . . . So I kind of learned to interact with people I don't know and how to work well with them."

"I want to be a social worker, and working at the science center helps me interact with a lot of different people and learn a lot of different stuff. So when I work at the information desk, I get a good chance to interact and like see how I can handle different problems."

"I got some leadership skills since [my worksite supervisor] said that I was going to be the supervisor for my group. . . . I'm not really such a good leader type, and I was really surprised, and it's been good. Like, people actually listened to me. . . . I'm good at following directions but wasn't used to giving them."

C. Matching Youth to Summer Experiences

To ensure a high-quality summer experience, local staff had to identify the most appropriate mix of services for each youth and match him or her to an academic program, an employer worksite, or both. This process was not trivial, given the volume of youth and the range of local experiences that were available. Many factors drove local decisions, including the personal interests of youth, the availability of worksites, and employer preferences.

1. Strategies to Match Youth to Academic Programs

Among the two-thirds of sites that offered academic programs either in addition to or instead of work experiences, youth were generally enrolled in academics based on an expressed interest or need. To match youth with occupational skills training, GED preparation, or postsecondary education, staff often identified appropriate academics based on interest inventories completed during the intake or orientation process. For example, a youth who expressed interest in becoming a nurse or doctor might be referred to a health care academy or training opportunity. In some cases, staff reviewed IEPs submitted by the local school district as part of eligibility determination to decide whether a youth was in need of school credit recovery or remediation. As mentioned earlier, three sites also placed younger youth in classroom activities based on their age and skill level.

Aside from age-based programs that engaged large numbers of younger participants in academics, most sites offered academics to only a limited number of summer participants. Even so, some sites had difficulty filling all of their academic slots. For example, one site offered up to 16 slots in each occupational skills training class but only enrolled 13 to 14 youth per class. Analysis of youth focus group transcripts suggest that some youth may not have been interested in attending school-based activities in a classroom setting during the summer months. Others appeared unaware of the availability of occupational skills training or other academic offerings.

2. Strategies to Match Youth to Summer Jobs

Ensuring a solid match between youth and employer was critical for both satisfying the employer's needs and maximizing the likelihood that the youth had a "meaningful" work experience. Sites reported that many employers had, for their new summer hires, specific requirements that had to be considered as sites determined their matching strategies. At least some providers in 10 sites reported that many worksites wanted older youth or youth with high school diplomas. As a result, it was more difficult to find placements for younger youth. Other employers had very specific requirements, such as hiring only youth residing in their municipality; youth with specific job skills such as computer literacy; youth with at least a 10th-grade reading level; or youth with a driver's license.

Given these factors and the volume of youth recruited for the SYEI, sites developed job-matching approaches that fell into four categories (see Figure VII.2). First, five sites required all or most youth to formally interview with prospective employers. Second, seven sites used matching processes that were driven largely by staff decisions but involved some interviewing based on employer requests. Third, another five sites empowered staff to match youth based on available information without any employer interviews. Finally, three sites had staff work directly with youth to select the most appropriate employer from the ones available.

Site administrators and staff in the 12 sites that conducted interviewing reported several reasons for using formal job interviews. The primary goals were (1) to simulate a real interview experience when applying for a job, (2) to ensure that the employer was comfortable with the match and was given the opportunity to choose the best candidate, and (3) to allow the youth to become familiar with the potential work environment.

Most interviewing involved one-on-one personal interactions between the employer and each interested youth. Site staff typically determined one or more potentially good employer matches for a given youth and then sent the youth on an interview with the worksite supervisor. The supervisor either hired the youth or asked to interview another candidate. One of these sites had staff accompany youth on their interviews to provide support, and two sites gave feedback to the youth based either on staff observation or the employer's feedback. In addition, two sites chose to hold site-wide job fairs for participating youth where employers interviewed multiple youth in the same day (see Box VII.4).

BOX VII.4. THE USE OF JOB FAIRS TO MATCH YOUTH TO EMPLOYERS

Athens, GA – At the start of the program, participating youth and employers attended a brief orientation session that ended with formal interviews. Youth were responsible for approaching worksite supervisors to initiate at least three interviews. Some interviews were held in small groups, while others were one on one. At the end of the job fair, each employer ranked his or her top three candidates. Staff then determined which youth would be placed with each employer.

Denver, CO – The site held three job fairs with the goal of having 95 percent of youth experience an interview. Youth were divided into groups by age and sent to a job fair with employers looking to hire from that age range. Employers were also color-coded by geographic region so the youth would interview with those close to their homes. During the job fairs, employers could either offer the job to a youth immediately or interview another youth.

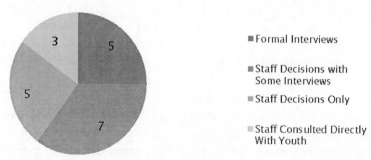

- Formal Interviews
- Staff Decisions with Some Interviews
- Staff Decisions Only
- Staff Consulted Directly With Youth

Source: Site visit interviews in 20 selected sites.
Note: N= 20 sites.

Figure VII.2. Job Matching Strategies

Respondents in the eight sites that chose not to conduct interviews said either that the time frame was too short or that it would have been logistically too difficult to interview all youth. Instead, these sites relied on staff either to review each youth's information or to talk directly with the youth before matching him or her to the most appropriate employer. Factors contributing to this matching process are discussed in detail below.

3. Factors Influencing the Job Matching Process

When asked what factors influenced their decisions to match youth with worksites, site staff reported four key considerations. First, 14 sites reported that youth interests expressed during application, orientation, or meetings with site staff drove the choice of employer. Second, 12 sites reported that the matching process was influenced by the job requirements based on age, experience, or skills or the types of employers available at the time of the matching. Third, 11 sites reported that direct employer feedback on candidates through the formal interviewing process was a major factor. Finally, 10 sites considered transportation needs and limitations when placing youth.

Six sites were not able to match youth with employers based on youth's expressed interests. Interviews with site staff and administrators revealed five main reasons.

1. **Timing of Employer Recruitment.** As discussed in Chapter VI, recruitment of employers typically began before youth recruitment, so available employers were not always the best fit based on youth interests.
2. **First-come, First-served Structure.** Most sites recruited enough employers given the total volume of enrolled youth. However, job matching was treated as first-come, first-served which may have limited the types of employers available to youth enrolled later in the summer.
3. **Need for Quick Placements.** Some local providers felt pressure to place youth quickly, which limited their time to make the best possible match.
4. **Employer Age Restrictions.** There were more limited opportunities for younger youth due to employer requirements.
5. **Lack of Communication.** Three sites reported that lack of communication resulted in difficulties matching youth to appropriate employers. In two of these sites, local providers were not given youth's intake paperwork and therefore did not know their interests before they arrived for service. The third site reported that youth recruitment and employer recruitment were conducted by completely separate staff, who did not coordinate efforts. As a result, there was a significant mismatch between the types of jobs that youth wanted and the employers that participated.

4. Challenges to Placing Youth in Jobs

Once youth were determined eligible and enrolled in the initiative, at least some in four sites were, after receiving orientation and work readiness training, not placed in jobs. In three of these sites, these youth interviewed poorly and were not selected or hired by any prospective employers. The fourth site reported that they enrolled more youth than could be matched given the number of appropriate employers that were available. None of these sites were able to provide solid estimates for the number of youth who were not placed.

Most of these youth were not provided with additional services and were not referred to other services within the community. One site notified the youth by mail that they would not receive further services from the initiative. Another site, however, reported that a small number of youth who interviewed poorly were hired directly by local service providers. This helped ensure that the youth were given the extra mentoring and guidance needed to have a successful experience and prevented the site from turning the youth away altogether.

D. Hours, Wages, and Process for Compensating Youth

The Recovery Act SYEI focused on putting money into the hands of youth. To balance their budgets, sites had to make trade-offs when identifying the number of youth to be served, the length of the summer initiative, the number of hours that each youth could participate, and the pay rate. Although generally successful when distributing their Recovery Act funds, most sites experienced at least some challenges in compensating youth.

1. Hours and Weeks Worked in Summer Jobs

The summer initiative ran from May through September 2009, for a total of 22 weeks. Most sites, however, did not begin serving youth until late June or early July. In determining the length of their initiatives, sites ultimately needed to weigh the pros and cons of providing more youth with less intensive experiences that lasted for fewer weeks or fewer youth with more intensive experiences that lasted more weeks.

Two sites discussed the challenges of determining the right initiative length. The LWIB in one site had to negotiate with a local provider as a result of differences in their service philosophies and developed a compromise on the number of youth that would be served and the number of weeks they could participate. The provider was accustomed to working intensively with at-risk youth over long periods of time. However, given the guidance provided by ETA to focus resources on summer 2009, the LWIB wanted the provider to enroll more youth for fewer weeks than what the provider wanted. In the second site, a LWIB administrator reported that the primary goal was to serve as many youth as possible in summer 2009, limiting the total number of work hours available to each youth. If the site were to implement the initiative again, the LWIB expected to serve fewer youth who could work more hours to maximize the benefit of their experience.

On average, summer experiences lasted seven weeks if a youth participated from start to finish. All but one initiative ranged from a minimum of 3 weeks to a maximum of 20. The one exception involved a provider that planned to continue serving its summer youth with Recovery Act funds through February 2010 even though it was not a regular WIA provider. Another site allowed a subset of youth who successfully completed their six-week work experience to work for additional weeks so the site could spend the rest of their Recovery Act allocation before the end of the summer.

On average, youth could work about 28 hours a week at their job placements, accumulating an average of just under 200 potential work hours if they completed the full initiative. One site paid youth for only 16 hours per week; seven sites paid youth full-time for 40 hours per week. Total hours ranged from 66 to 400 across the 20 sites. In three sites, the available work hours varied based on the age of the youth, with younger youth working fewer hours. Another site commented that older youth who were not governed by as many employer regulations were also able to work evening and overnight shifts.

Information gathered during youth focus groups reflects these same patterns. Focus group participants had been working for an average of just over five weeks by the time of our site visits in late July and August (see Table VII.6). On average, they worked 27 hours per week. Forty-five percent were working between 20 and 29 hours per week, with another 44 percent working 30 hours or more.

At least some youth in nine focus groups discussed the desire to work more hours for more weeks. The two primary reasons were (1) to continue participating in productive activities through the rest of the summer, and (2) to gain more work experience. A less-common reason was to earn more income.

2. Youth's Wages and Potential Earnings

On average, youth received $7.75 per hour for their summer work experience. Half the sites paid most or all youth the federal minimum wage of $7.25 per hour; two sites paid the state minimum wage of $7.40 and $7.75 per hour. Youth in another seven sites typically earned between $8.00 and $8.55 per hour. One site paid all youth $10 per hour.

Table VII.6. Work Hours and Wages of Focus Group Participants

	All Participants (Percentages Unless Specified)
Weeks Worked to Date	
1-2	7.3
3-4	25.0
5-6	27.4
7	31.5
Not Specified	8.9
Average (weeks)	5.4
Hours Worked/Week	
<20	11.3
20-29	45.2
30-34	25.0
35	18.6
Average (hours)	26.5
Hourly Wage	
$7.25	26.6
$7.26-$7.99	11.3
$8.00-$9.99	22.6
$10.00	10.5
Not Specified	29.0
Average (wage)	$8.33
Sample Size	**124**

Source: Information forms completed by youth who participated in site visit focus groups.
Note: Data pertain only to those youth focus group participants who reported working during the SYEI.

Subsets of youth in some sites, however, could earn more than their peers. For example, older youth sometimes earned more than younger youth. Two sites paid youth in supervisory roles additional wages, one offering an extra $1 per hour and the other offering between $9 and $12 for supervisors. Another paid some youth additional wages because one employer in the financial industry required a minimum of $12 per hour for entry-level positions. As discussed earlier, one site also paid an extra $1 per hour to those enrolled in a GED program or postsecondary education or agreed to conduct 20 hours of civic involvement.

Considering the average potential of 200 work hours, youth could earn total potential wages of about $1,526 over the summer.[19] Looking across sites, potential earnings ranged from a low of $986 to a high of $4,000 per youth. Seven sites had maximum earnings between $2,000 and $3,000. In 16 sites, however, the maximum earning potential varied across youth as a result of differences in the hours worked per week, the number of paid weeks, and the actual wage paid to each youth.

Members of our focus groups reported earning slightly more than the typical youth enrolled across all 20 sites. As shown in Table VII.6, focus group participants earned an average of $8.33 per hour. Just over one quarter earned the federal minimum wage of $7.25 per hour, and over 10 percent earned $10 or more. This may result from the fact that focus group participants were recruited by site staff and are not representative of any larger group.

3. Challenges to Payroll Processing

Responsible for paying wages to a large group of youth who served as new "summer employees," sites had to identify the best strategy to organize their payroll processing. Three organizational models emerged. First, half the sites chose to have local youth providers collect timesheets and issue paychecks to participating youth. Second, eight sites had the LWIB or its fiscal agent maintain responsibility for the process payroll. Finally, the LWIB's fiscal agent and the providers shared responsibility for payroll in the remaining two sites.[20]

Within these three basic payroll models, one LWIB and three local providers across four different sites contracted with an outside vendor to process payroll. In addition, at least one provider in two sites required that employers pay youth wages directly. Employers supplied documentation to the provider and were subsequently reimbursed with Recovery Act funds.

Challenges in the payroll process emerged quickly. Three sites reported that at least one provider had difficulty with cash flow. Under cost reimbursement contracts, providers in these sites were required to pay youth with their own funds, document the payments, and submit an invoice for reimbursement by the LWIB. This proved challenging for some small community-based providers. Providers in one of these sites also reported that they would not be reimbursed until the end of the initiative and therefore had to spend the bulk of their operating budgets to continue paying youth throughout the summer. To help prevent this problem, a different site gave providers the option of a 20 percent advance to cover initial wages before reimbursements began.

Scaling up local payroll systems to accommodate the volume of youth caused difficulties in seven sites. Providers were responsible for payroll in three of these sites, and the LWIB or its fiscal agent was responsible in the other four. A doubling of payroll in some locations created large workloads and significant stress among payroll staff. A small number of sites also experienced software or systems problems as they began processing the large increase in the payroll. These problems were generally resolved quickly.

Logistical problems in the flow and functioning of the payroll process arose in nearly three-quarters of local sites. Among these, eight reported issues with timesheet collection. In particular, four had difficulty collecting timesheets from some youth and employers in a timely manner, which resulted in delays in the processing of some paychecks. Another four sites reported errors or lack of signatures on some timesheets. Thinking forward to future summer initiatives, respondents from two of these sites reported that they would provide a more detailed timesheet orientation for both youth and employers. Respondents from another three sites also planned to consider electronic payroll systems or contracts with outside payroll vendors in the future.

Among those sites reporting logistical challenges, eight also experienced issues with paychecks. Three reported paycheck errors in the hours worked or amount paid to youth. Six of the eight also had problems distributing checks to youth. Among these, two reported that it was time-consuming and logistically challenging for provider staff to pick up paychecks from the LWIB's fiscal agent after payroll was processed and subsequently distribute checks to youth. Another reported that each youth had to sign a form documenting that he or she received the check. Two more sites reported that checks were often distributed late. Finally, one site said that youth did not receive their first paycheck until a month after the pay period ended. Most sites had already begun to remedy these problems by the time of the site visits; others were considering alternative strategies to help stem the problems in future summer initiatives.

When asked how they were able to process payroll without problems, the sites that did not experience challenges with payroll logistics simply reported that they had the existing infrastructure to handle the influx of youth or had efficient processes in place through previous WIA summer programming efforts. All of these sites required that employers sign youth timesheets. However, their processes for collecting timesheets varied with staff picking up timesheets from worksites, youth dropping off timesheets at the provider office, or employers sending or faxing timesheets to the provider. Paychecks were generally either distributed by staff through visits to the worksites or youth picked up their paychecks at the provider office.

Beyond payroll processing, 3 of the 20 sites reported that youth had to pay significant surcharges to cash their checks. In one of these sites, staff tried to educate youth about how to open a bank account to avoid these charges. However, staff reported that many youth were hesitant to do so either because of distrust of the banking system or concerns that their parents would access their wages through the account. Although many youth reported that their summer salaries helped support their household, staff members in another three sites also mentioned that youth expressed concern over the possibility that their parents would confiscate their wages.

VIII. ASSESSING YOUTH PROGRESS

Because the SYEI represented a significant investment of public resources, it was incumbent upon local sites to assess their progress and the progress of participating youth. Since most youth had little or no work experience, they naturally had to work on developing the attributes of good workers. Recognizing this, sites established procedures to provide assistance to youth both during and after their job placements and to track their progress over time. Furthermore, they needed to ensure that employers were meeting the expectations set for them based on their agreement to participate in the initiative.

This chapter discusses sites' efforts to track and document the progress of youth who participated in the SYEI. Section A discusses strategies sites used to monitor youth activities and employer compliance while youth were at their summer jobs. Section B then turns to data collection efforts to assess increases in the work readiness skills of participating youth and to gather feedback on program performance. Finally, Section C discusses the efforts sites made to ensure a smooth transition of youth to new opportunities after the SYEI came to an end.

KEY FINDINGS: ASSESSING YOUTH PROGRESS

- **Staff felt that in-person visits were critical to youth's retention and success in the workplace.** Sites used a combination of formal and informal monitoring techniques to assess youth progress at their jobs and proactively prevent major problems that could result in termination or drop-off.
- **Flexibility in the measurement of increases in work readiness resulted in inconsistency across sites and sometimes within sites.** To assess growth, most, but not all, sites measured work readiness skills before and after youth participated in activities. However, sites varied substantially in the timing of these assessments, the methods of capturing data (such as through staff observation, employer feedback, and testing of youth knowledge), and the types of skills assessed.
- **Sites planned to use established linkages with schools, regular WIA services, and other community partners to transition youth to post-summer activities.** However, respondents reported that budget constraints and other factors may have limited the number of youth who could be transitioned to the regular WIA youth and adult programs.
- **Local administrators, staff, and employers feared that the weak economy would diminish the number of participants placed in permanent jobs.** However, because site visits were conducted during the summer, the study was unable to assess the actual rates of permanent placement among SYEI participants.

A. Monitoring Worksite Experiences

Throughout the summer, staff spent significant time and energy following the progress of participating youth once they were placed at jobs. They sought to ensure that youth were receiving the mentorship they needed to learn and grow and were safe and productive in their workplaces. Although the study is not designed to measure their success in these efforts, site visit interviews examined the range of monitoring strategies that emerged across the sites.

YOUTH PERSPECTIVES: MENTORING BY WORKSITE SUPERVISORS

"I'm thinking about being a teacher when I'm older, so right now like interacting with kids, and even the teachers there, they help me. They give me lessons on how I should, like, talk to the kids and stuff, so that's helping me out a lot."

"There's a bunch of psychologists that are already there. They invite us to lunch, and we just talk, and I go over what steps they took to get to the position that they're in. And, you know, what I can do."

"I'll be like a step ahead of the game. [My supervisors] want to, like, sit down with me and like show me what classes I should be taking and what colleges I should be going to. . . . I'll actually be, like, ready to just go straight to [the local university]."

---

1. Adult Mentoring at Youth Worksites

Youth at all but one site were connected with an adult mentor at the start of their summer experience. At 12 sites, the worksite supervisor or a coworker at the job served as the youth mentor. At the other seven, worksite personnel and front-line staff shared responsibility for mentoring. As discussed in Chapter VI, sites discussed mentorship expectations with employers at the beginning of the summer, emphasizing that participants required more attention than regular employees. Many employers who were interviewed explained that their organizations had a vested interest in the success of these youth, and therefore they took their roles as mentors very seriously. Though the intensity of mentorship varied across sites, most youth were reported to interact with their worksite mentors daily and their program mentors less frequently.

Local staff and employers reported that mentoring relationships focused heavily on soft skills such as punctuality, work ethic, communication, and professionalism. Respondents felt that hard skills that were directly relevant for the job were easier to teach and, in some ways, less critical to the success of a youth's summer experience. Despite ETA guidance that participants should not be treated as "regular employees," respondents in seven sites stated that treating youth like "regular employees" was a valuable mentorship tool that taught them the importance of worksite performance and expectations.

2. Formal and Informal Monitoring of Worksites

To ensure that youth were having "meaningful" work experiences and receiving sufficient mentoring and oversight, sites expended significant staff resources monitoring youth activities once they were placed on a job. Although all 20 sites made in-person visits to worksites, two different approaches to monitoring emerged: (1) 11 sites used formal monitoring that involved site visits using a strict protocol, and (2) 17 sites used informal monitoring where staff informally dropped by employers to check in with youth and supervisors and to observe conditions at the site. Nine of these 17 used only informal monitoring; the remaining 8 used a combination of formal and informal.

Box VIII.1. Example of Formal Worksite Monitoring Activities

In *Hazard, KY,* youth providers across the site hired a total of 21 temporary summer employees as site monitors. The site monitors were responsible for visiting the worksites weekly. The providers were asked to target college students for the site monitor positions to further the mission of providing employment opportunities to young adults. Though some college students were hired, the monitors were mostly older adults, including school teachers and retirees. Site monitors were trained as a group by the lead agency using a manual that described the rules governing worksites. Monitors have three main responsibilities.

Worksite Checklists. Monitors completed a visual checklist containing 16 questions about the type of work youth were performing, the availability of adequate equipment, the number of youth assigned to the worksite, the number of youth present during the visit, safety concerns at the worksite, and whether youth were on-task.

Supervisor Interviews. Monitors conducted a supervisor interview using a list of 32 questions developed by the lead agency. The interview covered safety, child labor laws, the work activities for SYEI youth, procedures in case of an accident, employers' benefits from the SYEI, and any performance issues and resolutions. The supervisor was interviewed once over the course of the SYEI, and the interview took 10 to 15 minutes.

Youth Interviews. The lead agency randomly selected about 10 percent of each provider's participants to interview. Monitors reported trying to schedule these interviews near the end of a youth's work experience. Questions included the type of work performed, how the youth heard about the program, whether their supervisor was always on location while they were working, transportation issues, and any problems experienced.

Formal monitoring generally consisted of in-person visits to a worksite, during which a staff member used a standard protocol or monitoring checklist to assess quality (see Box VIII.1). Monitors followed three primary activities (1) speaking with the supervisor; (2) speaking with the youth, and (3) observing working conditions, safety, and compliance with child labor laws. The goal of these activities was to identify any workplace safety or compliance issues that needed to be resolved, as well as issues with the employer (such as inadequate supervision of youth activities), or the youth (such as chronic tardiness or poor attitude). One site also reported providing technical assistance to employers as needed. For example, one worksite lacked a sexual harassment policy, so the monitor helped the site develop one. At all but one of the sites that used this formal strategy, monitoring visits were the responsibility of the lead agency. In the last site, provider staff was responsible for monitoring activities.

Across the 11 sites that did at least some formal visits, only 3 sites visited worksites more than twice during the summer (see Table VIII.1). In these sites, visits occurred either weekly or every two to three weeks. In the other sites, visits occurred either once or twice over the course of the summer. In fact, four of these visited only 10 to 50 percent of participants' worksites. The remaining two sites did not specify frequency.

Informal monitoring was more casual and typically occurred as staff picked up youth timesheets or dropped off paychecks. While at the employer, monitors would ask both the employer and the youth if there were any issues or problems. They would also informally observe working conditions. Front-line staff from local providers in 15 sites and from the lead agency in 2 sites were responsible for these visits. Most monitoring visits took 30 minutes but took as little as 5 or as many as 90 minutes if there were issues at the worksite.

Though the frequency of informal visits varied across sites, most sites reported visiting worksites on either a weekly or a biweekly basis. One site did not visit all worksites; instead, staff visited employers with whom they had not worked in the past. Monitors from four sites reported that they would have liked either to visit more worksites or visit them more often. In two of these four sites, the sheer volume of youth and worksites prevented the intensity of monitoring that staff would have preferred. In the other two, monitors lamented that the rural nature of the local sites resulted in distances between employer locations that required up to three hours of driving, which made it difficult to visit worksites as often as desired.

Given the intensity of monitoring efforts, three sites hired new staff with the sole purpose of visiting and monitoring worksites. The monitors from at least two of these sites attended site monitor training and were furnished with a handbook. As discussed in Chapter III, another six sites hired staff members to serve as job coaches or case managers who also conducted informal monitoring visits as part of their responsibilities.

Table VIII.1. Types and Frequency of Monitoring Visits

	Number of Sites
Type of Monitoring	
Formal Monitoring Only	3
Informal Monitoring Only	9
Both Formal and Informal Monitoring	8
Frequency of Formal Visits	
None	9
Weekly to each worksite	1
Every 2-3 weeks to each worksite	2
Twice to each worksite	1
Once to each worksite	1
Once to only a subset of worksites	4
Unknown	2
Frequency of Informal Visits	
None	3
Daily	1
Weekly	4
Biweekly	5
As needed	5
Unknown	2

Source: Site visit interviews in 20 selected sites.
Note: N = 20 sites.

3. Importance of In-Person Monitoring Visits

Almost unanimously, respondents agreed that in-person visits to worksites were crucial to the success of the SYEI. Many sites described the visits as a way to proactively prevent major problems from occurring. Instead of waiting for a youth or an employer to contact staff with a large issue, staff were able to identify problems early and mediate to prevent youth from quitting or being removed or fired from a summer job. In addition to visiting worksites, many sites stayed on top of issues by maintaining regular phone or email contact with both employers and youth.

YOUTH PERSPECTIVES: THE BENEFITS OF STAFF MONITORING ACTIVITIES

"It's been nice that [the worksite monitor] comes by about every two weeks, just to say hi and see how everything is going. So, I mean, if we had a problem, whatever that may be, then we would be able to say, 'Hey, let's talk,' and not have to go find her."

"When [our supervisors] try to boss us around and we don't go for that, then they look at [the worksite monitor]. . . . I mean, like, with the job we just finished up today, putting the tar down, the guy, he was rude, disrespectful, had an attitude, but today he was cool, after him and [the worksite monitor] talked, and [the monitor] let him know, 'They're kids,' you know. 'Some of them are kids. Some are young adults. You have to treat them with respect. They see things differently than you see things.'"

Regular monitoring was also an effective way to build rapport with youth and employers. Staff reported, and employers confirmed, that most employers welcomed the help that worksite monitors could provide, including assistance with monitoring youth performance, tracking youth attendance, and addressing attitude issues. At one site, for example, provider front-line staff used the monitoring visits to discuss the potential for permanent placements for participating youth or additional training that youth might need.

None of the sites reported issues gaining access to worksites, with the exception of one instance in which a worksite was terminated for refusing to cooperate with the site's visitation policy. (This occurred before a youth was placed with the employer.) At most sites, providers told employers, either during employer recruitment and orientation or via the worksite agreement, that staff would be visiting throughout the summer. As a result, many sites reported being able to drop by worksites unannounced.

Only one site reported finding a major violation of an employer worksite agreement. A youth was being left unsupervised for long periods of time and had to be removed from the worksite. One site also encountered more minor violations that were quickly remedied, such as employer failure to post required child labor law posters or emergency evacuation routes. All other sites indicated that they did not encounter any violations.

To help prevent such violations, three sites also trained youth to identify worksite issues so they could serve as their own site monitors. These sites spent time explaining workplace safety and child labor laws to participating youth during orientation. They then instructed youth to contact staff if violations occurred.

4. Strategies to Handle Discipline and Poor Performance

Every site dealt with at least some youth who performed poorly on the job. However, these situations rarely resulted in youth being terminated from the initiative. As described above, sites made frequent visits to worksites and maintained regular communication with supervisors to help identify problems early and remediate them quickly. The most common worksite issues reported by staff were chronic tardiness, unexcused absences, poor work ethic, and poor attitude.

Sites addressed issues quickly, used conflicts as learning experiences, and gave youth second chances. When they encountered a workplace issue, staff worked with both the youth and the employer to formulate a solution. Often talking with the youth about the issue and the importance of proper worksite behavior was enough to solve the problem. One provider used a "three strikes, you're out" policy for minor offenses to allow youth an opportunity to correct inappropriate behaviors such as lateness or talking back to superiors. Other sites used more intense measures to deal with problematic behavior. For example, one provider used a one-day suspension policy to help youth "cool off" and reflect on their mistake before returning to work.

If a performance situation did not improve, or if the issue could not be resolved with mentoring and guidance, or if a youth was fired by an employer, youth were typically moved to another worksite or program activity. Two sites had specific plans for youth who were not successful at their first or second employers. One provider placed youth in a job at their own organization so staff could watch them closely and provide more intensive mentorship. At the other site, youth with chronic work behavior issues were placed in a training program aimed at helping to make behavioral adjustments that would aid in employment success.

Despite these staff efforts to mediate performance issues, all sites reported that a small portion of youth were terminated by the initiative, quit their jobs, or dropped out. Half the sites reported terminating at least some youth. This typically happened only after they attempted mediation between staff, the youth, and the employer; a change in worksite; and other avenues. At least two of these sites, however, reported that certain offenses, such as stealing and use of drugs, resulted in immediate termination. A small proportion of youth in all 20 sites also chose to drop out or quit their jobs during the course of the summer. Although data were not available on the proportion of terminations and dropouts in the study sites, anecdotal reports appear consistent with the national data presented in Chapter II that 82 percent of youth completed their summer work experience.

Three sites credited their emphasis on quality job-matching for youth's generally good worksite performance. Though overwhelmed by the number of youth and quick initiative start-up, these sites indicated that taking the time to match youth with the appropriate worksites was crucial to the success of placements. At one of the sites, staff also arranged a meeting with the youth and the employer prior to the start of the summer work experience. At this meeting, youth disclosed physical challenges and skills deficiencies so that the employer was aware of his or her strengths and weaknesses on the first day of work. Another site reported working closely with employers during the recruitment phase so "they knew what they were getting into" and were prepared for behavior challenges resulting from youthfulness and inexperience.

B. Assessment of Youth Experiences

To document their success in serving youth with Recovery Act funds, sites assessed the experiences of participants through a number of methods, including formal performance measures, additional data collection activities, and feedback from participants themselves. As discussed in Chapter II, ETA streamlined performance-reporting requirements so that sites were responsible for collecting only one outcome measure, namely the attainment of a work readiness goal. Sites were also required to report on the rate of completion of summer work experiences. Almost half the sites, however, chose to collect additional data beyond these two measures. More than three-quarters also solicited feedback from participants to promote continuous quality improvement.

1. Use of Standard Methods for Measuring Work Readiness Skill Increases

Administrators and front-line staff were overwhelmingly appreciative of the limited performance-reporting requirements for the SYEI. They often noted that the removal of other outcome measures made implementing the summer activities much more feasible. Given the tremendous effort required to ramp up efforts, engage youth and employers, and monitor youth activities, LWIB administrators reported that it would have been too difficult to track additional performance outcomes for such a large group of youth in such a short time. They also commented that the brevity of the summer initiative limited their ability to affect multiple dimensions of a youth's long-term success.

The measurement of success achieving work readiness goals was complicated and variable across sites.[21] The flexibility given to sites in the development of their work readiness measures resulted in inconsistency across and sometimes within sites. This was reported as an area for improvement in the GAO report, which suggested that "while many program officials, employers, and participants we spoke with believe the summer youth activities have been successful, measuring actual outcomes has proved challenging and may reveal little about what the summer activities achieved" (U.S. Government Accountability Office 2009). This study found similar results in the 20 selected sites.[22]

To maintain consistency, 15 sites established a standard measurement procedure for achievement of work readiness goals within their sites. Two additional sites individualized the work readiness measurement by youth based on needs for performance improvements. The final three sites allowed providers to decide on their measurement tool. Interestingly, these three sites involved a total of 25 providers, and thus potentially 25 variations in measurement. In describing the reasons for choosing this strategy, an administrator from one of these sites reported that it would be unfair to require providers serving special populations, such as English-language learners, to be judged on the same measure as other programs.

Among the 15 sites that used a standard measure, three administered the initiative through the lead agency with no subcontractors, two involved only a single subcontractor, and the remaining 10 contracted with multiple service providers. In those sites that involved multiple organizations, the lead agency typically defined the measurement tool and trained local staff either formally or informally on how to gather the appropriate information.

2. Timing of Work Readiness Skill Measurement

The work readiness outcome measure is intended to capture "a measurable increase in work readiness skills." To capture this increase, three-quarters of all sites performed pre-post tests of youth, where youth's work readiness skills were assessed initially as a baseline near the start of their participation and reassessed at a later stage to measure increases. Four sites used a post-only test, measuring work readiness skills at a single point in time near the end of the initiative. The final site conducted ongoing evaluations of youth performance throughout their summer experience to formally measure progress in work readiness skills. The obvious advantage of the pre-post design is the ability of sites to measure the difference in scores between two points in time using the same standard tool. Post-only tests do not include a consistent measurement of the youth's skills before participation in the initiative.

Despite the advantages of pre-post assessments, the timing of these assessments also played an important part in the quality of measurement. Five of the 15 sites that used pre-post tests conducted them at the beginning and end of the work readiness training component, generating results before youth were placed in a work experience. This could serve as an indicator of whether the youth was prepared for a worksite placement, serving as a "selling point" to potential summer employers. However, as a formal performance measure for federal reporting, this strategy could provide a reasonable assessment of whether youth learned the training material, but did not assess the youth's ability to implement that knowledge on the job. In addition, such testing practices could also measure learning from only a limited number of classroom hours, in some sites as little as 16 hours of work readiness training.

The remaining 10 sites that conducted pre-post tests assessed work readiness skills during the first or second week of the youth's participation and again toward the end of their work experience. Three of these sites also assessed skills at a midpoint in the initiative. The timing of tests in these sites potentially allowed sites to measure the gains in work readiness skills from both classroom activities, such as work readiness training and other academic experiences, and practical work experience at an employer.

3. Sources of Data for Work Readiness Skill Measurement

Staff, employers, and youth could each bring a unique perspective to the assessment of a participant's growth through the course of the SYEI. Administrators and staff across all 20 sites reported using different combinations of these three perspectives to assess youth progress (see Table VIII.2). First, 13 sites had local staff formally document observations or assessments of youth knowledge and performance. Second, 17 areas gathered written feedback from worksite supervisors. Third, nine sites conducted formal written tests of youth's work readiness knowledge. As shown in the table, however, not all of these assessments from the different perspectives were used in the formal calculation of work readiness sent to states for federal performance reporting. Although four sites collected data from all three sources, none used all three in their formal measurement tool.

A review of local measurement tools revealed eight key skill sets that were assessed among youth: (1) work habits, (2) attitude and interpersonal skills, (3) knowledge relevant for future employment, (4) communication, (5) portfolio development, (6) motivation and self-image, (7) job-specific skills, and (8) daily-living skills. More than three-quarters of sites measured youth progress in developing solid work habits (see Table VIII.3). More than half assessed work habits, attitudes, and interpersonal skills. The remaining skill sets were reported by smaller subsets of sites. One site gathered data about six of these eight categories in their assessment tool; the others measured four or fewer.

One-third of sites reported that they formally discuss the results of the work readiness assessment with each participating youth. These sites reported that this strategy allows staff to provide feedback to youth early in the initiative, based on the pre-test, on the areas where they need to continue improving. It also highlights youth's improvement when they were reassessed at the end of their experience. All these require youth to sign off on the assessment, indicating that they were informed of their progress.

Table VIII.2. Types of Methods Used to Assess Youth Progress

Assessment Method	Number of Sites Using This Method to Assess Youth Progress	Number of Sites Using This Method in Formal Measurement of Work Readiness Increases
Observation or assessment by staff	13	11
Feedback from worksite supervisors	17	9
Direct testing of youth knowledge	9	9
All three methods	4	0

Source: Site visit interviews in 20 selected sites.
Note: N = 20 sites.

Table VIII.3. Skills Assessed in Work Readiness Indicators

Skill Set	Specific Areas Covered in Assessment[a]	Number of Sites Measuring This Skill Set
Work habits	Exhibits appropriate dress and hygiene Attendance Punctuality Follows instructions/rules/procedures Works to best of ability Adheres to quality standards Organizational skills Initiative Time management and task completion Ability to work independently Works without distracting others	16
Attitude and interpersonal skills	Positive attitude toward supervisor, co-workers, and customers Accepts feedback constructively Contributes to team effort	11
Knowledge relevant for future employment	Career exploration Labor market information Job searching strategies Expectations of employer Interviewing skills Budgeting and finances	7

Table VIII.3. (Continued)

Skill Set	Specific Areas Covered in Assessment[a]	Number of Sites Measuring This Skill Set
Communication	Reading Writing Verbal	6
Portfolio development	Resume Cover letter Job applications List of references	6
Specific job skills	<As appropriate>	4
Motivation and self-image	Motivation Adaptability Effective coping skills Problem-solving skills Acquiring an improved self-image	3
Daily living skills	Using the phone Telling time Shopping Renting an apartment Opening a bank account Using public transportation	1

Source: Site visit interviews in 20 selected sites.

Notes: Skill sets shown in this table were developed from a review of local measurement tools. N = 20 sites.

[a] Assessments used by sites may not include all topics listed under a specific skill group.

4. Sites' Additional Data Collection Activities

Beyond the work readiness measure and completion rate for summer work experiences, states were required to report monthly on a small number of data items, including the number and characteristics of youth served under the Recovery Act and the services they received (discussed further in Chapter II). States and local sites, however, used data systems that could gather much richer information on youth experiences. These systems were used for regular WIA reporting requirements as well as state and local planning and management. Many sites chose to collect this additional information to support their local management of the SYEI, coordinate participant services effectively, and track overall progress of youth. This data could potentially be used in future evaluations to glean further insights into youth experiences and outcomes.

Administrators in 9 of the 20 sites reported collecting additional data on youth that were not required as part of federal performance reporting. Four sites chose not to collect additional data. In the remaining seven sites, it was unclear whether local staff consistently collected additional data that was required under the regular WIA program but were optional for the SYEI.

Sites most commonly collected additional data on services, participant outcomes, or both. Among the nine that collected additional data, seven chose to collect richer information on services, such as participation in each of the 10 service elements required under the regular WIA program or specialized services offered by the site. Six sites collected additional outcome measures; these could include return to school, permanent job placement, and receipt of educational certificates. Four sites also gathered additional data on youth's summer work experiences. The most common elements in this category included codes for employer, industry and occupation codes, hours worked, and wages. One of these four sites collected the additional worksite data through its accounting system rather than its WIA reporting system. Although many of these sites gathered data on common topics, their variable definitions and methods of measurement varied substantially, potentially limiting the feasibility of cross-site analysis if data were gathered for future evaluations.

5. Strategies to Gather Feedback from Youth

Seventeen sites implemented processes to gather feedback from all or some summer participants. In particular, 14 chose to conduct satisfaction or exit surveys with all or some of their participating youth. Of these sites, 10 conducted surveys with all participating youth. In the remaining four sites, some providers chose not to administer surveys or only a sample of youth was chosen to participate.

Three sites chose different methods of collecting feedback. One conducted focus groups with a subset of youth to get their verbal feedback on the summer experience. Another required site monitors to conduct one-on-one exit interviews with all youth. The last conducted in-person interviews with a randomly selected sample of 10 percent of youth.

Local administrators in the 17 sites that gathered feedback reported that the primary goal was to foster continuous program improvement for both summer initiatives and the regular WIA program. Some areas also used these instruments to assess employer performance to determine whether they were suitable for future youth placements. The remaining three sites that chose not to collect feedback from youth, reported they did not do so because of a lack of budget and a lack of time.

C. Youth Progress beyond Summer 2009

Once the summer initiative was over, youth moved to new phases and looked for new opportunities. The largest proportion of participants planned to return to school. Some youth could receive additional services from the workforce investment system and other organizations within the community. Still other youth sought to move into permanent jobs. As summer came to a close, sites had to decide how to transition participants into these various paths, as well as whether and how to track their progress throughout the school year. The timing of evaluation site visits prevented observations of what happened after the summer initiative ended; nonetheless, respondents were able to discuss their plans and expectations for the fall.

1. Transitioning Youth to Post-summer Activities

The goals and next steps of summer participants could differ substantially based on their age and education status. For most younger, in-school youth, the summer initiative served as an opportunity to use their summer break to earn money and gain work experience. A new semester at school began when the summer ended. For many older and out-of-school youth, there was no clear opportunity waiting at the end of the summer. As a result, sites had to tailor their strategies to help these different populations make meaningful transitions into the fall.

To facilitate transitions to post-summer activities for in-school youth, sites planned to use their established relationships with the public and private school systems and local WIA youth program. About half the sites reported plans to leverage their relationships with schools to assure that in-school youth returned to the classroom at the end of the summer. They also planned to use these connections to encourage out-of-school youth to seek educational services as needed. The local school district was a summer provider at four sites, and providers from six other sites reported having strong relationships with area schools. In two of these sites, for example, summer providers had front-line staff stationed in either a local public school or an alternative school building. This reportedly allowed frequent contact with youth and helped school officials coordinate services more effectively.

Budget constraints, however, may have influenced sites' ability to serve summer youth through regular WIA programs beyond September. As mentioned in Chapter III, many sites planned to spend all or most of their Recovery Act allocations during the summer. Most sites also reported that their regular WIA programs typically had waiting lists due to excess demand. As a result, six sites reported at the time of the study's site visits that financial constraints would limit referrals of summer youth to regular WIA youth and adult programs. Providers from all six of these sites indicated that staff would attempt to link youth with other, non-WIA programs when possible.

Sites also reported other reasons that would limit their ability to transition out-of-school youth 18 or older to the WIA adult program in the fall of 2009. Staff from five sites felt the youth program was more appropriate for most participants. They believed the adult program could be intimidating and placed less emphasis on critical services, such as mentoring, counseling, and intensive case management, that are vital to youth success. Administrators in one site added that co-enrollment in both the adult and the youth programs could be confusing and cause youth to be unsure of which front-line staff to contact when issues arise. Because of these various factors, administrators and staff in 14 sites expected that few or no participants would be enrolled in the adult program.

To encourage continued services for older youth, 12 sites reported that their states applied for and received waivers to use the work readiness indicator as the only performance measure for youth aged 18 to 24 who participate in only work experience beyond the summer months. Given the timing of our site visits during summer 2009, it is unclear whether these waivers had any influence on staff decisions to continue serving older youth into the fall.

Despite budget constraints and other inhibiting factors, connections to the WIA youth program were nevertheless expected to yield opportunities for at least some youth, both in and out of school, between the ages of 14 and 21. As noted in Chapter III, all or some summer providers in most sites administered the regular WIA youth program. As a result, summer staff were knowledgeable about WIA program eligibility requirements and services, familiar with regular WIA youth staff, and acquainted with enrollment procedures. They expected to be able to transition, to the WIA youth program, youth between the ages of 14 and 21 who needed assistance beyond the summer months. Staff from nine of these sites planned to meet with each youth toward the end of the summer experience to determine which, if any, WIA program was appropriate. Staff reported that the primary considerations in this decision were age, need, interest, and academic achievement. Importantly, nearly all sites also reported that a small portion of SYEI participants were already enrolled in regular WIA services before the summer months.

2. Challenges to Permanent Job Placements

Beyond services provided through WIA and other local programs, many youth, particularly those out of school, hoped to use their summer experience to transition into a permanent job. Statistics on the number of youth able to transition into permanent placements were unavailable during site visits. However, at least 17 sites reported that at least a small portion of youth would find steady jobs as a result of their summer experience (see Box VIII.2 for examples). As discussed in Chapter II, about 13 percent of all SYEI participants nationwide were reported to have been placed in work experience outside the summer months.

BOX VIII.2. EMPLOYERS THAT HOPED TO HIRE YOUTH PERMANENTLY

The supervisor of a day care center hoped, funds permitting, to offer jobs to two young men who worked at her center through the SYEI. She reported that these youth had worked hard all summer and were now trained for the position. She added that the youth might opt to pursue education instead, but that she hoped they would eventually return to work at the center. She explained that it is important for the children at the center to have more male role models and felt the SYEI was one way to encourage males to enter the childcare profession.

A local hospital hired 15 youth as part of the SYEI to serve as ward clerks (data entry), nutritional aides (food service, preparation, and cashiering), file clerks, admissions clerks, and maintenance workers. An administrator reported that because of the high cost of training youth just for the summer, the hospital would not have been able to offer summer employment without the Recovery Act. She strongly believed in the importance of summer employment because it offers the youth opportunities to explore career paths. She also felt the SYEI staff helped manage an otherwise burdensome application process, including performing background checks on behalf of the hospital. The hospital planned to hire one of the youth permanently as an admissions clerk, a position that is above entry level.

To facilitate permanent placements, almost half the sites reported that they relied on private for-profit companies to hire youth. As mentioned in Chapter VI, providers at four of these sites targeted private employers for recruitment as summer worksites because they were more likely to hire youth permanently. At least two of these sites also focused on matching older youth with private employers that were more likely to offer permanent jobs.

Respondents in seven sites did not expect public and nonprofit organizations to hire youth after the SYEI stopped subsidizing their wages. During focus groups, nonprofit and public employers at five of these sites stated that tight budgets and limited capacity typically precluded them from hiring youth permanently. At a sixth site, one provider did not speak with employers about permanent placements at all because most were nonprofits or public agencies that probably could not hire youth. At another site, where many providers directly employed youth, at least six nonprofit and public providers indicated that they would not be able to hire their youth permanently once the Recovery Act funds were gone.

Nine sites also expressed concern that the current recession would limit the number of permanent placements. For example, one private employer stated that they typically hire 25 percent of the youth they employ over the summer. This summer, however, they could not be able to hire nearly as many, a result of recession-related cutbacks. Front-line staff from these sites also stated that job opportunities in their local sites were limited, and that youth would probably not get hired over the more experienced out-of-work adults with whom they had to compete.

3. Plans to Conduct 12-Month Follow-ups of Summer Youth

To assess youth's progress over time, local sites are required as part of the regular WIA program to follow youth for a full year after they exit the program. Under the Recovery Act, however, ETA gave local sites the flexibility to decide whether they would conduct a 12-month follow-up with summer participants. At least one provider in three sites planned to follow up with all or a portion of summer youth after the initiative concluded. The LWIB in one rural site required that the local provider track 20 percent of summer youth from each county through quarterly follow-ups. Individual providers in two other sites intended to formally follow youth, though they were not obligated through their contracts with the LWIB to do so.

The remaining 17 sites chose not to conduct the 12-month follow-up. While data were not available from all sites, six of these sites reported financial constraints, a lack of staff capacity, and the volume of youth as barriers to following youth over time. However, providers in at least four sites planned to informally check in with some or all participants. In addition, those that are enrolled in the regular WIA youth or adult programs will continue to receive services from many of these same SYEI providers. Staff also reported that many youth are likely to seek their assistance with referrals to other programs and services.

IX. Reflections on the 2009 SYEI and Future Considerations

The American Recovery and Reinvestment Act of 2009 (Recovery Act) posed a new and exciting opportunity for local workforce investment areas to develop or reinvigorate their summer youth employment initiatives (SYEIs). Once a large component of the workforce investment strategy for youth, these programs received reduced emphasis within the previous decade. During their monumental efforts in the summer of 2009 in response to the Recovery Act, local areas reported tremendous successes as well as some significant hurdles. This evaluation report has documented their experiences, painted an in-depth picture of implementation, and given a voice to the youth and employers who were at the core of this effort.

Drawing information from across the report, this final chapter distills the main lessons learned by the 20 sites studied during the summer of 2009 as well as the challenges they faced along the way. Section A provides overall impressions of implementation and how the initiative unfolded over time. Section B summarizes the key factors that contributed to both the successes and challenges of the summer experience. Finally, Section C looks to the future, discussing considerations for the future of participating youth and the initiative as a whole.

A. Overall Impressions of the Summer Experience

The evaluation captured the perspectives of more than 600 administrators, staff members, youth, and employers who took part in the SYEI. Respondents discussed the successes and challenges of the 2009 effort. Based on this feedback, the study distilled several key impressions of the summer experience.

1. Effects of the Size of the Initiative and Timeframe for Implementation

Given the state of the United States economy early in 2009, Congress emphasized urgency when it passed the Recovery Act. Federal guidance encouraged the workforce investment system to focus on spending Recovery Act youth funds on summer employment in 2009. As a result, parties at all levels of the workforce investment system—Federal, state, and local—had to act quickly to ensure that the SYEI could get off the ground in time. Once the Act was signed into law in mid-February, the Department of Labor (DOL) quickly developed guidance and distributed it to states and local areas in mid-March. The Employment and Training Administration (ETA) also followed the guidance with a series of technical assistance webinars on the Recovery Act vision and expectations, effective program models, and tips on measuring work readiness. During this same timeframe, funding was being distributed to states, which then had to determine local allocations. Local areas often began planning before they received final guidance or their funding allocations, adjusting their plans as necessary over time.

The size of the initiative and the quick timeframe affected every aspect of planning and implementation. Many local areas were starting from scratch, having to build the SYEI from smaller scale summer programs or no existing program. All sites hired at least some temporary workers to help recruit, enroll, and serve the high volume of youth. To implement the initiative by May, planning had to begin early and quickly. As a result, some sites reported having to make compromises along the way, including curbing the extent of innovation and choosing to implement some practices without exploring all possible options. For example, some sites chose not to develop procurement procedures that would allow new and diverse local organizations to compete for SYEI contracts, and others felt they did not have sufficient time to properly vet worksite opportunities. Despite these limitations, administrators and staff reported pride in what they were able to accomplish in the summer of 2009.

2. Overall Success Despite Inevitable Challenges

Despite the tremendous pressure, sites succeeded in implementing the SYEI without any major problems. They were able to recruit sufficient numbers of youth, place them in employment, and provide additional services. There were aspects of the initiative that could inevitably be improved, but sites reported accomplishing their major goals and quickly spent a significant portion of their Recovery Act funds.

Across the nation, the workforce investment system served more than 355,000 youth between the ages of 14 and 24 from May through November 2009. Of these, more than 88 percent were placed in summer jobs. Many received additional services, including academic help, support services, and leadership development opportunities. More than 82 percent of participating youth successfully completed their work experiences, and nearly 75 percent achieved a measurable increase in work readiness during the summer.

Administrators and staff at the 20 study sites reported a perceived threefold effect from the SYEI. First, they got money into the hands of needy families. Second, youth and their families spent this new disposable income in a depressed economy. Third, youth gained valuable work experience, increasing their human capital and long-term job prospects. Although the study was unable to assess how meaningful youth experiences were or how their experiences could affect them and their communities over time, site visits revealed many interesting, creative, and innovative activities.

3. Youth Appreciation for Summer Experiences

The study gathered data from only a small, nonrandom subset of participants, but the 149 youth who participated in the study through focus groups were overwhelmingly positive about their summer experiences. They appreciated the opportunity to hold a job, gain work skills, and build their résumés. Many were enthusiastic about having money in their pockets for the first time and about being able to help their families in tough economic times. Many reported that, in the absence of the initiative, they would have been competing for jobs with more experienced adult workers or doing nothing productive over the summer. Although youth had some important feedback on key ways to improve the initiative, their most common complaint was that the initiative was too short and offered few work hours.

4. Positive Employer Feedback

Most sites were able to recruit enough worksite opportunities for participating youth. Employers appeared motivated by a sense of altruism and a desire to give back to their communities. Some employers also saw the SYEI as an opportunity to take advantage of cost-free summer assistance during lean times or to train and vet potential future employees. Employers interviewed for this study felt that the experience was worth the effort of mentoring youthful employees and almost unanimously agreed that they would participate again if given the opportunity.

B. Implementation Challenges and Lessons

Despite the positive feedback from staff, youth, and employers, implementation of the SYEI was not without its challenges. Every new initiative evolves over time as local implementers gain a better understanding of what works best. At the time of the site visits, SYEI sites and providers had just begun to reflect on how stumbling blocks could have been avoided or traversed more smoothly. Based on those reflections, as well as observation of initiative practices across all 20 sites, the study identified seven key lessons from SYEI implementation.

1. Enrollment and Eligibility Determination

Staff across all sites struggled to handle the increased volume of youth, particularly the process of determining their eligibility. The volume strained local capacity, created large workloads for staff, and, in some sites, created delays in youth enrollment. For future summer initiatives, local areas should consider providing more training to less experienced staff members to prepare them for summer tasks. As did some sites in 2009, local areas should also consider relying more heavily on experienced staff to perform more complex tasks, such as eligibility determination. Local areas should also examine other possible strategies to reduce workloads and maximize staff resources such as streamlining intake procedures through prescreening applications and coordinating with schools and social service agencies to determine youth eligibility.

2. Recruitment of Veterans and Older Youth

Although overall youth recruitment efforts proved very successful, sites had difficulty reaching older youth between the ages of 22 and 24 as well as veterans and their spouses. Given that these target populations were new for local youth programs, they had to modify their recruitment strategies to reach them. For future summers, sites should think beyond "youth" when designing and promoting youth activities, given that many veterans and young adults have children, household responsibilities, and significant work experience. Sites that had success with these groups reported that it was important to avoid alienating older youth by characterizing the SYEI as a youth program. Local areas should also consider developing new partnerships or reframing old partnerships with organizations that already serve these young adults. Finally, they should consider implementing strategies to differentiate services based on the unique needs of these older participants.

3. Recruitment of Private Sector Employers

Although federal guidance encouraged the involvement of private employers, some sites were hesitant about including them. Sites raised three concerns: (1) the advisability of choosing one private employer over another for a government-subsidized job, (2) the lack of sufficient information on the quality of private sector jobs, and (3) the age and background restrictions imposed by private employers. While not necessarily appropriate for all youth, the private sector can be a good source of high quality jobs for many participants, particularly older, more experienced youth. Most sites did successfully engage at least some private employers, and the private employers involved in the study appreciated the opportunity to participate and support local youth. About one-third of sites felt that private employers were more likely to hire participants permanently and were a better fit based on youth interests. In addition, sites did not report any problems or conflicts related to equity among local businesses. With sufficient planning time, local areas can address concerns about the quality of private sector jobs by sufficiently vetting potential employers and training worksite supervisors to ensure that they can provide quality tasks and professional mentoring.

4. Green Jobs

While more than half of sites reported at least some success placing youth in green industries and jobs, administrators and staff across sites and even within sites often did not use a common definition for green jobs. Respondents in three sites explicitly expressed confusion over the definition. To further expand youth opportunities in this emerging field, sites require additional guidance from ETA on what constitutes a green job. The Bureau of Labor Statistics as well as several states, foundations, and private organizations have already begun efforts to define the concept of green jobs more clearly and conduct inventories of these jobs across the country.

5. Job Matching

Some sites felt—and youth agreed—that job matching of youth to employers could have been improved by either aligning employer recruitment to the interests of youth or more closely considering data from youth intake and assessments when determining the most appropriate employer. To the extent possible, local areas should match youth to employers based on their interests and career goals to help maximize the potential for a valuable summer experience that may lead to better employment opportunities. To help achieve this goal, sites should consider using information on the types of jobs that best suited the interests of youth enrolled in the summer of 2009 to help focus initial employer recruitment efforts in future summers. In addition, if sites chose to recruit employers before enrolling youth, they should consider continuing employer recruitment as needed once youth are enrolled to accommodate the interests of as many participants as possible. Given that all matches may not be ideal, staff should also work to ensure that both employers and youth have reasonable expectations for the summer experience. In particular, staff should stress to youth that, no matter what their work assignment, they will be able to build their résumés and can learn important work skills.

6. Measurement of Work Readiness Increases

Sites varied dramatically in their measurement of work readiness increases among youth and sometimes used different approaches within a site. These inconsistencies make it difficult to assess the true meaning of the national performance measure. To ensure the use of a valid measure across all local areas, sites require additional guidance from ETA on standards and best practices in measuring increases in work readiness skills. This includes guidance on the timing and frequency of youth assessments, the most appropriate sources of data on youth performance, and the types of skills that should be assessed.

7. Innovation

Variations in the local infrastructure and economy of study sites clearly affected their implementation of the SYEI. For instance, one site reported denying services to some youth who did not live near a participating employer because the youth's community lacked a good public transportation system. However, other sites with youth in similar situations either developed their own van routes or recruited businesses within the communities where youth lived to allow them to participate. As another example, administrators in some areas said they could not place significant numbers of youth into green jobs given the lack of green industry in their local economies. Other sites in similar situations, however, developed their own green projects or tapped into the public sector for green opportunities. Addressing local circumstances may require innovation. When encountering an implementation challenge, administrators should consider new or innovative models, including looking to other sites with similar local circumstances for potential solutions.

C. Looking beyond the Summer of 2009

Although the SYEI of 2009 was a monumental effort, it was not the end of the road for participating youth. Many participants came out of the initiative looking for new opportunities to expand on their experiences. How they fared beyond the summer and what effect the SYEI had on their employment prospects can only be determined through further research. During the evaluation site visits, some administrators and staff were still overwhelmed by the task at hand. However, others had already begun reflecting on what worked and what could be improved.

1. New Opportunities for Youth in the Fall

Most sites planned to use established linkages with other local organizations and partners to transition youth to new opportunities when the summer ended. The largest proportion of participants planned to return to school. Some youth could receive additional services from the workforce investment system, including regular WIA youth and adult programs and other organizations within the community. Still other youth sought to move into permanent jobs.

The evaluation was not designed to examine what opportunities youth were able to seize, but respondents mentioned several issues that could potentially limit these chances. Although the regular WIA programs for youth and adults might yield services for some SYEI participants, sites were concerned that most Recovery Act funding was spent on the SYEI and that the regular WIA programs already had waiting lists due to excess demand. In addition, administrators worried that the state of the economy would limit the extent of job opportunities that could become permanent placements.

2. The Need for Future Evaluations

This study provided rich information on the implementation of the SYEI funded by the Recovery Act in 2009. It examined national patterns of participation and explored the experiences of 20 sites through qualitative data collection and analysis. The study could not, however, assess the quality of youth experiences, examine what strategies sites implemented with Recovery Act funding in the fall and spring, or track participants to assess their longer-term progress. Future evaluation efforts are necessary to study those aspects of the Recovery Act effort. Long-term follow up or better efforts to track future participants can provide more insight into how this youth population fares beyond the summer. The extent of waiting lists and excess demand for the SYEI that sites in this study reported may also suggest that a random assignment evaluation to assess the impact of the SYEI on youth outcomes is possible if funding is available to serve sufficient numbers of youth in future summers.

3. Site Readiness for Summer Initiatives in 2010

During the summer of 2009, sites worked through many of the challenges inherent in the implementation of a new initiative and learned lessons that can be used to inform future efforts. As they reflected on their experiences, some administrators were already developing plans to improve certain aspects of their initiatives. With sufficient funds and time for planning, sites looked forward to offering summer work opportunities to youth in 2010. Even if dedicated funding were not available, a few sites felt the success of the SYEI in helping youth gain a better understanding of the world of work would prompt them to consider dedicating a larger portion of their WIA-formula funds to developing summer initiatives for youth.

REFERENCES

Bloom, H. S., Orr, L. L., Cave, G., Bell, S. H. & Doolittle, F. (1993). *"The National JTPA Study: Title II-A Impacts on Earnings and Employment at 18 Months."* Bethesda, MD: Abt Associates.

Center for Labor Market Studies. (2009). *"Dire Straits for Many Workers: The Economic Case for New Job Creation and Retraining Strategies in 2010 for the Nation's Young, and Dislocated Blue Collar Workers."* Boston, MA: Center for Labor Market Studies.

CTB McGraw-Hill. (2010). *Tests of Adult Basic Education (TABE).* Retrieved from http://www.ctb.com on January 8.

Comprehensive Adult Student Assessment Systems. (2010). *"CASAS."* Retrieved from http://www.casas.org on January 8.

Eurostat. (2009). *"The Environmental Goods and Services Sector."* Luxembourg: Office for Official Publications of the European Communities.

Graybill, Bonnie. (2009). *"California's Green Economy."* Presentation to the Green Collar Jobs Council, California Labor Market Information Division, December 8.

Hardcastle, Alan. (2008). *Green Economy Jobs in Washington State.* Washington State University, Extension *Energy Program.* (2009). Prepared for the Washington State Employment Security Department, January.

Jolly, Nicholas A. (2008). "How "Green" is Connecticut's Economy?" *The Connecticut Economic Digest,* vol. *13,* no. 12, pp. 1–3, 5.

McLaughlin, J., A. Sum & O'Brien, S. (2009). *"Nation's Teen Summer Employment Rate Hits New Post-World War II Low: Effects of Federal Jobs Stimulus Overwhelmed by Private Sector Declines."* Boston: Center for Labor Market Studies.

Michigan Department of Energy & Labor and Economic Growth. (2009). *Michigan Green Jobs Report.* Bureau of Labor Market Information and Strategic Initiatives, May. (2009).

New York State Department of Labor. (2009). *New York State's Clean Energy Industry: Labor Market and Workforce Intelligence.* Albany, NY: NYS Department of Labor, May 2009.

Oates, Jane, Assistant Secretary for Employment & Training, U.S. Department of Labor. (2009). *Testimony before the Committee on Education and Labor,* U.S. House of Representatives, Washington, DC, October 1.

Oregon Employment Department, Workforce & Economic Research Division. (2009). *The Greening of Oregon's Workforce: Jobs, Wages, and Training.* Salem, OR: Oregon Employment Department, June.

Pew Charitable Trusts. (2009). *The Clean Energy Economy.* Washington, D.C.: The Pew Charitable Trusts, June.

Psychological Assessment Resources, Inc. (2010). *"Wide Range Achievement Test (WRAT)."* Lutz, FL: PAR, 1005. Retrieved from http://www.parinc.com on January 8.

Social Policy Research Associates. (1998). *"Technical Assistance Guide: Providing Educational Services in the Summer Youth Employment and Training Program."* Waltham, MA: SPR and the Center for Human Resources, Brandeis University.

Social Policy Research Associates. (2004). *"The Workforce Investment Act After Five Years: Results from the National Evaluation of the Implementation of WIA."* Waltham, MA: SPR and TATC Consulting for the U.S. Department of Labor.

Statistics Canada. (2007). *Environment Industry: Business Sector 2002 (revised) and 2004.* Ottawa: Minister of Industry, September.

Sum, Andrew. (2009). "The Crisis in the Black Youth Labor Market: A True Depression." In *The Defenders Online,* retrieved from http://www.thedefendersonline.com/ on December 15.

U.S. Census Bureau. (2009). *"State and County Quick Facts."* Washington, DC: U.S. Census Bureau. Retrieved from http://quickfacts.census.gov on December 15, 2009.

U.S. Congress. (1999). "How is the summer employment opportunities element administered?" *Code of Federal Regulations* Title 20, Pt. 664.610. Washington, DC: Code of Federal Regulations.

U.S. Congress. (2009). "American Recovery and Reinvestment Act of 2009." Pub. Law No. 111-5, February 17. Retrieved from U.S. Government Printing Office, http://frwebgate.access.gpo.gov/cgi-bin/getdoc.cgi?dbname=111_cong_bills&docid=f:h1enr.txt.pdf   on September 10, 2009.

U.S. Congress. (2009). "Workforce Investment Act of 1998." Pub. Law No. 105-220, August 7, 1998. Retrieved from http://www.doleta.gov/USWORKFORCE/WIA/ wialaw.txt on September 10,.

U.S. Congress. (2000). "What definitions apply to this part?" *Code of Federal Regulations* Title 29, Pt. 37.4.

U.S. Congress. (1999). "What safeguards are there to ensure that participants in Workforce Investment Act employment and training activities do not displace other employees?" *Code of Federal Regulations* Title *20*, Pt. 667.270.

U.S. Department of Labor. (2006). *"Training and Employment Guidance Letter No. 17-05 Attachment B."* Washington, DC: DOL, February 17.

U.S. Department of Labor. (2009). *Program Year 2008 Workforce Investment Act Title I Annual Report.* Washington, DC: DOL.

U.S. Department of Labor. (2009a). *Performance and Accountability Report FY 2009.* Washington, DC: DOL.

U.S. Department of Labor, Bureau of Labor Statistics. (2009b). *"The Employment Situation."* Washington, DC: DOL,.

U.S. Department of Labor. (2009c). *"Training and Employment Guidance Letter No. 13-08."* Washington, DC: DOL, March 6.

U.S. Department of Labor. (2009d). *"Training and Employment Guidance Letter No. 14-08."* Washington, DC: DOL, March 18,.

U.S. Department of Labor. (2009e). "Training and Employment Guidance Letter No. 24-08." Washington, DC: DOL, May 21.

U.S. Government Accountability Office. (2004). *Workforce Investment Act: Labor Actions Can Help States Improve Quality of Performance Outcome Data and Delivery of Youth Services.* Washington, DC: GAO, February.

U.S. Government Accountability Office. (2009). *Recovery Act: Funds Continue to Provide Fiscal Relief to States and Localities, While Accountability and Reporting Challenges Need to Be Fully Addressed.* Washington, DC: GAO, September.

APPENDIX A. DETAILED LIST OF RESEARCH QUESTIONS

The evaluation answers a set of six research questions and related subtopics:

1. *How did the selected sites plan for and organize summer youth initiatives with funding from the Recovery Act?* What was the organizational structure of summer youth initiatives?.How did sites identify and select summer youth providers? How did the summer initiative fit within the larger context of the regular WIA youth program and within existing summer youth programs? What processes did sites use to design their initiatives? What proportion of funds from the Recovery Act was allocated for summer activities?

2. *How did selected sites identify, recruit, and enroll at-risk youth?* How many and what types of youth did sites target for their summer initiatives? Did sites have procedures for identifying and recruiting youth most in need of services, such as out-of-school youth and those most at risk of dropping out, youth in and aging out of foster care, youth offenders and those at risk of court involvement, homeless and runaway youth, children of incarcerated parents, migrant youth, Indian and Native American youth, and youth with disabilities? How did sites provide priority service for veterans and their eligible spouses? What challenges did sites face in identifying and recruiting youth? What challenges emerged in determining eligibility and conducting youth enrollment? What strategies worked well?

3. *What were the characteristics of participants nationwide?* How many youth participated in summer youth initiatives funded by the Recovery Act? What were the background characteristics of participating youth? How many youth completed summer work experiences? What growth did states report that youth achieve in work readiness skills? To help inform the national statistic, how did selected sites determine whether a measureable increase in work readiness skills for summer youth participants has occurred?

4. *What services were offered in the summer months in selected sites?* How were participants oriented to the initiative? Did sites use a group orientation process for youth prior to the start of the summer initiative? What types of assessments and Individual Service Strategies (ISS) did sites use for youth served with Recovery Act funds? Which of the 10 youth program elements were offered to summer participants?[23] How was work readiness preparation integrated into the initiative? Did sites integrate work-based and classroom-based learning activities and how? What is the typical duration and intensity of services? How did services differ for youth of different ages? How did sites determine whether a 12-month followup should or should not be used for youth served with Recovery Act funds during summer months? How and under what circumstances do sites transition youth to the regular WIA youth program? Did states plan to use a waiver of regular reporting

requirements to keep serving older youth? Does this appear to encourage services to older youth? What successes and challenges did sites encounter in offering summer services to at-risk youth? What promising strategies do they identify?

5. *What types of work experiences were offered to participating youth in selected sites?* What was the breakdown between public sector, private sector, and nonprofit summer employment opportunities offered in the summer youth initiative? How were employers recruited, assessed, selected, and oriented to the initiative? To what extent was the Work Opportunity Tax Credit promoted as an incentive to hire disconnected youth? What were the connections to registered apprenticeship or pre-apprenticeship programs? Did sites use project-based community service learning opportunities that are not conducted at an employer worksite? Did sites consider and/or use transitional job approaches that combined short-term subsidized work experience with support services and career counseling? To what extent did sites develop work experiences and other activities that exposed youth to opportunities in "green" educational and career pathways? How were youth matched to work experiences? How were worksites supervised, and what was the participant-to-staff ratio? To what extent and how did initiatives support the transition of older youth to permanent placement? What successes and challenges did sites encounter in developing and implementing summer work experiences for at-risk youth? What promising strategies did they identify?

6. *What lessons can be drawn about the implementation of summer youth initiatives?* What implementation strategies appeared to work well? What challenges did sites encounter and how did they overcome those challenges? How has the current economic context influenced implementation? How did sites' experiences vary based on their location in urban and rural areas? How did their experiences vary based on other site characteristics (for example, size, prior summer youth programs, organizational structure)?

APPENDIX B. CHARACTERISTICS OF YOUTH FOCUS GROUP PARTICIPANTS

	Percentage of All Participants
Age at Time of Site Visit	
14–15	20.7
16–17	35.2
18–21	35.2
22–24	9.0
Male	48.0
Race	
White	11.4
Black or African American	20.8
Multiracial	6.7
Other	39.6

(Continued)

Not Specified	21.5
Latino or Hispanic Origin	28.9
Education Status	
Enrolled for 2009–2010 school year	81.9
Not enrolled for 2009–2010 school year	18.1
Grade for Those Enrolled for 2009–2010 School Year	
8–9	5.4
10	15.4
11	14.1
12	20.1
College/Vocational School	26.9
Educational Attainment of Those Not Enrolled for the 2009–2010 School Year	
High school diploma	11.4
GED	3.4
Associates degree	0.7
None	2.7
Mental, Physical, or Emotional Health Problems	9.4
Sample Size	**149**

Source: Information forms completed by youth who participated in site visit focus groups.

APPENDIX C. RECOVERY ACT ALLOCATIONS AND DRAW DOWNS BY STATE

	Funding Allocation	Draw Downs through November 2009	Percentage of Allocation Drawn Down through November 2009
Total [a]	**$1,188,000,000**	**$717,299,355**	**60.4**
Alabama	$11,647,403	$6,907,116	59.3
Alaska	$3,936,018	$1,782,928	45.3
American Samoa	$170,030	N.A.	N.A.
Arizona	$17,830,637	$8,740,869	49.0
Arkansas	$12,065,555	$8,097,148	67.1
California	$186,622,034	$90,934,238	48.7
Colorado	$11,874,970	$7,553,078	63.6
Connecticut	$11,034,723	$7,720,153	70.0
Delaware	$2,918,025	$989,503	33.9
District of Columbia [b]	$3,969,821	$0	0.0
Florida	$42,873,265	$31,260,046	72.9
Georgia	$31,361,665	$21,877,460	69.8

Table. (Continued)

	Funding Allocation	Draw Downs Through November 2009	Percentage of Allocation Drawn Down Through November 2009
Guam	$1,383,998	N.A.	N.A.
Hawaii	$2,918,025	$962,798	33.0
Idaho	$2,918,025	$2,702,489	92.6
Illinois	$62,203,400	$41,108,830	66.1
Indian and Native Americans	$17,820,000	N.A.	N.A.
Indiana	$23,677,573	$14,451,625	61.0
Iowa	$5,172,183	$3,729,683	72.1
Kansas	$7,121,714	$3,572,925	50.2
Kentucky	$17,709,821	$12,388,656	70.0
Louisiana	$20,012,271	$12,459,616	62.3
Maine	$4,293,710	$2,324,563	54.1
Maryland	$11,585,610	$6,760,700	58.4
Massachusetts	$24,838,038	$15,187,870	61.1
Michigan	$73,949,491	$47,957,332	64.9
Minnesota	$17,789,172	$12,064,000	67.8
Mississippi	$18,687,021	$14,626,657	78.3
Missouri	$25,400,077	$19,662,596	77.4
Montana	$2,918,025	$1,976,125	67.7
Nebraska	$2,944,616	$2,367,115	80.4
Nevada	$7,570,212	$4,489,715	59.3
New Hampshire	$2,918,025	$1,398,671	47.9
New Jersey	$20,834,103	$11,017,481	52.9
New Mexico	$6,235,678	$4,089,402	65.6
New York	$71,526,360	$38,215,020	53.4
North Carolina	$25,070,698	$15,216,257	60.7
North Dakota	$2,918,025	$2,372,760	81.3
Northern Marianas	$512,149	N.A.	N.A.
Ohio	$56,158,510	$37,250,239	66.3
Oklahoma	$8,708,036	$5,811,533	66.7
Oregon	$15,068,081	$11,586,865	76.9
Palau	$86,779	N.A.	N.A.
Pennsylvania	$40,647,780	$19,910,754	49.0
Puerto Rico	$42,456,987	$26,189,294	61.7
Rhode Island	$5,611,097	$3,549,668	63.3
South Carolina	$24,712,293	$14,230,501	57.6
South Dakota	$2,918,025	$2,422,337	83.0
Tennessee	$25,099,116	$17,502,348	69.7
Texas	$82,000,708	$59,095,423	72.1
Utah	$5,067,154	$4,065,703	80.2
Vermont	$2,918,025	$2,262,337	77.5

Table. (Continued)

	Funding Allocation	Draw Downs Through November 2009	Percentage of Allocation Drawn Down Through November 2009
Virgin Islands	$817,044	N.A.	N.A.
Virginia	$12,982,612	$7,320,015	56.4
Washington	$23,445,432	$14,645,836	62.5
West Virginia	$5,343,318	$3,362,290	62.9
Wisconsin	$13,808,812	$10,012,084	72.5
Wyoming	$2,918,025	$1,116,703	38.3

Source: Training and Employment Guidance Letter No. 13-08 and state performance reports for WIA youth initiatives supported by the Recovery Act submitted to the U.S. Department of Labor as of December 31, 2009.

N.A. = not available.

[a] Total draw downs and percentage of funds drawn down do not include data from outlying areas or from Indian and Native American grantees.

[b] Draw down reports show that Washington, DC has not yet begun to draw down its Recovery Act allocation. It is unclear whether this reflects actual initiative status or a reporting error.

APPENDIX D. KEY PERFORMANCE STATISTICS BY STATE

	Total Number of Participants Enrolled through November 2009	Percentage Employed During Summer	Percentage Completing Summer Employment[a]	Percentage Achieving Work Readiness Goal[b]	Percentage Employed Outside the Summer Months
Total[c]	**355,320**	**88.3**	**82.4**	**74.8**	**12.8**
Alabama	5,367	64.6	75.9	80.5	0.0
Alaska	972	97.3	95.9	84.2	4.9
American Samoa	N.A.	N.A.	N.A.	N.A.	N.A.
Arizona	3,404	87.6	89.0	86.8	0.9
Arkansas	3,475	97.3	85.2	90.1	0.0
California	45,267	92.9	86.7	73.7	6.8
Colorado	3,328	94.3	79.6	78.5	5.5
Connecticut	4,066	100.0	94.1	84.2	1.8
Delaware	1,071	99.6	69.4	65.1	0.0
District of Columbia[d]	94	0.0	N.A.	N.A.	100.0
Florida	14,548	93.8	92.4	86.7	3.2
Georgia	11,192	98.5	91.1	90.9	7.5
Guam	357	100.0	100.0	100.0	0.0
Hawaii	626	94.7	79.8	80.5	1.9

Table. (Continued)

	Total Number of Participants Enrolled Through November 2009	Percentage Employed During Summer	Percentage Completing Summer Employment[a]	Percentage Achieving Work Readiness Goal[b]	Percentage Employed Outside the Summer Months
Idaho	848	99.1	85.1	76.4	0.0
Illinois	17,868	93.0	81.0	80.2	0.4
Indian and Native Americans	3,763	84.8	85.0	79.0	N.A.
Indiana	2,603	98.4	70.8	79.8	0.0
Iowa	1,375	92.4	80.3	78.8	7.2
Kansas	1,920	89.2	75.1	61.0	1.4
Kentucky	6,051	99.9	98.0	80.1	0.0
Louisiana	5,762	93.3	86.6	79.6	5.6
Maine	1,544	45.3	59.1	71.0	5.8
Maryland	4,438	81.4	98.8	90.8	1.1
Massachusetts	6,917	98.2	91.8	85.2	2.9
Michigan	20,649	88.9	68.2	67.6	28.6
Minnesota	6,031	92.1	88.9	85.8	3.2
Mississippi	6,742	97.0	75.2	72.3	1.6
Missouri	9,447	91.9	78.5	74.6	6.4
Montana	819	84.2	58.7	56.6	23.2
Nebraska	1,062	98.9	77.6	71.3	0.0
Nevada	1,560	96.3	76.4	84.2	30.5
New Hampshire	585	88.2	89.7	94.0	0.0
New Jersey	6,195	95.0	31.9	21.9	0.0
New Mexico	1,831	96.3	36.5	82.8	6.0
New York	25,323	94.3	85.2	83.2	3.8
North Carolina	6,436	100.0	71.1	62.2	3.7
North Dakota	817	73.4	67.3	48.8	7.7
Northern Marianas	N.A.	N.A.	N.A.	N.A.	N.A.
Ohio	17,861	58.7	85.4	89.5	13.6
Oklahoma	1,847	89.9	71.0	64.1	14.4
Oregon	4,251	85.3	94.6	66.4	1.1
Palau	N.A.	N.A.	N.A.	N.A.	N.A.
Pennsylvania	9,359	98.7	73.5	71.8	0.8
Puerto Rico	25,627	61.6	N.A.	21.7	100.0
Rhode Island	1,665	98.7	84.3	95.9	0.8
South Carolina	7,235	89.4	80.5	84.2	7.7
South Dakota	721	100.0	88.5	88.3	0.0
Tennessee	12,577	92.9	75.1	72.5	2.0
Texas	24,669	88.6	87.4	83.3	2.4

Table. (Continued)

	Total Number of Participants Enrolled Through November 2009	Percentage Employed During Summer	Percentage Completing Summer Employment[a]	Percentage Achieving Work Readiness Goal[b]	Percentage Employed Outside the Summer Months
Utah	847	87.1	43.0	44.6	8.9
Vermont	808	98.9	100.0	59.0	9.0
Virgin Islands	314	89.2	67.9	27.5	0.0
Virginia	3,968	95.5	79.7	75.7	8.0
Washington	5,913	92.1	91.2	77.4	7.9
West Virginia	2,501	56.4	96.2	78.9	0.4
Wisconsin	4,071	99.7	89.0	91.0	0.0
Wyoming	496	76.0	79.4	65.8	13.3

Source: Training and Employment Guidance Letter No. 13-08 and state performance reports for WIA youth initiatives supported by the Recovery Act submitted to the U.S. Department of Labor as of December 31, 2009.

Note: ETA defined "summer" as May 1 through September 30. N.A. = not available.

[a] Pertains only to those youth who were employed during the summer and for whom data are available.

[b] Pertains only to those youth who participated during the summer months and for whom data are available.

[c] Statistics in the total row do not include youth from outlying areas or those served by Indian and Native American grantees.

[d] Draw down reports show that Washington, DC has not yet begun to enroll youth with its Recovery Act allocation. It is unclear whether this reflects actual initiative status or a reporting error.

End Notes

[1] JTPA's predecessor, the Comprehensive Employment and Training Act (CETA), also provided for summer youth employment through block grants to state and local governments.

[2] An out-of-school youth is an eligible youth who has either dropped out of school or received a high school diploma or General Educational Development (GED) credential but is deficient in basic skills, underemployed, or unemployed (U.S. Congress 1998).

[3] Washington, D.C., and Puerto Rico are counted among the states. Outlying areas include American Samoa, Guam, Northern Marianas, Palau, and the Virgin Islands. Indian and Native American grantees were also required to report on program performance.

[4] ETA defined "summer" as May 1 through September 30 (U.S. Department of Labor 2009d).

[5] Dividing total expenditure by the number of enrolled youth results in a higher cost per participant for the regular WIA youth compared to Recovery Act youth. This may result from the fact that most of the youth served by the Recovery Act participated only during the summer months, whereas the regular WIA youth program serves youth for significantly longer periods of time. Note that some youth enrolled through the Recovery Act may continue to be served beyond November 2009, increasing the actual cost per participant.

[6] States submitted their first performance reports in June with aggregate information for May and June.

[7] Although older youth can also be considered for the WIA dislocated worker program, few are likely to be eligible to be classified as dislocated workers, given the criteria used for each program.

[8] The study used respondents' reports on their sites' area types and unemployment rates because many of the local workforce investment areas do not directly correspond to census areas for which systemically collected information is available.

[9] Within a local area, the Workforce Investment Board (WIB) can hire professional staff and be the administrative and fiscal agent for WIA funds. Alternatively, the LWIB can designate one or more contractors to operate the WIA program. For simplicity, unless otherwise specified, the remainder of this chapter uses the term "lead agency" to refer to either the LWIB or the administrative agency operating the SYEI.

[10] Although administrators in these study sites stated that they had not exercised a waiver, two of the three sites were located in states that had been granted procurement waivers.

[11] These included one site that exercised a waiver. In this site, the WIA administrative agency operated the summer youth program and also contracted with three providers—one of which was new to the WIA procurement system—to run two-week academies.

[12] It is important to note that higher enrollment numbers could indicate more demand than anticipated or higher drop-off rates of youth during the program.

[13] It is important to remember that counts from youth focus groups are not representative of all youth within the site. In addition, although moderators encouraged all focus group members to participate, time limitations and group dynamics may have prevented some participants from expressing their views.

[14] Providers in three of these sites grouped youth by more than one characteristic.

[15] Work readiness training was not discussed in focus groups in two sites. However, these sites were two of the four that did not require work readiness training.

[16] According to instructions on the Internal Revenue Service Forms 5884 and 8850, employers can claim up to $1,200 for a summer youth employee living in an empowerment or renewal zone and performing services between May 1 and September 15. However, employers participating in the SYEI would not qualify for this credit while Recovery Act funds were used to pay youth wages.

[17] Focus group information forms did not capture the non-employment activities that the remaining 13 percent of respondents were engaged in. However, focus group discussions revealed that most of these youth were in education programs.

[18] Recognizing the growing emphasis on green jobs, recent public, nonprofit, and private sector efforts are under way to define the concept of green jobs more clearly. In addition to efforts by the Bureau of Labor Statistics, several states have conducted surveys and analytic studies of green jobs (Graybill 2009; Hardcastle 2009; Jolly 2008; Michigan Department of Energy 2009; New York State Department of Labor 2009; Oregon Employment Department 2009). Additional studies have been conducted by the Pew Charitable Foundation, Statistics Canada, and Eurostat (Pew Charitable Trusts 2009; Statistics Canada 2007; Eurostat 2009).

[19] These figures include hourly wages for both work and academic experiences but do not include additional supportive service payments or one-time stipends or incentives for the completion of academic activities.

[20] In one of these two sites, the fiscal agent was an education agency and processed the majority of payroll. However, the agency could not assume payroll responsibility for those youth who did not clear a background check, so the providers were responsible for paying this subset. In the other site, most providers handled payroll, but the LWIB's fiscal agent processed payroll for two providers who did not have the internal capacity.

[21] The ETA definition of this measure is presented in Chapter II.

[22] Given findings from the GAO and Mathematica studies, ETA began to gather input from local areas on potential improvements in performance measurement. ETA solicited feedback from local practitioners through two Recovering America's Youth Summits in fall 2009 and plans to provide further written guidance on performance measurement for future summer programs in spring 2010.

[23] The 10 youth program elements offered through the regular WIA program include (1) tutoring, study skills training, and instruction leading to secondary school completion; (2) alternative secondary school offerings; (3) summer employment opportunities directly linked to academic and occupational learning; (4) paid and unpaid work experience, including internships and job shadowing; (5) occupational skill training; (6) leadership development opportunities; (7) supportive services; (8) adult mentoring for a duration of at least 12 months; (9) follow-up services; and (10) comprehensive guidance and counseling, including drug and alcohol abuse counseling (Workforce Investment Act of 1998).

CHAPTER SOURCES

The following chapters have been previously published:

Chapter 1 – This is an edited, excerpted and augmented edition of a United States Congressional Research Service publication, Report Order Code R40929, dated May 10, 2010.

Chapter 2 – This is an edited, excerpted and augmented edition of a United States Congressional Research Service publication, Report Order Code R40930, dated November 18, 2009.

Chapter 3 – This is an edited, excerpted and augmented edition of a United States Congressional Research Service publication, Report Order Code R40830, dated June 2, 2010.

Chapter 4 -This is an edited, excerpted and augmented edition of a Mathematica Policy Research, Inc. publication, dated February 26, 2010.